ANGLAIS

DISCOVERING

# Literature

PREMIÈRES • TERMINALES

SÉRIE L

Programme 2011

W0362446

Françoise GRELLET

Professeur agrégé

Moira KENNEDY

B.Ed., Glasgow University

Professeur certifié

Nathan

**Cover photos**
**Top:** Whoopy Goldberg, in *Color Purple*, directed by Steven Spielberg, 1985 ph© Collection Christophel
**Bottom:** 'Alice', illustration by John Tenniel for the 1921 edition of *Alice in Wonderland and Through the Looking-Glass*, Lewis Carroll ph© Mary Evans/Rue des Archives

Edition : Anne-Sophie Cayrey
Iconographie : Sophie Suberbère
Conception de la couverture et de la maquette : Favre & Lhaïk

Le papier de cet ouvrage est composé de fibres naturelles, renouvelables, fabriquées à partir de bois provenant de forêts gérées de manière responsable.

# Avant-propos

Ce livre est destiné aux élèves de premières L et de terminales L qui suivent l'enseignement de littérature anglaise en langue anglaise.

Cet ouvrage se veut une introduction à la littérature des pays anglophones. Il est constitué de quatre parties qui se complètent et se répondent, mais qui sont utilisables indépendamment les unes des autres.

## Landmarks

La première partie, *Landmarks*, a pour but de donner quelques repères chronologiques. Pour chacune des grandes périodes de l'histoire littéraire de la Grande-Bretagne et des États-Unis, ainsi que pour les principaux pays du Commonwealth, il est proposé :

› une chronologie des événements historiques majeurs et des œuvres essentielles ;

› la liste des mouvements littéraires les plus importants.

L'objectif n'est pas de proposer une histoire littéraire, mais de permettre d'associer auteurs et mouvements littéraires, artistiques ou historiques, de créer associations et mises en regard.

On pourra consulter cette partie avant ou après l'étude d'un texte, en guise d'introduction, ou encore d'ouverture sur d'autres auteurs ou tendances de la même période.

## Literary Trails

La seconde partie, *Literary Trails*, est composée de neuf dossiers autour de genres ou de thèmes typiquement anglo-saxons. La liste n'est pas exhaustive et nous avons par exemple laissé de côté certains genres caractéristiques de cette littérature, tels que roman policier ou science-fiction, assez bien représentés dans les manuels existants.

L'objectif de cette partie n'est pas d'offrir l'étude approfondie d'un genre en quelques pages. Notre intention est plutôt de faire découvrir certains aspects importants de la littérature anglo-saxonne afin de donner l'envie d'aller plus loin et, peut-être, de lire une œuvre complète.

Les genres et thèmes choisis reflètent l'apport de la littérature anglo-saxonne dans les domaines qui touchent à l'imagination, qu'il s'agisse du fantastique, du gothique, du nonsense, de l'utopie, ou de l'absurde, de tout ce qui relève du mystérieux ou de l'extraordinaire. C'est peut-être la souplesse de la langue anglaise ou l'excentricité bien connue de nombre d'Anglo-saxons qui peuvent expliquer cette tendance. Nous avons cependant inclus quelques thèmes tels que *Political and social statements* et *Feminine voices*, moins spécifiquement anglo-saxons, mais pourtant largement présents dans cette littérature.

Chacun des dossiers de cette partie comprend :

› une courte introduction, qui explique l'importance du genre ou du thème ainsi que ses caractéristiques principales ;

› plusieurs textes anglais ou américains, représentatifs de diverses périodes. Chaque texte est suivi de quelques questions ou activités (*Zooming in*) qui proposent des pistes pour entrer dans le texte.

› à la fin de chaque dossier, quelques suggestions de films, livres, tableaux ou enregistrements (*Moving on*) permettant d'aller plus loin.

## Tools

La troisième partie, *Tools*, doit aider à la révision ou à la découverte d'un vocabulaire critique de base. Il s'agit, pour la plupart, de termes déjà connus en français, mais qui ne sont pas toujours maîtrisés en anglais. Ces termes sont présentés sous forme de courts exercices qui pourront accompagner l'étude d'un texte.

## Tasks

La dernière partie, *Tasks*, propose un certain nombre d'activités à partir de textes littéraires. Ces derniers sont donnés uniquement à titre d'exemple, les activités n'étant pas liées à un texte précis. Elle peuvent donc être utilisées plusieurs fois à partir de textes différents.

Cet ouvrage peut servir de manuel de classe, le travail se faisant à partir des textes proposés, ou bien de livre d'accompagnement, qui pourra être utilisé parallèlement à tout autre travail littéraire.

Nous espérons avant tout que cet ouvrage donnera l'envie de lire, d'aller plus loin, de découvrir d'autres aspects de la littérature et de la culture anglo-saxonnes.

# Sommaire

## Landmarks



## Literary Trails

# From the Renaissance to the Elizabethan Age

## HISTORY

- **1337-1453** Hundred Years' War
- **1455-1485** Wars of the Roses
- **1509** Accession of Henry VIII
- **1534** Break with Rome
- **1558** Accession of Elizabeth I
- **1588** Spanish Armada defeated
- **1603** Accession of James I
- **1605** Gunpowder Plot

## POETRY

- **1386-1400** **CHAUCER** *The Canterbury Tales* Stories told by pilgrims and ironically reflecting character and society
- **1590-1596** **SPENSER** *The Faerie Queene*
- **1591** **SIDNEY** *Astrophel and Stella*
- **1609** **SHAKESPEARE** *Sonnets*

Pastoral and allegorical poems; imitation and renewal of Petrarchan sonnets

## PROSE & FICTION

- **1516** **MORE** *Utopia* Description of a an ideal system of government

## THE THEATRE

- **1508** *Everyman* A Morality play (a Christian allegorical play about the fight between good and evil)
- **1588** **MARLOWE** *Doctor Faustus*
- **1590** **SHAKESPEARE** *First plays*
- **1606** **JONSON** *Volpone*
- **1612** **SHAKESPEARE** *Last plays*

The Golden age of drama

## PAINTING

◆ Portraits and allegories (HOLBEIN)

**HOLBEIN** (1497-1543)
*The Ambassadors*, 1533

◆ Miniatures (HILLIARD)

**HILLIARD** (1547-1619)
*Unidentified Woman*, 1580

◆ Portraits (VAN DYCK)

**VAN DYCK** (1599-1641)
*Three Children and a dog*

## The Elizabethan World Order

• The Renaissance was marked by invention, discovery and change at all levels.
In the field of astronomy, people had known since 1541 that the sun – and no longer the earth – was at the centre of the universe.
Alchemy, and its attempt to transform base[1] metals into gold, was giving way to chemistry.
It was the beginning of the exploration of the earth and of colonization.
The rigid social hierarchy which had so far prevailed[2] (the sovereign › the nobility › the gentry[3] › citizens › yeomen[4] › labourers and workmen) was beginning to be challenged[5] with the rise of Parliament.

• Yet it would take time for mentalities to change and in many people's minds, as well as in Shakespeare's plays, it was the old conception of the universe which was the true one. People's lives were thought to be influenced by the stars with clear parallels between the whole cosmos (the macrocosm) and the world of man (the microcosm) since man was made up of the same elements (earth, water, air and fire) as the universe.

• People also believed that everything (men, animals, inanimate objects) had a fixed place in the pattern[6] of the world. At all levels, there was a **hierarchy** or a chain – socially (from the king to the lowest beings), among animals (from the lion to the oyster[7] clinging to the rock and therefore close to the mineral world) as well as among abstract notions (justice being considered as the highest virtue). As for man, he was in a central position between angel and beast.

• Such a conception of the world led the Elizabethans to see the universe in terms of **analogy** and corresponding planes: there were parallelisms between the macrocosm, the microcosm (man) and the body politic (the state). Storms and strange occurrences[8] against nature accompany disasters on the earth – for instance the killing of a king.

Such a vision of an ordered universe was a reminder that God's creation was harmonious and should not be thrown into confusion.

Note the pearls (symbolic of purity), the globe and the queen's hand on America. In the background, there are scenes of the defeat of the Armada in 1588.

Georges GOWER, *Elizabeth I, Armada Portrait*, c. 1588
National Portrait Gallery, London

## Politics

The Elizabethans and Jacobeans were afraid of instability and civil war (the wars of the Roses were not so far behind them), just as they feared a plot against the sovereign (in 1605 the Gunpowder Plot had been an attempt to blow up[9] the Houses of Parliament to re-establish a Catholic king).
This explains the belief that a sovereign should be an absolute one, who must preserve stability and order, and be the representative of God on earth.

1. **base**: *inférieur*
2. **to prevail**: *régner*
3. **the gentry**: *la petite noblesse*
4. **a yeoman**: *un franc-tenancier*
5. **to challenge**: *contester*
6. **the pattern**: *la structure*
7. **an oyster**: *une huître*
8. **an occurrence**: *un événement*
9. **to blow up**: *faire exploser*

## The Elizabethan theatre

• The very popular Elizabethan theatre (Christopher Marlowe, William Shakespeare, Ben Jonson) derives from short religious plays acted out in church then in the open air and inspired by the Bible (Mystery plays) or by the lives of Saints (Miracle plays). They later developed into Morality plays, in which Good and Evil fought in order to possess someone's soul. In the second half of the 15th century, the theatre was no longer linked with the church and included comedy, history plays and revenge tragedies, influenced by Seneca and showing bloody deeds[7] and the need to avenge[8] them.

• Elizabethan theatres were built around an inner yard[9] See p. 144, like the Globe reconstruction, making for close contact with the audience. A soliloquy was therefore quite natural since the actor addressed the audience. The audience was mixed, made up of both better educated or wealthier people in the galleries and of people standing in the yard, where you could attend the play for a mere penny. A play therefore had to appeal to[10] a large range of people. There were no women actresses. Women's parts were played by boys, thus creating sexual ambiguity when, as was often the case in comedies, women were disguised as men.

## Shakespeare's plays

Shakespeare wrote:

- history plays (showing the rise and fall of kings, the necessity for authority and a strong government, the qualities that make a good sovereign),
- comedies (using disguise, mistaken identity and even farce, but also developing more serious themes such as a reflection upon love and theatrical illusion),
- tragedies (with their heroes the victims of their own 'tragic flaws[11]' – ambition, jealousy or blindness – and beset[12] by doubts and questioning),
- romances (set in pastoral or exotic places, they deal with forgiveness, reconciliation and reunion).

## Why were his plays so popular and why have they remained so?

- Shakespeare did not respect the Aristotelian division into genres and his plays often unite tragedy and comedy, which appeals to different types of public.
- The themes of his plays are universal: politics, love, death, illusion, ambition.
- His characters range[13] from kings, noblemen and courtiers to simple servants and tradesmen.
- The plays are complex, open to different interpretations, both conservative and provocative, which is why they lend themselves to such a variety of productions.
- The language is rich in metaphors and images, which are both visual and symbolic and can be appreciated at different levels.

7. **a deed**: *un acte*
8. **to avenge**: *venger*
9. **a yard**: *une cour*
10. **to appeal to**: *plaire à*
11. **a flaw**: *un défaut*
12. **to beset**: *assaillir*
13. **to range from ... to ...**: *aller de ... à ...*

### SHAKESPEARE'S MAJOR PLAYS

| TRAGEDIES | HISTORY PLAYS | COMEDIES | ROMANCES |
|---|---|---|---|
| **1595**: *Romeo and Juliet* | **1591-2**: *Henry VI* | **1590-1**: *The Two Gentlemen of Verona* | **1607**: *Pericles* |
| **1599**: *Julius Caesar* | **1592-3**: *Richard III* | *The Taming of the Shrew* | **1609**: *The Winter's Tale* |
| **1600-1**: *Hamlet* | **1595**: *Richard II* | **1594-5**: *Love Labour's Lost* | **1610**: *Cymbeline* |
| **1603-4**: *Othello* | **1596-8**: *Henry IV* | **1595**: *A Midsummer Night's Dream* | **1611**: *The Tempest* |
| **1605-6**: *King Lear* | **1598-9**: *Henry V* | **1596-7**: *The Merchant of Venice* | |
| **1606**: *Macbeth* | | **1597-8**: *The Merry Wives of Windsor* | |
| **1606**: *Antony and Cleopatra* | | **1598**: *Much Ado About Nothing* | |
| **1608**: *Coriolanus* | | **1599-1600**: *As You Like It* | |
| | | **1601**: *Twelfth Night* | |
| | | **1604-5**: *All's Well that Ends Well* | |

## The heyday[14] of the sonnet

• Under the influence of Dante and Petrarch, the sonnet became very popular during the Renaissance and in the late 16th century was adapted to English in a form with fewer rhymes See p. 146.

• Both Sidney and Spenser wrote collections of sonnets describing their love and emotions. As for Shakespeare's *Sonnets* (1609), some of them are addressed to a young man, some of them to a lady. They are far more original in their themes and imagery and depart from Petrarchism. The poet goes through all the range of emotions in his relationship with the young man – love, passion, despair, jealousy – and expresses his carnal desire for the lady.

Shakespeare's sonnet 71, p. 149

14. **the heyday**: *l'âge d'or*

### Sir Philip SIDNEY, *FROM ASTROPHEL AND STELLA*, XLI, 1591

Having this day my horse, my hand, my lance
Guided so well, that I obtained the prize,
Both by the judgment of the English eyes,
And of some sent from that sweet enemy, France;
Horsemen my skill in horsemanship advance[1],
Townsfolks my strength; a daintier[2] judge applies
His praise to sleight[3], which from good use doth[4] rise;
Some lucky wits[5] impute it but to chance;
Others, because of both sides I do take
My blood from them who did excel in this,
Think Nature me a man of arms did make.
How far they shot awry[6]! the true cause is,
Stella looked on, and from her heavenly face
Sent forth the beams[7] which made so fair my race.

Paolo UCCELLO, *St George and the Dragon*, c. 1460
Musée Jacquemart-André, Paris

1. **advance:** *faire les éloges de* 2. **dainty:** *délicat, difficile* 3. **sleight:** *l'habileté* 4. **doth :** does *(archaïsme)* 5. **a wit:** *un homme d'esprit* 6. **shot awry:** *se trompaient* 7. **the beams:** *les rayons*

### William SHAKESPEARE, *MACBETH*, 1606

Prompted by his ambition, his wife and the prophecy of three witches, Macbeth – a victorious general – is led to kill king Duncan in order to become king himself. The murder leads to further killings, then to civil war and social and cosmic disruption. As he is about to be defeated, and learns of his wife's death, Macbeth has a sudden understanding of the futility and absurdity of life.

She should have died hereafter[1]
There would have been a time for such a word.
Tomorrow, and tomorrow, and tomorrow
Creeps[2] in this petty[3] pace from day to day
To the last syllable of recorded time;
And all our yesterdays have lighted fools
The way to dusty death. Out, out, brief candle,
Life's but a walking shadow, a poor player
That struts[4] and frets[5] his hour upon the stage
And then is heard no more. It is a tale
Told by an idiot, full of sound and fury
Signifying nothing.

Orson WELLES, in *Macbeth*, 1948

1. **heareafter:** *un jour ou l'autre ou plus tard* 2. **to creep:** *ramper* 3. **petty:** *insignifiant* 4. **to strut:** *se pavaner* 5. **to fret:** *s'inquiéter*

# The 17th century

## HISTORY

- **1625** Accession of Charles I
- **1629** Parliament abolished
- **1642-48** Civil War
- **1649** Execution of Charles I
- **1649-1660** Commonwealth (Cromwell)
- **1660** Restoration of Charles II
- **1665-66** Great Plague and Great Fire of London
- **1688** The Glorious Revolution

## POETRY

- **1633** **DONNE** *Poems* Metaphysical poetry: religious and love poetry developing paradoxes and unexpected images
- **1667** **MILTON** *Paradise Lost* A defence of Puritanism A didactic epic about the creation of the world and the fall of man
- **1681** **MARVELL** *Poems* **DRYDEN** *Absalom and Achitophel*

## PROSE & FICTION

- **1611** *Authorized Version of the Bible*
- **1625** **BACON** *Essays*
- **1644** **MILTON** *Areopagitica* An attack against censorship
- **1651** **HOBBES** *Leviathan* A justification of absolute governments
- **1660-69** **PEPYS** *Diary* A day-to-day account of life during the Restoration
- **1678** **BUNYAN** *The Pilgrim's Progress* An allegory of a Christian's progress through life

Political and religious work (1644–1678)

## THE THEATRE

- **1700** **CONGREVE** *The Way of the World*
- **1707** **FARQUHAR** *The Beaux' Stratagem*

RESTORATION COMEDY
Humorous satire of the manners of the time

## PAINTING

◆ Portraits (LELY, KNELLER)

LELY (1618-1680)
*Portrait of George Monck*, 1665-1666

KNELLER (1673-1721)
*Portrait of James Stanhope*, 1705-1710

Marked by two revolutions, the 17th century was dominated by political and religious controversies, which are reflected in its literature.

## Political writings

- **John Milton** wrote many pamphlets to support Cromwell's government: he advocated[1] education for women, divorce, and the liberty of the press in his well-known *Areopagitica* (1644).
- As for **Thomas Hobbes**'s *Leviathan* (1651), it starts from the thesis that men are selfish and that the 'state of nature' is one of war. Men should therefore choose a strong government which will have absolute control over all aspects of their lives.

## Religious works

It was during the 17th century that three religious works were published that would remain extremely popular for at least two centuries and were sometimes the only books to be found in many people's homes.

- *The Authorized Version of the Bible* (also called *King James Bible* since James I had commissioned it), a highly poetic text published in 1611.
- **Bunyan**'s *Pilgrim's Progress*, (1678) is an allegory of a Christian soul in its journey from the City of Destruction (the corruption and evil in this world) to the Celestial City (Heaven). What made the book so popular was the simplicity and realism of the incidents Christian, the protagonist, is confronted with in his journey (crossing a bog[2], physical obstacles, deciding who is a true and who is a false friend).
- **Milton**'s *Paradise Lost* (1667).

## Restoration theatre

- In 1642, Parliament, which was controlled by the Puritans, closed all theatres, which only reopened in 1660, at the end of the Commonwealth. The new theatres were different, showing the influence of the French theatre (Charles II had been in exile in France): only one side of the stage was close to the audience, the stage was lit by candles and women could now act as well as men. The theatre had lost its universal appeal, and was now mainly attended by the nobility and the middle class.
- The dominant genres showed a reaction against Puritanism:
  - heroic dramas, like those of **Dryden**, are written in a melodramatic and bombastic[3] style and show epic heroes torn between their passion and their duty or honour,
  - comedies of manners, like those of **Farquhar** and **Congreve**, use wit[4] and cynicism to satirize a sophisticated society obsessed with sex and money.

## Poetry

- In the early 17th century, a group of poets called Metaphysical Poets (**John Donne**, **George Herbert**) wrote both religious and love poems based on logical reasoning, concision, striking[5] images and directness of expression.
- The second half of the century is dominated by **John Milton**. *Paradise Lost* (1667) is an epic poem which he wrote to 'justify the ways of God to man'. It relates Satan's fall, God's creation of the earth and of Adam and Eve, Satan's temptation of Eve and their expulsion from the Garden of Eden. The poem is written in very musical verse and long, balanced syntax.

**John MILTON,**
**'Satan's words' in *Paradise Lost*, 1667**

So farewell hope, and with hope farewell fear,
Farewell remorse! All good to me is lost;
Evil, be thou[1] my good; by thee[2] at least
Divided empire with heaven's king I hold...

**1. thou:** you **2. thee:** you

**1.** to advocate: *plaider en faveur de*
**2.** a bog: *un marécage*
**3.** bombastic: *grandiloquent*
**4.** wit: *l'esprit, le fait d'être spirituel*
**5.** striking: *frappant*

# The 18th century

## HISTORY

- **1701** Act of Settlement
- **1714** Accession of George I
- **1745** Jacobite rebellion
- **1776** American Declaration of Independence; Steam engine invented
- **1789** French Revolution

## POETRY

- **1730** THOMSON *The Seasons*
- **1734** POPE *Essay on Man*
- **1742** YOUNG *Night Thoughts*
- **1757** GRAY *Odes*

Poetry of melancholy

## PROSE & FICTION

- **1719** DEFOE *Robinson Crusoe* — A realistic description of survival through hard work
- **1726** SWIFT *Gulliver's Travels* — A political satire of Britain through the description of imaginary worlds
- **1747-49** RICHARDSON *Clarissa* (epistolary); FIELDING *Tom Jones* (picaresque)
- **1760-67** STERNE *Tristram Shandy* — A digressive and sentimental novel

THE RISE OF THE NOVEL

## THE THEATRE

- **1773** GOLDSMITH *She Stoops to Conquer*
- **1777** SHERIDAN *The School for Scandal*

Witty comedy of manners

## PAINTING

◆ Social satire (HOGARTH)
Conversation pieces (family portraits)

▸ **HOGARTH** (1697-1764)
*Heads of Six of Hogarth's Servants*, 1750-1755

◆ Portraits (REYNOLDS),

▸ **REYNOLDS** (1723-1792)
*The Children of Edward Holden Cruttenden*, 1763

◆ Portraits and landscape (GAINSBOROUGH)

▸ **GAINSBOROUGH** (1727-1788)
*Conversation in a Park*, 1745

## From reason to sensibility

The 1688 Glorious Revolution led to the modern English parliamentary democracy by limiting the powers of the sovereign and reinforcing those of Parliament. As for the 1701 Act of Settlement, it stipulated that the monarch must belong to the Church of England and led to the union of Scotland with England and Wales to form Great Britain. The Hanoverian dynasty came onto the throne, and with it came a period of relative stability and tolerance during which literature flourished[1].

- The first half of the century showed the influence of classicism: it was the Age of Enlightenment[2], with its respect for conventions, tolerance, reason and morality. Social satire was expressed through the use of wit and irony (for example in the poems of **Alexander Pope** or in **Jonathan's Swift**'s *Gulliver's Travels*, 1726).
- In the second half of the century an interest in melancholy, sentimentality and picturesque or wild nature announced pre-romanticism. This is reflected in the poetry of **Collins, Gray, Thomson** and **Goldsmith**.

## The rise of the novel

Several factors can explain the birth of this new literary genre:

The engravings and paintings of William Hogarth also satirize contemporary life. In *Marriage à la Mode*, for example, he shows the disastrous consequences of a marriage based not on love but on economic interests. It is a series of six paintings, each presented like a stage. In the first one, we find the concluding stages of the negotiations of a marriage agreement. The earl's son will marry a rich merchant's daughter. The earl will gain money, the merchant's daughter a title.

William HOGARTH, *Marriage A la Mode*, c. 1743, National Gallery, London

› the increase of literacy[3] and the rise of a middle class who wanted to be both edified and amused,

› the desire to see literature reflect contemporary society – not the lives of heroes or princes,

› a new interest in feelings and psychology (showing the influence of the philosophers **Locke** and **Hume**).

## The main novelists

- **Daniel Defoe** (*Robinson Crusoe*, 1719; *Moll Flanders*, 1722) describes with realism the lives of characters who fight to survive (Robinson Crusoe because he has been shipwrecked[4] on a desert island, Moll Flanders because she has been reduced to stealing and prostitution by poverty). His characters reflect the Puritan faith in hard work and the possibility of economic progress.
- **Samuel Richardson** developed the genre by choosing the epistolary mode, which lends itself to subtle psychological analysis. He was a moralist who wanted to reform as well as entertain and his hugely popular novels (*Pamela*, 1740-41; *Clarissa*, 1747-48) describe virtuous heroines who refuse to be seduced by libertines.
- The novels of **Henry Fielding** also reflect the society of the time but in a very different way. It is no longer in the boudoir but along the road that his picaresque heroes (*Joseph Andrews*, 1742; *Tom Jones*, 1749) discover life and gain experience. Their adventures lead them to meet a whole range of characters who allow the author to present a satire of selfishness and hypocrisy and to praise benevolence and charity.
- As for **Laurence Sterne**, his masterpiece *Tristram Shandy* (1760-67) is a comic and sentimental novel which challenges fictional illusion and already mocks all the conventions of the new genre. With its lack of chronology, its digressions and its diagrams, it is concerned with the subjectivity of perception, with the association of ideas and with the relativity of the passing of time.

1. **to flourish:** *prospérer, s'épanouir*
2. **the Age of Enlightenment:** *le Siècle des lumières*
3. **literacy:** *le fait de savoir lire et écrire*
4. **to be shipwrecked:** *faire naufrage*

# The Romantic Age

## HISTORY

- **1793** – The Terror in France. France and Britain at war
- **1805** – Trafalgar
- **1813** – Napoleon defeated at Waterloo
- **1825** – First railway
- **1832** – Reform Act (extends the right to vote)

## POETRY

- **1789** – **BLAKE** *Songs of Innocence*
- **1798** – **WORDSWORTH AND COLERIDGE** *The Lyrical Ballads*
- **1805** – **WORDSWORTH** *The Prelude*
- **1812** – **BYRON** *Childe Harold's Pilgrimage*
- **1816** – **COLERIDGE** *Kubla Khan*, *Christabel*
- **1819-24** – **BYRON** *Don Juan*
- **1820** – **KEATS** *Odes*; **SHELLEY** *Prometheus Unbound*

PRE-ROMANTICISM (1789) — FIRST GENERATION OF ROMANTIC POETS (1798–1805) — SECOND GENERATION OF ROMANTIC POETS (1819–1820)

## PROSE & FICTION

- **1794** – **RADCLIFFE** *The Mysteries of Udolpho*
- **1813** – **AUSTEN** *Pride and Prejudice*
- **1814** – **SCOTT** *Waverley* (Historical novels)
- **1816** – **AUSTEN** *Emma*
- **1818** – **WOLLSTONECRAFT SHELLEY** *Frankenstein*

Austen: lucid and ironic novels of manners

Gothic novels: a study of the effect of terror on sensitive minds

## PAINTING

◆ Visionary and Gothic (BLAKE, FUSELI) ◆ Landscape painting (CONSTABLE, TURNER)

**CONSTABLE** (1776-1837)
*Boat-building near Flatford Mill*, 1815

**TURNER** (1775-1851)
*Yacht approaching the coast*, 1840-1845

## A turbulent age

The period which began around 1780 and ended with the accession of Queen Victoria (1837) was a turbulent age marked by three revolutions: the American Revolution (1776), the French Revolution, and the Industrial Revolution. It was therefore an age of controversy.

- The French Revolution was criticized by some but defended by others, who saw it as the triumph of justice and equality, before the Reign of Terror turned idealism into disillusion. But it had led to hope and dreams which had an impact on the literature of the time.
- As for the Industrial Revolution, it brought dramatic[1] changes to the country. New machinery changed the means of production, so that the old cottage industry[2] began to disappear, replaced by large factories. As the process of enclosures[3] grew, many people left their villages to find work in large cities (Manchester, Birmingham, Liverpool, Nottingham), where the working and living conditions in overcrowded[4] slums[5] were often horrifying. Social reform was only being introduced gradually, but political reform started with the 1832 Reform Bill – a first attempt to bring more justice to Parliamentary representation.

## The Romantic movement

It was first of all a reaction against the Age of Reason which had marked the early 18th century, with its respect for literary conventions and traditions.

On the contrary, the Romantics:

- privileged instincts and passions,
- put the subjectivity of the individual or of the writer himself, his inner vision, the exploration of the human mind, at the heart of the text,
- affirmed the creative and regenerative powers of the imagination,
- saw nature – unspoilt[6] by civilization – as divine, and, in a more general way, anything simple and natural as a proper subject for literature.
- admired all forms of idealism or rebellion, which explains their interest in the quest-romance – the journey in search of an ideal.

**William Wordsworth**'s Preface to the 1800 edition of *The Lyrical Ballads* is usually considered as the poetic manifesto of the Romantics. In it, Wordsworth explains that:

- essential passions are best found among rustic and humble life,
- the language of poetry should be that of ordinary men,
- poetry is a "spontaneous overflow[7] of powerful feelings".

William BLAKE engraved his own paintings, then painted them. This is his engraving of 'The Chimney-sweeper[1]', from his *Songs of Experience*. The poem condemns a society which allows such child labour (the child is carrying a bag of soot[2].)

William BLAKE, 'The Chimney-sweeper', plate 37 from *Songs of Innocence and of Experience*, c. 1815-1826, Fitzwilliam Museum, University of Cambridge, UK

1. a chimney-sweeper: *un ramoneur* 2. soot: *la suie*

1. **dramatic:** *spectaculaire*
2. **cottage industry:** *l'industrie familiale, chez soi*
3. **enclosure:** *le fait de clore, d'entourer de haies, des espaces autrefois publics*
4. **overcrowded:** *surpeuplé*
5. **a slum:** *un taudis*
6. **unspoilt:** *non gâché par*
7. **the overflow:** *le débordement*

Constable's paintings capture the mood of a place, particularly the effects of light on sky and water.

John CONSTABLE, *The Hay Wain*, 1821, National Gallery, London

## Poetry

• **William Blake**, both a poet and a painter, was an early Romantic who attacked rationality, materialism and all that restrains[10] imagination and instincts, which alone can help us be reunited with the divine. A radical and visionary poet, he developed his own complex mythology. In his *Songs of Innocence* (1789) and *Songs of Experience* (1794), he was particularly concerned with the condition of children such as chimney-sweepers who were the innocent victims of industrialisation.

### The first generation of Romantic poets

• **William Wordsworth**'s lyrical poetry is concerned with the development of the inner self (the subject of his long poem *The Prelude*, 1805) and with man's relationship with nature.

• **Samuel Taylor Coleridge** was attracted to the mysterious and the supernatural and his poems show the influence of the Gothic movement See p. 60 and of German legends.

*The Rime of The Ancient Mariner* (1798) is a ballad – a form privileged by the Romantics because it was considered as simple and authentic. The poem is the story of a mariner who shoots an albatross. This brings a curse[11] upon the ship, which will only start moving again when the mariner blesses[12] nature.

**S. T. COLERIDGE,**
**'The Rime of The Ancient Mariner',**
***in The Lyrical Ballads*, 1798**

Day after day, day after day,
We stuck[1], nor breath nor motion;
As idle[2] as a painted ship
Upon a painted ocean.

Water, water, every where,
And all the boards did shrink[3];
Water, water, every where,
Nor any drop to drink.

The very deep did rot[4]: O Christ!
That ever this should be!
Yea, slimy[5] things did crawl with legs
Upon the slimy sea.

1. **we stuck:** *nous restâmes immobiles* 2. **idle:** *oisif*
3. **to shrink:** *rétrécir* 4. **to rot:** *pourrir* 5. **slimy:** *visqueux*

10. **to restrain:** *réprimer*
11. **a curse:** *une malédiction*
12. **to bless:** *bénir*

Turner was fascinated by the effects of light, colour and movement in nature.
William TURNER, *Rain, Steam and Speed, The Great Western Railway*, 1844, National Gallery, London

### The second generation of Romantic poets

• **George Gordon Byron** was more a classicist at heart, as is shown by his love of satire and comedy in his poem *Don Juan* (1819-1824), which reverses the traditional story as it is Don Juan who is seduced. But the hero of *Childe Harold* (1812-1818) is a typical Romantic hero, who travels restlessly to escape his own weariness[13].

**G. G. BYRON, *Childe Harold*, 1812-18**

Where rose the mountains, there to him were friends;
Where rolled the ocean, thereon was his home;
Where a blue sky, and glowing clime[1], extends,
He had the passion and the power to roam[2]
The desert, forest, cavern, breaker[3]'s foam[4],
Were unto him companionship; they spake[5]
A mutual language...

1. **clime:** *contrée (littéraire)* 2. **to roam:** *errer*
3. **a breaker:** *une grosse vague* 4. **foam:** *l'écume*
5. **spake:** *forme achaïque de 'spoke'*

• **Percy Bysshe Shelley** was an idealist and a revolutionary who refused institutions and laws as well as conventional morality. In his poem *Prometheus Unbound* (1820), the hero who stole fire from the Gods is a rebel who eventually brings love to the world.

• **John Keats**'s poetry is highly sensuous and inspired by beauty, which he saw as threatened[14] by both time and the evils of the world.

## The novel

The Gothic novel See p. 58 remained very popular, but two new forms appeared.

• **Walter Scott**'s historical novels are often set in the past of Scotland and show heroes torn[15] between idealism and the forces of history.

• As for **Jane Austen**'s novels, they are not romantic in spirit but mock any excess of sentimentality See p. 61, 91. They are novels of manners, which examine the society of her time with irony and detachment, condemning pretension and hypocrisy, while defending moral values, common sense, compassion and love. By the end of the novels, her heroines have reached self-knowledge, love and marriage.

13. **weariness:** *la lassitude*
14. **to threaten:** *menacer*
15. **torn:** *déchiré*

# The Victorian Age

## HISTORY

- **1837** Accession of Queen Victoria
- **1838** Beginning of the Chartist movement
- **1851** Great Exhibition
- **1854** Crimean War
- **1876** Queen Victoria Empress of India
- **1880** First Boer War
- **1901** Accession of Edward VII

## POETRY

- **1832** TENNYSON *Poems*
- **1855** BROWNING *Men and Women*

VICTORIAN POETRY (questionings and anxiety about man's place in the universe)

## PROSE & FICTION

- **1847** BRONTE E. *Wuthering Heights*; BRONTE C. *Jane Eyre*
- **1848** THACKERAY *Vanity Fair*
- **1850** DICKENS *David Copperfield*
- **1861** DICKENS *Great Expectations*
- **1865** CARROLL *Alice's Adventures*
- **1872** ELIOT *Middlemarch*
- **1886** STEVENSON *Dr Jekyll and Mr Hyde*
- **1894** KIPLING *The Jungle Book*
- **1896** HARDY *Jude the Obscure*
- **1900** CONRAD *Lord Jim*

Imaginative tales of passionate love

Realism, social and moral study of society

Novels of adventure and action

Determinism, tragic view of man as a victim of circumstances

## THE THEATRE

- **1894** SHAW *Arms and the Man* — Social concerns
- **1895** WILDE *The Importance of Being Earnest* — Witty comedies

A criticism of conventional morality

## PAINTING

- The Pre-Raphaelites (MILLAIS, ROSSETTI, BURNE-JONES)
- Art nouveau (MORRIS, BEARDSLEY)
- Aestheticism (WHISTLER)

**MILLAIS** (1829-1896) *Ophelia*, 1851

**BURNE-JONES** (1833-1898) *The Wedding of Psyche*, 1895

**WHISTLER** (1834-1903) *Symphony in White*, 1864

## A period of profound changes

The Victorian age (Queen Victoria reigned from 1837 to 1901) was a period of enormous changes:

• Britain was fast becoming a rich and powerful nation, the financial centre of the world, with an empire on which "the sun never set[1]". But the change from an agricultural to an industrial society, the overcrowded urban centres, the difficult economic situation and poor harvests[2] in the 1830s and 1840s, led to a growing division between the rich and the poor, the "Two Nations" Disraeli wrote about. The Chartist movement was an attempt to introduce more political justice, but it was abandoned (although most of its propositions were later adopted).

• All through the 19th century, social reforms helped to improve the electoral system, the situation of women, education, justice and particularly the working conditions of factory workers.

• Charles Darwin's *Origin of Species* (1859) challenged the traditional views of the church and led to a public debate over evolution.

Such changes were accompanied by contradictions:

• The feeling of wealth and progress often resulted in pride in the Puritan ideals and respectability of the middle class, in complacency[3] and self-confidence. It is often associated with hypocrisy and sexual repression.

• Yet there was also an increasing sense of anxiety in the last two decades of the century, reflected for example in the sombre view of fate to be found in Thomas Hardy's novels.

## Poetry

• The poetry of **Tennyson**, **Browning** and **Arnold** reflects the Victorians' doubts and anxiety about man's place in the universe.

*Capital and Labour*: a cartoon from *Punch* (published in the 1840s) showing the wealthy upper classes at the top and the poor working class at the bottom.

1. **to set:** *se coucher (soleil)*
2. **a harvest:** *une récolte*
3. **complacency:** *la suffisance*

This painting was inspired by Tennyson's 1830 poem *Mariana*, whose main character is taken from Shakespeare's *Measure for Measure*. Mariana's fiancé, Angelo, has abandoned her, and she lives alone and miserable in an isolated grange.

> She only said, "My life is dreary[1],
> He cometh[2] not," she said;
> She said, "I am aweary[3], aweary;
> I would that I were dead!"

Like all Pre-Raphaelite painters, Millais was inspired by literature and heroic scenes from the past.

Sir John Everett MILLAIS, ***Mariana***, 1851, Tate Gallery, London

1. **dreary:** *morne* 2. **cometh:** 'comes' *(archaïque)*
3. **aweary:** 'weary' *(archaïque)*: *lasse*

## The novel

The novel became very popular during the Victorian age, often appearing in serialized[4] form. It provided entertainment but also often sensitized[5] readers to social problems.

• **Charlotte**, **Emily** and **Anne Brontë** were brought up by their father in a parsonage[6], near the wild Yorkshire Moors. Their novels show the influence of the Romantic and Gothic movements. They describe complex, passionate characters,

4. **serialized:** *publié en feuilletons*
5. **to sensitize:** *sensibiliser*
6. **a parsonage:** *un presbytère*

### Charlotte BRONTË, *Jane Eyre*, 1847

Jane Eyre, a poor, ill-treated orphan, finds a place as a governess at Thornfield Hall, and falls in love with its master, Mr Rochester. Unknown to her, his wife, who has become mad, is kept locked up upstairs. Jane and Rochester decide to get married, but during the church service, a lawyer will explain the marriage is impossible for Rochester is already married. They will finally be reunited after a series of incidents. This passage takes place on the morning of the planned wedding: Jane explains to Rochester that a woman she does not know entered her bedroom during the night.

"Ghosts are usually pale, Jane."
"This, sir, was purple: the lips were swelled and dark; the brow furrowed: the black eyebrows widely raised over the bloodshot eyes. Shall I tell you of what it reminded me?"
"You may."
"Of the foul German spectre - the vampire."
"Ah! – what did it do?"
"Sir, it removed my veil from its gaunt head, rent it in two parts, and flinging both on the floor, trampled on them."
"Afterwards?"
"It drew aside the window-curtain and looked out; perhaps it saw dawn approaching, for, taking the candle, it retreated to the door. Just at my bedside the figure stopped: the fiery eyes glared upon me – she thrust[1] up her candle close to my face, and extinguished it under my eyes. I was aware her lurid[2] visage flamed over mine, and I lost consciousness; for the second time in my life – only the second time – I became insensible from terror."

1. **to thrust:** *projeter* 2. **lurid:** *épouvantable*

often in desolate settings. In **Charlotte Brontë**'s *Jane Eyre* (1847), a poor governess asserts her independence as a woman and falls in love with her employer. Emily Brontë's *Wuthering Heights* (1847) relates the violent love between Catherine and Heathcliff amid[7] wild, primitive nature. See p. 140

- **Charles Dickens**'s novels contain both humour and tragedy See p. 71. Many of his characters are picturesque or grotesque, close to caricature. But Dickens also wanted his novels to reform society and used them to criticize poverty, overcrowded slums, the exploitation of children, the absurdities of the law – any form of cruelty or social injustice.

- Many other novelists wrote about the society of the time. **William Makepeace Thackeray** directed his satire against the selfishness, vanity and corruption of his contemporaries, as in *Vanity Fair* (1847-1848). **George Eliot** portrayed provincial life and the way education, religion and social environment can stifle[8] someone's development (*Middlemarch* (1871-1872), *The Mill on the Floss*, 1860).

- Later in the century, **Thomas Hardy**'s novels describe the close relationship between man and nature and see men as the victims of economic and social changes which they are not strong enough to fight (*Tess of the D'Urbervilles*, 1891).

- As for **Rudyard Kipling**, he was a very popular poet and novelist, who mainly wrote about India and is often considered as the "voice of imperialism".

### CHARLES DICKENS, *Oliver Twist*, Chapter 2, 1837-38

Oliver Twist is an orphan[1] who, at the age of nine is sent to a workhouse, where children work for very little food. One day they decide that they will draw lots[2] and one of them will ask for more food, something unheard of before.

Child as [Oliver] was, he was desperate with hunger, and reckless[3] with misery. He rose from the table; and advancing to the master, basin and spoon in hand, said, somewhat alarmed at his own temerity:
"Please, sir, I want some more."
The master was a fat, healthy man; but he turned very pale. He gazed in stupefied astonishment on the small rebel for some seconds, and then clung for support to the copper[4]. The assistants were paralysed with wonder; the boys with fear.

"What!" said the master at length, in a faint voice.

"Please, sir," replied Oliver, "I want some more."

The master aimed a blow at Oliver's head with the ladle[5]; pinioned[6] him in his arms; and shrieked[7] aloud for the beadle[8].

The board[9] were sitting in solemn conclave, when Mr. Bumble rushed into the room in great excitement, and addressing the gentleman in the high chair, said,

"Mr. Limbkins, I beg your pardon, sir! Oliver Twist has asked for more!" Horror was depicted on every countenance[10].

1. **a orphan:** *un orphelin* 2. **to draw lots:** *tirer au sort* 3. **reckless:** *imprudent* 4. **the copper:** *la marmite de cuivre* 5. **the ladle:** *la louche* 6. **to pinion:** *tenir les bras derrière le dos de qqn* 7. **to shriek:** *hurler* 8. **the beadle:** *le bedeau* 9. **the board:** *le comité* 10. **the countenance:** *le visage*

## The theatre

- **Oscar Wilde**'s novel(*The Picture of Dorian Gray*, 1891) and plays See p. 87 (*The Importance of Being Earnest*, 1895) reflect the art for art's sake movement. They combine wit, humour and social concerns – an attack against Victorian conventions and hypocrisy.

- The plays of **George Bernard Shaw** provide another challenge to conventional bourgeois ideas.

Lord LEIGHTON was the best representative of the Aesthetic movement in painting.

Lord LEIGHTON, *Flaming June*, c. 1895
Museo de Arte de Ponce, Puerto Rico

7. **amid:** *au milieu de*
8. **to stifle:** *étouffer*

# The 20th century: until World War II

## HISTORY

- **1901** Accession of Edouard VII
- **1910** Accession of George V
- **1914-18** First World War
- **1916** Irish Easter Rising
- **1919** Treaty of Versailles
- **1921** Partition of Ireland
- **1928** Women get full voting rights
- **1929** New York Stock Exchange Crash
- **1933** Hitler takes power in Germany
- **1936** Accession of George VI

## POETRY

- **1914-1920** First World poets: **OWEN, BROOKE, SASSOON, THOMAS**
- **1922** **ELIOT** *The Waste Land*
  Modernist poetry (collage, different voices, striking images to convey the chaos of modern society)
- **1928** **YEATS** *The Tower*
  The poet of the Irish Renaissance
- **1930** **AUDEN** *Poems*
- **1933** **SPENDER** *Poems*

The thirties' Poets political and social concerns

## PROSE & FICTION

- **1907** **CONRAD** *The Secret Agent*
- **1913** **LAWRENCE** *Sons and Lovers*
- **1922** **JOYCE** *Ulysses*
- **1924** **FORSTER** *A Passage to India*
- **1927** **WOOLF** *To the Lighthouse*
- **1932** **HUXLEY** *Brave New World*
  Satire of Society
  a warning of the dangers of science

Experimentations with stream of consciousness (Woolf, Joyce), narrative technique (Conrad) and a study of relationships (Lawrence, Forster)

## THE THEATRE

- **1907** **SYNGE** *The Playboy of the Western World*
- **1912** **SHAW** *Pygmalion*
  Social concerns
- **1924** **O'CASEY** *Juno and the Paycock*
- **1935** **ELIOT** *Murder in the Cathedral*

The Irish Renaissance (an attempt to reawaken Irish consciousness)

## PAINTING

- Post-impressionism (GORE, JOHN)
- The Bloomsbury Group (FRY, GRANT, BELL)
- Vorticism (NEVINSON)
- Surrealism (NASH)

▸ **NASH** (1893-1977) *Over the Top*, 1918

▸ **NICHOLSON** (1894-1982) *Lime Green*, 1952

| 1936-39 | 1939-45 | 1940 | 1941 | 1944 |
|---|---|---|---|---|
| Spanish Civil War | Second World War | Battle of Britain | Pearl Harbour | D-Day |

**1940**

**GREENE**
*The Power and the Glory*
Moral concerns with good and evil, guilt and salvation

◆ Visionary paintings (SPENCER)

◆ Abstraction (NICHOLSON)

The sense of anxiety and gloom resulting from the horrors of World War I did not end with Armistice Day. Unemployment, labour disputes[1], and tensions abroad, where there were demands for independence in many parts of the Empire (the south of Ireland became a free state in 1921) made the years between the two world wars difficult and often dismal[2] ones. This is reflected in literature by anguish and ironical distance.

## The War Poets

The deaths and mutilations, the landscape of the trenches with their shells[3] and fire had a lasting impact on people's imagination and inspired a group of poets.

- **Rupert Brooke** expressed romantic, patriotic feelings about the honour of fighting for one's country.
- But the poetry of **Wilfred Owen** and **Siegfried**

WILFRED OWEN,
***Dulce et Decorum Est*[1], 1917**

Men marched asleep. Many had lost their boots
But limped on, blood-shod[2]. All went lame[3];
all blind;
Drunk with fatigue; deaf even to the hoots[4]
Of tired, outstripped[5] Five-Nines[6] that dropped behind.

**1.** It is sweet and honourable to die for one's country (Horace): an ironic title **2. blood-shod:** *chaussés de sang* **3. lame:** *estropié, éclopé* **4. a hoot:** *un sifflement* **5. to outstrip:** *dépasser, devancer* **6. five-nines:** shells containing poison gas

**1. a labour dispute:** *un conflit social*
**2. dismal:** *sombre, maussade*
**3. a shell:** *un obus*

Paul NASH, *We are Making a New World*, 1918,
The Stapleton Collection

**Sassoon** is a poetry of protest against the absurdity, the waste, the "pity of War".

## Modernism

Modernism is a term which can be applied to many experimentations with writing in the first decades of the 20th century. It was influenced by post impressionist art, which led to a fragmentation of perspective. Modernism is characterized by:

- a break with Victorian tradition,
- radical experiments with language,
- a focus on the study of inner life and perceptions partly due to Freud's discoveries about the workings of the human mind.

See p. 114

• **T. S. Eliot**'s poetry (*The Waste Land*, 1922) uses collage, multiplicity of voices and numerous allusions to convey the sense of anguish, dislocation and the loss of spiritual values at the beginning of the 20th century.

Nevinson's paintings are influenced by cubism and futurism.
Christopher NEVINSON, *Bursting Shell*, 1918,
The Stapleton Collection

• **Joseph Conrad**'s novels take place at sea and in exotic countries and explore moral conflicts, in particular man's reactions to unfamiliar or hostile surroundings. Conrad was a moralist, for whom courage, honesty and self-respect were essential values. But his novels (*Heart of Darkness*, 1899; *Lord Jim*, 1900) are modernist because of their innovative narrative technique: broken-up chronologies and multiple points of view.

• Both **James Joyce** and **Virginia Woolf** experimented with stream of consciousness.

See p. 116, 136, 157.

› **Joyce** turned his back on the paralysis, conformity and stifling[4] Catholicism of Ireland but kept writing about Dublin, which fascinated him. His novels (*Ulysses*, 1922) use myth, inventive language and interior monologue to render the complexity of reality.

› **Woolf**'s novels (*Mrs Dalloway*, 1925) try to convey all the fleeting[5] perceptions and ideas that go through someone's mind at any one time. Together with interior monologue, her novels show how one's subjectivity can make time expand or contract.

Like Virginia Woolf, Vanessa Bell was a member of the Bloomsbury group, a group of writers and artists who rejected the conventions and inhibitions of Victorian England and celebrated friendship, loyalty and sexual freedom.

*Virginia Woolf in a deckchair*, by Vanessa BELL (her sister), 1912, Sotheby's London

### V. WOOLF, 'Modern Fiction' in *The Common Reader*, 1925

Life is ... a luminous halo, a semi-transparent envelope surrounding us from the beginning of consciousness to the end... Is it not the task of the novelist to convey this varying, this unknown and uncircumscribed[1] spirit, whatever aberration and complexity it may display...?

1. **uncircumscribed:** *sans limite*

• Another member of the Bloomsbury Group was **E. M. Forster**. His novels show the clash between love and spontaneity on the one hand and the weight of conventions, propriety and class on the other. In *A Passage to India* (1924), he examines the racial, religious and cultural divisions between the Indian community and the British colonizers. See p. 138

### E. M. FORSTER, *A Passage to India*, 1924

Mrs Moore, who has just arrived from England, meets an Indian doctor in a mosque.

"You understand me, you know what I feel. Oh, if others resembled you!"
Rather surprised, she replied: "I don't think I understand people very well. I only know whether I like or dislike them."
"Then you are Oriental."
She accepted his escort back to the Club, and said at the gate that she wished she was a member, so that she could have asked him in.
"Indians are not allowed into the Chandrapore Club even as guests," he said simply.

4. **stifling:** *étouffant*
5. **fleeting:** *fugitif, éphémère*

• **D. H. Lawrence** passionately defended instincts, emotions and sexuality since they alone could counter rationality, materialism and industrialisation, which kill human relationships, (*Women in Love*, 1920). His prose is marked by repetition and imagery often close to expressionism.

## The Irish Renaissance

• The Irish fight for independence was accompanied by a literary revival. It focused on the romantic past of Ireland, with its Celtic myths, as well as on the political struggle for freedom. This is reflected in the novels of **James Joyce** See p. 136, in the poetry of **William Butler Yeats**, in the plays of **John Millington Synge** and **Sean O'Casey**.

## The 1930s: Social and moral concerns

The depression of the 1930s and the rise of totalitarianism in Germany deepened the sombre mood of the nation. This led to more committed[6] writing.

• Many of **Graham Greene**'s novels are influenced by his Catholic faith and show moral dilemmas. They are concerned with good and evil, guilt and grace, often with corrupt characters who are shown to be still capable of redemption (*The Power and the Glory*, 1940).

• **George Orwell** and **Aldous Huxley** wrote satires of their society, and turned the utopian genre into dystopias See p. 53.

• The poetry of **W. H. Auden** was influenced by Marxism and Brecht and mainly deals with social and political issues. He often used traditional poetic form such as the ballad in order to appeal to a larger public. The following poem by Auden is a cry of despair, a poem of mourning for the death of a friend.

6. **committed:** *engagé*

### W. H. AUDEN, 'Funeral Blues', in *Collected Shorter Poems*, 1966

Stop all the clocks, cut off the telephone.
Prevent the dog from barking with a juicy bone,
Silence the pianos and with muffled[1] drum[2]
Bring out the coffin[3], let the mourners[4] come.

Let aeroplanes circle moaning[5] overhead
Scribbling in the sky the message He is Dead,
Put crêpe bows[6] round the white necks of the public doves[7],
Let the traffic policemen wear black cotton gloves.

He was my North, my South, my East and West,
My working week and my Sunday rest
My noon, my midnight, my talk, my song;
I thought that love would last forever, I was wrong.

The stars are not wanted now; put out every one,
Pack up the moon and dismantle the sun.
Pour away the ocean and sweep up the wood;
For nothing now can ever come to any good.

1. **muffled:** *étouffé* 2. **a drum:** *un tambour* 3. **a coffin:** *un cercueil* 4. **mourners:** *ceux qui pleurent un mort* 5. **to moan:** *gémir* 6. **a bow:** *un nœud* 7. **a dove:** *une colombe*

In 1941 the sculptor Henry Moore made this drawing of people sheltering from bombings.

Henry MOORE, *Pink and Green Sleepers*, 1941, Henry Moore Foundation

## D. H. Lawrence, *Women in Love*, 1920

They turned off the main road, past a black patch of common-garden, where sooty[1] cabbage stumps[2] stood shameless. No one thought to be ashamed. No one was ashamed of it all.

"It is like a country in an underworld," said Gudrun. 'The colliers[3] bring it above-ground with them, shovel it up[4]. Ursula, it's marvellous, it's really marvellous – it's really wonderful, another world. The people are all ghouls[5], and everything is ghostly. Everything is a ghoulish replica of the real world, a replica, a ghoul, all soiled, everything sordid. It's like being mad, Ursula.'

Spencer Gore, *The Beanfield*, Letchworth 1912, Tate Gallery, London

The sisters were crossing a black path through a dark, soiled[6] field. On the left was a large landscape, a valley with collieries, and opposite hills with cornfields and woods, all blackened with distance, as if seen through a veil of crape[7]. White and black smoke rose up in steady columns, magic within the dark air. Near at hand came the long rows of dwellings, approaching curved up the hill-slope, in straight lines along the brow[8] of the hill. They were of darkened red brick, brittle[9], with dark slate[10] roofs. The path on which the sisters walked was black, trodden-in by the feet of the recurrent colliers, and bounded from the field by iron fences; the stile[11] that led again into the road was rubbed shiny by the moleskins of the passing miners. Now the two girls were going between some rows of dwellings, of the poorer sort.

1. **sooty:** *couvert de suie* 2. **a stump:** *une souche, un moignon* 3. **the colliers:** *les mineurs* 4. **to shovel up:** *remonter quelque chose à la pelle* 5. **a ghoul:** *un déterreur de cadavres* 6. **soiled:** *souillé* 7. **crape:** *du crêpe* 8. **the brow of the hill:** *le sommet de la colline* 9. **brittle:** *cassant* 10. **slate:** *l'ardoise* 11. **the stile:** *le tourniquet (porte)*

# The 20th century: after World War II

## HISTORY

- **1945-51** Labour government, Nationalizations, National Health Service
- **1947** India Independent
- **1949** NATO created
- **1951** Churchill Prime Minister
- **1952** Accession of Elizabeth II
- **1956** Suez
- **1961** South Africa becomes a Republic
- **1964-70** Wilson's Labour government

## POETRY

- **1952** THOMAS D. *Collected poems* – Lyrical oneness with nature
- **1955** LARKIN *The Less Deceived*
- **1958** BETJEMAN *Collected Poems*
- **1966** HEANEY *Death of a Naturalist*
- **1970** HUGHES *Crow*

Larkin, Betjeman: Detached, ironic, but compassionate view of life

Heaney, Hughes: The violence and mystery of the natural world

## PROSE & FICTION

- **1945** WAUGH *Brideshead Revisited*
- **1949** ORWELL *1984*
- **1952-69** LESSING *The Children of Violence*
- **1954** GOLDING *Lord of the Flies*
- **1957** MURDOCH *The Sandcastle*
- **1957-60** DURRELL *The Alexandria Quartet*
- **1959** SILLITOE *The Loneliness of the Long Distance Runner*
- **1962** BURGESS *A Clockwork Orange*
- **1969** FOWLES *The French Lieutenant's Woman*

## THE THEATRE

- **1953** BECKETT *Waiting for Godot*
- **1956** OSBORNE *Look Back in Anger*
- **1958** ARDEN *Live Like Pigs*; WESKER *Chicken Soup With Barley*
- **1960** PINTER *The Dumb Waiter*, *The Caretaker*
- **1966** STOPPARD *Rosencrantz and Guildenstern are Dead* – "Philosophical Farces"

Osborne, Arden, Wesker: Angry Youg Men (working class setting and concerns)

Beckett to Pinter: THE THEATRE OF THE ABSURD

## PAINTING

- Industrial scenes (LOWRY)
- Pop Art (BLAKE, HAMILTON, HOCKNEY)
- Op Art (RILEY)
- Expressionism (BACON, HODGKIN)

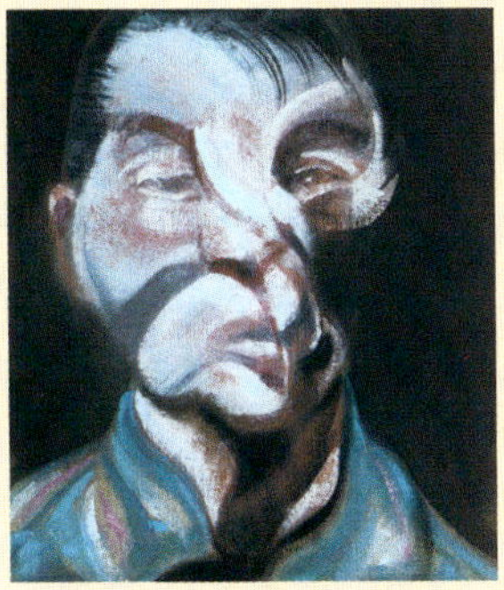

BACON (1909-1992)
*Study Portrait*, 1970

RILEY (born1931) *Nataraja*, 1993

1973 — Britain joins the EEC
1979-90 — Mrs Thatcher's Conservative government
1982 — Falklands War
1985 — Anglo-Irish agreement
1997 — Tony Blair's New Labour government
2003-4 — Iraq War
2010 — Conservative Lib-dem government

1981 — **RUSHDIE** *Midnight's Children*
1984 — **SWIFT** *Waterland*
1989 — **ISHIGURO** *The Remains of the Day*

1971 — **BOND** *Lear*

Violence to reflect the brutality of society

## Profound changes

- The war, the holocaust and the atomic bomb left deep traumas in Britain. When the war ended in 1945, the country started to rebuild itself on all fronts, particularly thanks to an ambitious plan of social reforms, which became the basis of the Welfare State[1] for the improvement of education, health, social insurance and pensions.
- But other events also led to profound changes:
  - the independence of many former colonies in the late 1940s (India in 1947),
  - Britain's entry into the EEC in 1973,
  - the unemployment and strikes of the 1970s,
  - the Troubles in Northern Ireland in the 1970s and 1980s,
  - the more recent 'war on terror'.
- All of them are reflected in various ways in the literature of the second half of the 20th century: through guilt or cynicism, through anxiety or rebellion, through lyricism or ironic detachment.
- It is difficult to find clear literary movements in this post-war period, so these pages will mainly focus on a few major writers.

## Poetry

- **Dylan Thomas**'s poems are rhetorically exuberant and lyrical, and celebrate man's mysterious relationship with nature.
- **John Betjeman** and **Philip Larkin** describe post-war Britain (consumerism, ugliness, lack of faith, loneliness) with detachment, scepticism and irony, but always with compassion.

**1. the Welfare State:** *l'État providence*

**Philip Larkin, 'This be the Verse', in *Collected Poems*, 1988**

They fuck you up, your mum and dad.
They may not mean to, but they do.
They fill you with the faults they had
And add some extra, just for you.

But they were fucked up in their turn
By fools in old-style hats and coats,
Who half the time were soppy[1]-stern[2]
And half at one another's throats[3].

Man hands on misery to man.
It deepens like a coastal shelf[4].
Get out as early as you can,
And don't have any kids yourself.

1. **soppy:** *sentimental* 2. **stern:** *sévère* 3. **at one another's throats:** *à se battre* 4. **a coastal shelf:** *un écueil le long de la côte*

• **Ted Hughes**'s poetry describes the mystery and violence of the natural world in an attempt to bring man closer to his mythical past, his instincts and his imagination.

• **Seamus Heaney**'s early poems show his interest for his Irish roots and farming background. But many of his later poems also refer to the political tensions in Northern Ireland and to the difficulty for a poet of taking sides.

Lowry's paintings reflect the monotony and sadness of working class lives and what he called 'the apocalypse of grime[1]'.

L. S. Lowry, *The Canal Bridge*, 1949
Southampton City Art Gallery Hampshire

1. **grime:** *la saleté*

## The theatre

• The movement of the **Angry Young Men** (**John Osborne**, *Look Back in Anger* (1957); **John Arden**, **Shelagh Delaney**, (*A Taste of Honey*, 1958) addresses social questions and symbolises the doubts and the anger of a new generation who refused middle-class conventions. Their plays are set among the working class and often use slang[2] and crude[3] language, which is why they are also called 'kitchen sink'[4] dramas.

*A taste of Honey* is set in the industrial north, where a girl of 17 is made pregnant by her black lover and has a difficult relationship with her mother and a homosexual friend.

From Tony Richardson's film, *A Taste of Honey*, 1958

• **The Theatre of the Absurd: Samuel Beckett, Harold Pinter** See p. 124.

• The plays of **Tom Stoppard** are very close to those of the Theatre of the Absurd, but also use wit, parody and metatextuality to present philosophical questions (*Rosencrantz and Guildenstern Are Dead* 1966, *The Real Thing* 1982, *Arcadia* 1993).

2. **slang:** *l'argot*
3. **crude:** *grossier*
4. **a kitchen sink:** *un évier de cuisine*

**Tom STOPPARD, *Rosencrantz and Guildenstern Are Dead*, 1966**

Rosencrantz and Guildenstern are two minor characters in Shakespeare's *Hamlet*; they are friends of Hamlet and have been introduced by the king in order to find out whether Hamlet is mad. In Stoppard's play roles are reversed and they become the main characters, who are killed at the end. They are lost in a world they cannot understand. The play is therefore a reflection on determinism and the quest for meaning.

GUIL: But for God's sake what are we supposed to *do*?!

PLAYER: Relax. Respond. That's what people do. You can't go through life questioning your situation at every turn.

GUIL: But we don't know what's going on, or what to do with ourselves. We don't know how to *act*.

PLAYER: Act natural. You know why you're here at least.

GUIL: We only know what we're told, and that's little enough. And for all we know it isn't even true.

PLAYER: For all anyone knows, nothing is. Everything has to be taken on trust[1]; truth is only that which is taken to be true...

1. **trust:** *la confiance*

• **The Theatre of Violence:** In the plays of **Edward Bond**, physical violence (the lapidation of a baby in *Saved*, 1965) represents the victimization of human beings in a capitalist society.

## Fiction

• The movement of the **Angry Young Men** also concerns fiction, for instance with **Kingsley Amis**'s *Lucky Jim* (1954) or **Alan Sillitoe**'s *The Loneliness of the Long-Distance Runner* (1959), the story of a teenager in a prison school for delinquent youths. He has a gift for long-distance running, competes in an importance race, but decides to lose in order to defy the prison authorities.

• **The moralists:** The novels of **William Golding** explore the nature of evil and savagery, often using parody to do so. *Lord of the Flies* (1954) parodies the traditional view that human nature outside any contact with civilisation is good (as in R. M. Ballantyne's *The Coral Island*, 1857). The boys in *Lord of the Flies* are left on a desert island in the middle of a nuclear war and descend into barbarism.

• **Iris Murdoch**'s novels also deal with philosophical questions of good and evil, to which the reader often has to find an answer on his own: *The Bell* (1958), *A Severed Head* (1961).

• **The post-modernists: John Fowles**'s novels often associate realism and fantasy, so that he is one of the first British writers to have used magic realism. *The French Lieutenant's Woman* (1969) is a pastiche of a Victorian novel and the narrator constantly comments on the contrast between Victorian manners and our own. The reader is reminded that this is fiction and with multiple endings, it is a typical work of postmodern metafiction.

**Salman Rushdie** (*Midnight's Children*, 1981) also has recourse to magic realism and myth to describe the relations between India and Britain. See p. 142

• **Feminist voices: Doris Lessing**'s novels address the questions of apartheid, political commitment and women's attempts to free themselves in a male-dominated world (*The Golden Notebook*, 1962).

**Angela Carter**'s novels and short stories combine magic realism with Gothic elements. In *The Bloody Chamber* (1979) she revises traditional fairy tales, transforming them into feminist stories for our time. See p. 66

• **History and Memory: Graham Swift** explores the role of history and of place upon our lives. (*Waterland*, 1983)

**Kazuo Ishiguro**'s characters remember their past and are full of delusions and longing (*The Remains of the Day*, 1989).

# From the Colonial Age to 1900 (US)

## HISTORY

- **1607** First English settlement at Jamestown
- **1620** Mayflower Compact
- **1775-83** War of Independence
- **1776** Declaration of Independence
- **1791** Bill of Rights
- **1803-04** Louisiana Purchase Lewis and Clark expedition reaches the Pacific
- **1848** Gold Rush
- **1861-65** Civil War
- **1865** Slavery abolished

## POETRY

- **1845** **POE** *The Raven*
- **1847** **LONGFELLOW** *Evangeline* Moralistic poetry
- **1855** **WHITMAN** *Leaves of Grass* Prophetic poetry

## PROSE & FICTION

- **1771-93** **FRANKLIN** *Autobiography*
- **1776** **PAINE** *Common Sense* (a defence of the Revolution)
- **1826** **COOPER** *The Last of the Mohicans*
- **1840** **POE** *Tales of the Grotesque and the Arabesque*
- **1841-44** **EMERSON** *Essays*
- **1850** **HAWTHORNE** *The Scarlet Letter*
- **1851** **MELVILLE** *Moby Dick*; **STOWE** *Uncle Tom's Cabin* (a denunciation of slavery)
- **1854** **THOREAU** *Walden*

THE AMERICAN RENAISSANCE
Sombre, symbolic and imaginative works

TRANSCENDENTALISM
A celebration of the divinity of man and his oneness with nature

## PAINTING

- Portraits (SMIBERT, FEKE)
- Historical paintings (COPLEY, PEALE, STUART)
- Landscapes (DURAND, COLE, CHURCH)
- Genre painting (MOUNT, BINGHAM)
- Landscapes: the luminists

**COPLEY** (1738-1815)
*Watson and the Shark*, 1778

**CHURCH** (1826-1900)
*Niagara*, 1857

1865-77 — Reconstruction
1890 — Frontier closed
1907 — Peak immigration year

1890-91 — DICKINSON

1881 — JAMES *The Portrait of a Lady*
1884 — TWAIN *The Adventures of Huckleberry Finn* A humorous novel of initiation and a satire on Southern society
1895 — CRANE *The Red Badge of Courage*
1900 — DREISER *Sister Carrie*
1905 — WHARTON *The House of Mirth*
NATURALISM
Psychological realism

◆ Aesthéticism (WHISTLER) ◆ Portraits (SARGENT, CASSATT) ◆ Realism (HOMER, EAKINS)

EAKINS (1844-1916)
*Max Schmitt in a single scull*, 1871

## The colonies

The immigrants who arrived in the new world in the 17th century faced many hardships and had little time to read anything but the Bible. It was only in the 18th century that the growth of immigration, the improved living conditions and increased religious tolerance led to a more diversified cultural life. The theatre was banned by the Puritans, but people read sermons and religious works, historical essays, biographies, newspapers, poetry and many books imported from England.

## The new nation

By the end of the 18th century, Puritan ideas of predestination were being challenged by a belief in rationality, tolerance and the laws of nature. Science and reason could help to improve men and politics. Resistance against injustice was now justified, which led to the Revolutionary War, the Declaration of Independence and the writing of the Constitution.

## The early 19th century

With new waves of immigrants causing a sharp increase in population, the frontier[1] kept moving west. The vastness of the land and the spirit of individualism and democracy associated with the frontier became a major theme in American literature.

1. **The frontier:** *la Frontière, la limite des terres colonisées*

• The country also became more and more urban and industrialized, so that the gap between the rich and the poor increased too, leading to the creation of humanitarian societies. But it was the subject of slavery which most divided the nation: the Southern states considered they needed slavery for their economy, while the north was mainly abolitionist, influenced by some popular books like **Harriet Beecher Stowe**'s *Uncle Tom's Cabin* (1852). The controversy led to the Civil War.

## After the Civil War

• The growth of industry, the railways and the development of big business encouraged both:

› a feeling of self-satisfaction: America was indeed the land of opportunity,

› inequalities and corruption, which would lead to Darwinist ideas of a 'struggle for life' and to naturalism in literature.

## Literary independence

• It took some time for the new republic to produce a literature of its own. At first, the main works were political essays reflecting the controversies of the time. The most influential book in these early years is **Benjamin Franklin**'s *Autobiography* (1791), in which he tells how hard work, self-reliance and pragmatism led him to rise to power gradually.
Although some pre-romantic poetry was published, it was mainly through the novel that America gained literary independence.

• **James Fenimore Cooper**'s frontier novels are adventure stories set in the American wilderness (*The Last of the Mohicans*, 1826, *The Deerslayer*, 1841). They reflect the conflict between man and society by addressing such themes as the destruction of the Prairie and the white man's violation of Indian land.

F. E. Church painted dramatic landscapes which suggest the sublime and the Romantic movement. This painting also evokes "Manifest Destiny", the idea that the expansion westward was the will of God.

Frederic Edwin CHURCH, *Our Banner in the Sky*, 1863, Private Collection

Heade's paintings reflect the Transcendentalists' interest in peaceful landscapes, the softness of light and the harmony of nature.

Martin Johnson HEADE, *Salt Marsh Hay*, c. 1865, Butler Institute of American Art, Youngstown

## Transcendentalism

• Transcendentalism was a romantic philosophical and literary movement based on the idea that each soul² is divine and one with nature, with which it shares a universal soul. People should therefore trust their own selves, their intuitions and reject authority if they do not agree with it. Transcendentalism was extremely influential, encouraging the idea of self-reliance³ as well as that of civil disobedience.

• **Ralph Waldo Emerson** developed this idea in his essays (*Nature*, 1836), while **Henry David Thoreau** tested it by spending two years in the woods, observing nature in all its details and changes, an experience he recorded in *Walden* (1854).

• The poetry of **Walt Whitman** was also influenced by Transcendentalism. It is a celebration of America, its people and its land, of democracy and of the self, particularly in terms of sexual freedom. Although his poetry shocked his contemporaries at first, they later came to see *Leaves of Grass* as an epic⁴ of America.

## The American Renaissance

The works of **Poe**, **Hawthorne** and **Melville** are darker, more imaginative and symbolic.

• **Edgar Allan Poe** wrote poetry and short stories; some are a study in terror, others are detective stories which show the importance of reasoning.

See p. 64

• **Nathaniel Hawthorne**'s novels and short stories examine moral conflicts and the darkness of the human mind: sin, guilt and evil. They are often set in colonial America and Hawthorne criticizes the hypocrisy and intolerance of the Puritans, as in *The Scarlet Letter* (1850), in which

### Walt WHITMAN, 'O Captain! My Captain!', 1865

This is the first stanza of Whitman's poem 'O Captain! My Captain!', a poem about Lincoln's death. He is compared to the captain of the ship America.

O Captain! My Captain! our fearful trip is done,
The ship has weathered[1] every rack[2], the prize we sought[3] is won,
The port is near, the bells I hear, the people all exulting,
While follow eyes the steady keel[4], the vessel grim[5] and daring[6];
But O heart! heart! heart!
O the bleeding drops of red,
Where on the deck[7] my Captain lies,
Fallen cold and dead.

1. **weather'd:** *réchappé à* 2. **a rack:** *un écueil* 3. **sought:** *prétérit de 'seek', chercher* 4. **the keel:** *la quille du bateau* 5. **grim:** *sombre, sévère* 6. **daring:** *audacieux* 7. **the deck:** *le pont du bateau*

2. **the soul:** *l'âme*
3. **self-reliance:** *l'autonomie*
4. **an epic:** *une épopée*

the heroine, who has committed adultery, has to wear a scarlet letter 'A' on her clothes.

• **Herman Melville** too had none of the optimism of the Transcendentalists and his novels, set at sea, are darkly symbolic. *Moby Dick* (1851) relates the hunting of the white whale[5] which bites off[6] one of the captain's legs. The voyage becomes a mythic one, which can be read at different levels; it can represent the American frontier and a religious quest for the meaning of the universe.

• The novels of **Mark Twain** (*Huckleberry Finn*, 1884) are humorous satires of Southern society, with its slavery and hypocrisy.

## Naturalism

Towards the end of the 19th century, realism became darker, turning to naturalism. People's lives are described in Darwinian terms; they are determined by heredity and environment; the world is a jungle in which only the fittest survive.

• In **Theodore Dreiser**'s *Sister Carrie* (1900), for example, people are obsessed with material success and social climbing.

• **Stephen Crane**'s *The Red Badge of Courage* (1895) is an attack against heroism. The novel takes place during the Civil War, and the sensitive hero who starts with dreams and illusions is soon faced with chaos and absurdity until he flees[7], terrified.

## Psychological realism

The novels of **Henry James** and **Edith Wharton** are set in wealthy[8] circles and analyze the moral dilemmas of sensitive and intelligent characters.

• **James**'s technique is often close to stream of consciousness (*The Portrait of a Lady*, 1880; *The Turn of the Screw*, 1898), while his main subject is the contrast between the innocence and vitality of the New World and the corruption and materialism of Europe.

• **Wharton**'s novels (*The House of Mirth*, 1905) satirize the ambition, hypocrisy and stifling[9] conventions of fashionable society. See p. 96

• The poetry of **Emily Dickinson** consists in the anatomy of a mind, its moods, perceptions, moral and religious explorations.

Whistler's paintings belong to the "art for art's sake" movement. What matters is not what is represented but the effect, the harmony of colours created.

James Abbot McNeill Whistler
*Nocturne in Black and Gold, The Falling Rocket*, 1875, Institute of Art, Detroit

**5. a whale:** *une baleine*
**6. to bite off:** *emporter d'un coup de dent*
**7. to flee:** *fuir*
**8. wealthy:** *riche*
**9. stifling:** *étouffant*

# The 20th century: until World War II (US)

## HISTORY

- **1917** US declares war on Germany
- **1919** Prohibition
- **1929** Wall Street crash leads to Depression years
- **1933** Roosevelt President: the New Deal
- **1941** The US enter WWII
- **1944** Allied landing in Normandy
- **1945** US bomb on Hiroshima Yalta

## POETRY

- **1916** **SANDBURG** *Chicago Poems*
- **1922** **ELIOT** *The Waste Land* (modernism and imagism)
- **1926** **HUGHES** *The Weary Blues*

The Harlem Renaissance: Black cultural movement also reflected in the novels of Richard Wright: 1945, *Black Boy*

## PROSE & FICTION

- **1919** **ANDERSON** *Winesburg, Ohio*
- **1922** **LEWIS** *Babbitt*

A satire of the narrow-mindedness of small-town America

- **1925** **FITZGERALD** *The Great Gatsby*
- **1929** **FAULKNER** *The Sound and the Fury*
  **HEMINGWAY** *A Farewell to Arms*

Fitzgerald, Hemingway, Dos Passos
THE LOST GENERATION
Modernist techniques to reflect a sense of emptiness and loss

- **1936** **DOS PASSOS** *USA*
- **1939** **STEINBECK** *The Grapes of Wrath*

Social awareness

The Southern Renaissance: Violent and grotesque characters reflecting guilt about and nostalgia for the Southern past

## THE THEATRE

- **1931** **O'NEILL** *Mourning Becomes Electra*
  Plays which unite realism and symbolism

## PAINTING

- The Ash Can School (HENRI, SLOAN)
- The Modernists (O'KEEFFE, STELLA, DAVIS)
- The precisionists (DEMUTH, SHEELER)
- The urban scene (HOPPER)
- The regionalists (BENTON, WOOD)

**DEMUTH** (1883-1935) *My Egypt*, 1927

**HOPPER** (1882-1967) *Nighthawks*, 1942

The years that followed World War I, with the sense of disillusionment it led to, can be divided into two very different periods.

## The Jazz Age or Roaring Twenties (until 1929)

This period was marked by growing prosperity: the car, the radio, the cinema and the telephone... began to transform people's lives. Credit and advertising encouraged consumption[1] and

*Tales of the Jazz Age*, cover of the 1922 first edition

the business boom encouraged speculation. It was accompanied by changes in manners: flappers (young women who cut their hair, wore short skirts, smoked and behaved unconventionally), bootleggers (who made illegal alcohol in those years of Prohibition[2]), dissipation – all showing individualism and the need to rebel against conventions and taboos. This liberation is reflected in the novels of the 'Lost Generation' (see below).

## Social concerns

The economic crisis brought about by the Wall Street crash in 1929 forced the nation to face unemployment and poverty and resulted in a stronger sense of community, which reached a climax[3] with Roosevelt's programs of federal involvement[4].

## Poetry

The poetry of **Robert Frost** does not experiment with form but mirrors[5] the disenchantment of the age through detachment and irony. It mainly describes the nature and activities of New England, which become the starting point of a reflection, as in the poem 'The Road Not Taken'.

**Robert Frost,**
**'The Road not Taken', in 1920**
**in *Complete Poems of Robert Frost*, 1967**

Two roads diverged in a yellow wood,
And sorry I could not travel both
And be one traveler, long I stood
And looked down one as far as I could
To where it bent in the undergrowth[1];

Then took the other, as just as fair,
And having perhaps the better claim[2],
Because it was grassy and wanted wear[3];
Though as for that the passing there
Had worn them really about the same,

And both that morning equally lay
In leaves no step had trodden[4] black.
Oh, I kept the first for another day!
Yet knowing how way leads on to way,
I doubted if I should ever come back.

I shall be telling this with a sigh
Somewhere ages and ages hence:
Two roads diverged in a wood, and I—
I took the one less traveled by,
And that has made all the difference.

**1. the undergrowth:** *le sous-bois* **2. having the better claim:** *il peut mieux y prétendre* **3. wanted wear:** *n'était pas piétiné* **4. trodden:** *participe passé de 'tread', piétiner*

**1. consumption:** *la consommation*
**2. prohibition:** *l'interdiction de la vente d'alcool*
**3. a climax:** *un point culminant*
**4. involvement:** *participation, engagement*
**5. to mirror:** *refléter*

As for **T. S. Eliot**, he was a modernist, who used collages of images and allusions to convey[6] the chaos and lack of spiritual values of contemporary civilization. His poetry shows the influence of Cubism, Futurism and cinematic techniques.

## The theatre

The plays of **Eugene O'Neill**, the first major American playwright, are realistic since they describe tragic characters who cannot reconcile their dreams and illusions with reality. But O'Neill also uses expressionistic techniques such as the use of dance, masks or choruses.

## The novel

### The Lost Generation

The expression describes a group of American writers who turned their backs on the values of America in the 1920s to find a more cosmopolitan life in Paris. Their sense of moral loss and meaninglessness is expressed through experimental narrative techniques influenced by painting or the cinema.

- **Ernest Hemingway** used a concise, laconic and detached style to describe heroes confronted with death and suffering. All that matters is to face them with stoicism and dignity. The world of his novels and stories is therefore one of violence: bullfights[7], hunting or war. (*A Farewell to Arms*, 1929; *The Old Man and the Sea*, 1952)
- **Francis Scott Fitzgerald**'s heroes are typical of the Jazz Age: their glamorous and dissipated lives and their obsession with money express their quest[8] for an unattainable American Dream. But they too often end up in depression, alcoholism and despair. (*The Great Gatsby*, 1925)

**6. to convey:** *exprimer*
**7. a bullfight:** *une corrida*
**8. a quest:** *une quête*

Hopper's paintings suggest the sadness and loneliness of urban life.
Edward HOPPER, *Automat*, 1927,
Des Moines Art Center, James D. Edmundson Foundation

• **John Dos Passos**'s *USA* (1938) is a trilogy which presents a social and political panorama of the United States between WWI and the Depression years. Using fragmentation and multiple voices, it alternates the biographies of well-known figures, fictional narratives, stream of consciousness sections and montages of headlines, songs or advertisements.

### John Dos Passos, "The Big Money", in *USA*, 1936

*USA* contains several biographies of influential or well-known people in America between the two wars. This is part of a biography of the actor Rudolph Valentino.

Valentino spent his life in the colorless glare[1] of krieg lights[2], in stucco villas obstructed with bricabrac, Oriental rugs, tiger-skins, in the bridal suites[3] of hotels, in silk bathrobes in private cars.

He was always getting into limousines

or getting out of limousines, or patting the necks of fine horses.

Wherever he went the sirens of the motorcyclecops screeched[4] ahead of him,

flashlights flared[5],

the streets were jumbled with hysterical faces, waving hands, crazy eyes; they stuck out their autographbooks, yanked his buttons off[6], cut a tail off his admirablytailored dress-suit[7]; they stole his hat and pulled at his necktie; his valets removed young women from under his bed; all night in nightclubs and cabarets actresses leching for[8] stardom made sheepseyes[9] at him under their mascaraed lashes.

He wanted to make good[10] under the glare of the million-dollar searchlights

of El Dorado:

the Sheik, the Son of the Sheik;

personal appearances.

**1. the glare:** *l'éclat aveuglant* **2. krieg lights:** spotlights **3. the bridal suite:** *la suite nuptiale (d'un hôtel)* **4. to screech:** *hurler* **5. to flare:** *briller, éclater* **6. to yank off:** *arracher* **7. a dress suit:** *une tenue de soirée* **8. to lech for:** *désirer, courir après* **9. to make sheep's eyes at:** *faire les yeux doux à* **10. to make good:** *réussir*

## The satire of provincial life

In novels such as *Babbitt* (1922), **Sinclair Lewis** attacks the hypocrisy, conformity, self-satisfaction and lack of cultural pursuits of small-town America. His characters are often close to caricature.

## Social concerns

During the Depression years, most writers abandoned their interest in experiment and became more concerned with the living conditions of ordinary Americans. Many of the novels of **John Steinbeck** (*The Grapes of Wrath*, 1939; *Of Mice and Men*, 1937) are about the tragedies which

A still from John Ford's *The Grapes of Wrath*, with Henry Fonda, 1940

resulted from the Great Depression. *The Grapes of Wrath* follows a group of Okies (inhabitants from Oklahoma) who lose everything during dust storms[9] and have to move to California to try and find work. They are exploited there by capitalism but become closer as a group through courage, solidarity and friendship. See p. 73

**9. a dust storm:** *une tempête de poussière*

**Langston HUGHES, 'Mother to Son', in *Selected Poems*, 1926**

Well, son, I'll tell you:
Life for me ain't been[1] no crystal stair.
It's had tacks[2] in it,
And splinters[3],
And boards[4] torn up[5],
And places with no carpet on the floor—
Bare[6].
But all the time
I'se[7] been a-climbin' on,
And reachin' landin's,
And turnin' corners,
And sometimes goin' in the dark
Where there ain't been no light.
So boy, don't you turn back.
Don't you set down[8] on the steps
'Cause you finds it's kinder[9] hard.
Don't you fall now—
For I'se still goin', honey,
I'se still climbin',
And life for me ain't been no crystal stair.

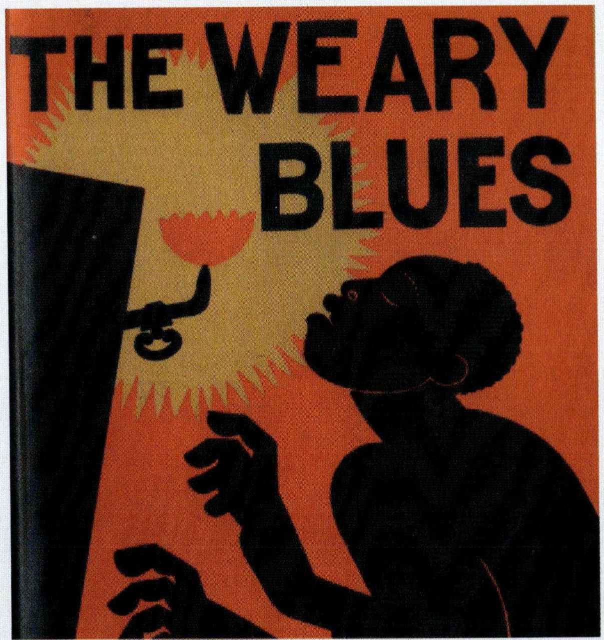

*The Weary Blues*, cover of the 1926 edition

**1. ain't been:** 'hasn't been' *(familier)* **2. tacks:** *des punaises, clous* **3. splinters:** *des échardes* **4. a board:** *une planche* **5. torn up:** 'to tear up': *arracher* **6. bare:** *nu* **7. I'se:** 'I've' *(familier)* **8. to set down:** to sit down **9. kinder:** 'kind of' *(familier)*

## The Harlem Renaissance

This cultural and literary movement appeared in Harlem in the 1920s, around a group of black writers, artists and musicians who took pride in their African identity. The poetry of **Langston Hughes** describes the struggles, the longings and the frustrations of poor Black Americans. Its rhythms are inspired by blues and jazz. See p. 104

## The Southern Renaissance

Haunted by its defeat in the Civil War, by racism (the Ku Klux Klan) and by religious intolerance, the South had for a long time been culturally isolated.

In the 1930s, a reaction took place, led by **William Faulkner**. His characters are obsessed by the past and by guilt, and the South is threatened by commercialism and corruption. This is conveyed by an atmosphere of violence: rape, incest or murder. Faulkner's novels are also experimental, using dislocated time, stream of consciousness and multiple points of view to render the complexity of thought. (*The Sound and the Fury*, 1929).

# The 20th century: after WW II (US)

## HISTORY

- **1947** Beginning of Cold War
- **1950-53** Korean War
- **1953** Anti-communist crusade
- **1955-56** Montgomery bus boycott
- **1960** Kennedy president: New Frontier
- **1963** Equal Rights march on Washington; Kennedy assassinated
- **1964-73** Vietnam War
- **1969** First landing on the moon

## POETRY

- **1946** **BISHOP** *North and South*
- **1951** **RICH** *A change of World*
- **1956** **GINSBERG** *Howl* — The Beat poets: A reaction against mainstream values and culture
- **1959** **LOWELL** *Life Studies*
- **1965** **PLATH** *Ariel*

Bishop, Rich, Lowell, Plath: Confessionnal poets (lyrical and intimate expression of feeling)

## PROSE & FICTION

- **1948** **MAILER** *The Naked and the Dead*
- **1951** **SALINGER** *The Catcher in the Rye*; **McCULLERS** *The Ballad of the Sad Café*
- **1952** **ELLISON** *Invisible Man*
- **1955** **NABOKOV** *Lolita*
- **1957** **KEROUAC** *On the Road*; **MALAMUD** *The Assistant*
- **1960** **UPDIKE** *Rabbit, Run*
- **1961** **HELLER** *Catch-22*
- **1964** **BELLOW** *Herzog*
- **1965** **O'CONNOR** *Everything that Rises Must Converge*
- **1966** **CAPOTE** *In Cold Blood*
- **1966** **ROTH** *Portnoy's Complaint*; **VONNEGUT** *Slaughterhouse-Five*

## THE THEATRE

- **1947** **WILLIAMS T.** *A Streetcar Named Desire*
- **1953** **MILLER** *The Crucible*
- **1962** **ALBEE** *Who's Afraid of Virginia Woolf?*

1947–1953: Individuals crushed by materialism and conformity

1962: The theatre of the Absurd

## PAINTING

- **Realism** (WYETH)
- **Abstraction** (POLLOCK, KLINE, DE KOONING, NEWMAN, ROTHKO)
- **Pop Art** (JOHNS, RAUSCHENBERG, WARHOL, LICHTENSTEIN, ROSENQUIST)

**Pollock** (1912-1956) *Number 4*, 1949

**Rothko** (1903-1970) *Untitled*, 1953-1954

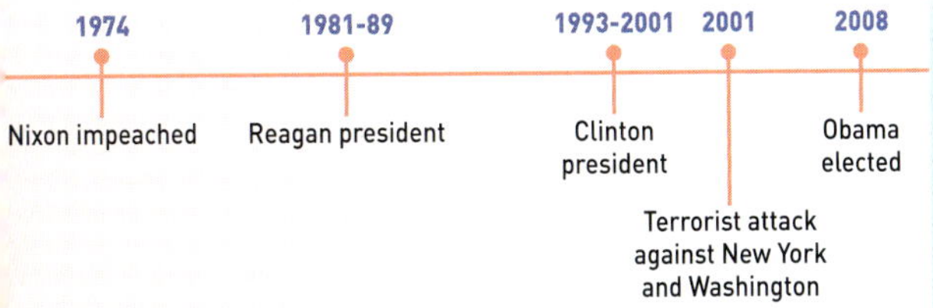


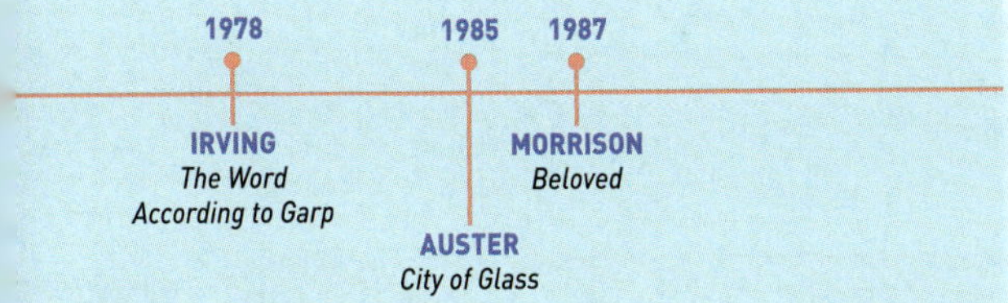


Many political and social events influenced literature in the second half of the 20th century:

- the Holocaust and the scars left by World War II,
- the Cold War and the anti-Communist persecutions of the McCarthy years,
- the protests and civil rights marches of the 1960s,
- the Vietnam War,
- the Watergate affair and the impeachment of President Nixon,
- more recently the 9/11 attacks upon the United States and the war on terrorism.

Here are the major literary trends[1] since 1945.

## The theatre

The plays produced after WWII show the way human beings can become the victims of society.

- In the plays of **Tennessee Williams** (*A Streetcar Named Desire*, 1947), violence, rape and incest are the result of the frustrations of characters who cannot live out[2] their illusions, who are dreamers obsessed by the past. The plays use symbolism and many theatrical effects (lighting and sound effects).
- **Arthur Miller**'s plays show simple, ordinary Americans and the clash between their private and public lives. In *Death of a Salesman* (1949), Willy believes in the success myth, in the American Dream until, old and exhausted, he loses his job as a salesman. *The Crucible* (1953), inspired by the McCarthy witch-hunts, is about the persecution of witches in 17th century Salem. See p. 77

1. **a trend:** *une tendance*
2. **to live out:** *accomplir*

## 'The Beat writers'

The 'Beat writers' were rebels against capitalism, the consumer society and Cold War politics. In their search for an interior truth, any means was acceptable: sex, hallucinogens but also meditation and religious mysticism. They also believed in spontaneous writing to convey the intensity of experience without the intervention of reason. This is clear in the poetry of **Lawrence Ferlinghetti**, in **Allen Ginsberg**'s poem 'Howl' (1956), which shocked America, and in **Jack Kerouac**'s novel *On the Road* (1957), an endless journey through America.

## Southern literature

The decline of the Old South is still the theme of many novels by Southern novelists. It is reflected by violence, grotesque characters and lack of communication. In the novels of **Carson Mc Cullers**, love is always one-sided and therefore doomed[3] (*The Heart is a Lonely Hunter*, 1940, *The Ballad of the Sad Café*, 1951). **Harper Lee**'s *To Kill a Mockingbird* (1960) is about a white lawyer who defends a black man accused of rape[4] in Alabama.

**3. doomed:** *condamné*
**4. a rape:** *un viol*

**Lawrence FERLINGHETTI,**
**'I am waiting', stanza I,**
**in *A Coney Island of the Mind*, 1958**

I am waiting for my case[1] to come up
and I am waiting
for a rebirth of wonder[2]
and I am waiting for someone
to really discover America
and wail[3]
and I am waiting
for the discovery
of a new symbolic western frontier
and I am waiting
for the American Eagle[4]
to really spread its wings
and straighten up and fly right
and I am waiting
for the Age of Anxiety
to drop dead
and I am waiting
for the war to be fought
which will make the world safe
for anarchy
and I am waiting
for the final withering away[5]
of all governments
and I am perpetually awaiting
a rebirth of wonder

**1. a case:** *procès* **2. wonder:** *l'émerveillement* **3. to wail:** *hurler*
**4. an eagle:** *un aigle* **5. to wither away:** *s'étioler, se fâner*

Rauschenberg was one of the pop artists who mocked the vulgarity of American culture. His paintings often contain collages of three dimensional objects which evoke real life rather than art.

**Robert RAUSCHENBERG, *Axle*, 1964**
**Museum Ludwig, Cologne**

The banality of the US map is rendered vibrant and original through Jasper Johns's expressionist technique.

Jasper JOHNS, *Map*, 1963, Museum of Modern Art, New York

The stories of **Flannery O'Connor** show how violence and the evils of society can still lead to redemption and grace.

## Non-fiction

In the 1960s, several writers explored the relationship between fiction and journalism. You find such neo-realism, for instance, in many of **Norman Mailer**'s novels as well as in **Truman Capote**'s *In Cold Blood*, the story of a mass-murder in Kansas.

## New voices

After WWII, several groups, minorities and ethnic communities began to establish their identity and to be more widely represented in literature. The themes of suffering, estrangement[5] and of a search for recognition[6] are common ones in their works.

**5. estrangement:** *la séparation*
**6. recognition:** *le fait d'être reconnu*

[redacted]

**1. a spook:** *un fantôme*

- **Black voices:** **Ralph Ellison**'s *Invisible Man* (1952); **James Baldwin**'s *Go Tell It on the Mountain* (1953); **Toni Morrison**'s *The Bluest Eye* (1970) or *Beloved* (1987).
- **Women's voices:** **Joyce Carol Oates** (*We Were the Mulvaneys*, 1996); **Grace Paley** (*The Little Disturbances of Man*, 1959).
- **Jewish voices** (the traumas left by the Holocaust, the tense relationship between Jews and Gentiles, often related with distance and humour): **Saul Bellow**'s *Herzog* (1964); **Philip Roth**'s *The Human Stain* (2000).

## Novels of Manners

Such novels focus on the lives of a social group, with their frictions, tensions and doubts, often with a satirical point of view. The main characters of **J. D. Salinger**'s short stories and only novel (*The Catcher in the Rye*, 1951) are idealistic and sensitive children and adolescents who are confronted with the hypocrisy and self-interest of society.

**John Updike**'s novels and stories are set in suburban communities and show the changes brought about by materialism, infidelity, and lack [redacted]

## Postmodernist fiction

In order to renew and mock the form of fiction and to express the emptiness and confusion of society, several writers in the 1960s and 1970s used farce, parody and absurdity. The novels of **Vladimir Nabokov**, **Joseph Heller**, **Kurt Vonnegut** and **Paul Auster** all reflect this tendency in different ways. See p. 121

**John UPDIKE, *Rabbit, Run*, 1961**

"I'll be right back," he says.

As he goes down the stairs worries come as quick as the clicks of his footsteps. Janice, money, Eccles's phone call, the look on his mother's face all clatter[1] together in sharp dark waves; guilt and responsibility slide together like two substantial shadows inside his chest. The mere engineering[2] of it – the conversations, the phone calls, the lawyers, the finances – seems to complicate, physically, in front of his mouth, so he is conscious of the effort of breathing, and every action, just reaching for the doorknob, feels like a precarious extension of a long mechanical sequence insecurely linked to his heart. The doorknob's solidity answers his touch, and turns nicely.

Outside in the air his fears condense.

1. **to clatter:** *résonner* 2. **to engineer:** *concevoir, manigancer*

Warhol's repetitions of well-known objects or people force us to view them in a different way and are a reflection on mass-production.
Andy WARHOL, Colored Campbell's Soup Can, 1965
Museum of Modern Art NY

# Canada

It was in 1867 that the British North America Act turned Canada into a federal dominion. But it was only after 1920 that a real Canadian literature – not influenced by Europe or the United States – appeared. Large waves of immigrants coming from non-European countries after 1970 also brought new questions about Canadian culture and identity.

In the early 20th century, the 'Group of Seven' was a group of painters who used bold colours and rugged[1] shapes to paint the Canadian landscape.

Lawren HARRIS, *Algoma Country*, 1920-1921
Gallery of Ontario, Toronto

## Recurrent themes

In Canadian literature they are:

› the huge expanse of land and space: the prairie, lakes and forests, life in isolated small towns, the severe, inhospitable climate,

› the multicultural background since Canada is a land of immigration, but also the relationship between the French and English communities and the place of native Indians in society,

› the search for a Canadian identity, free from the influence of English and French colonialism, but also from the economic and cultural domination of the neighbouring United States.

For the reasons given above, **Margaret Atwood** explained that the central symbol of Canadian literature was survival.

## Major writers

• **Margaret Atwood**'s poems and novels are often about women who have been victimized by society – by men, by colonialism, by immigration – and who try to free themselves See p. 53 (*Alias Grace*, 1996).

• **Michael Ondaatje**'s novels are highly lyrical and poetic and explore the nature of identity. (*The English Patient*, 1992).

1. **rugged:** *rude, sauvage*

**Margaret ATWOOD, 'The Immigrants', last stanza, in *Eating Fire*, 1998**

my mind is a wide pink map
across which move year after year
arrows and dotted lines[1], further and further,
people in railway cars
their heads stuck out of the windows
at stations, drinking milk and singing,
their features hidden with beards or shawls[2]
day and night riding across an ocean of unknown
land to an unknown land.

1. **dotted lines:** *des pointillés* 2. **a shawl:** *un châle*

# Australia and New Zealand

Australia became independent in 1901 and New Zealand became a dominion in 1907. Both countries also reached literary maturity in the early 20th century.

The Australian painter Sir Sidney Nolan was inspired by Australian history and painted several pictures of Ned Kelly behind his helmet.
Sir Sidney NOLAN, *Ned Kelly*, 1955, Private Collection

## Australia

The main themes to be found in Australian literature are:

- the difficulty of accepting the past as a penal colony,
- the desolate wilderness of the bush, but also the sense of adventure it evoked with the free and open life of the bushrangers, and the spirit of mateship[1] (equality and friendship) it led to – a central concept in Australian culture, becoming an 'Australian myth'.

• The figure of Ned Kelly in particular is central to Australian history and literature. He was a 19th century bushranger who became an outlaw and the leader of a gang, but also a folk hero for his rebellion against British authority. He inspired **Robert Drewe**'s *Our Sunshine* (1991) and **Peter Carey**'s *True History of the Kelly Gang* (2001).

## New Zealand

The main themes to be found in New Zealand literature are:

- the beauty of the natural landscape,
- the condition of the Maoris.

## Major writers

• The novels of **Patrick White** (*Voss*, 1957) are about individuals alienated from others and having to cope with an inhospitable environment. They are studies in suffering and redemption.

• The major New Zealand writer is **Katherine Mansfield**, who at the beginning of the 20th century wrote short stories (*The Garden Party and other stories*, 1922) describing the subtle feelings of sensitive people confronted with selfishness or indifference.

1. **mateship:** *la camaraderie (en anglais australien)*

# The Caribbean

There is little political, ethnic, cultural or literary unity in the various islands which form the Caribbean, or West Indies. But this very diversity has led to:

- a concern with identity, with a sense of estrangement[1], a major theme in Caribbean literature,
- an interest in local culture, with its myths and rituals, even its belief in the supernatural,
- a satire of colonialism.

## Major writers

### • Jean Rhys

Her novels often portray women who are lonely, sensitive and vulnerable. Away from their homeland they feel alienated and are sexually exploited. In *Wide Sargasso Sea* (1966), Jean Rhys imagines the story of Bertha, the mad wife of Mr Rochester in Charlotte Brontë's *Jane Eyre*. Bertha, or rather Antoinette in the novel, is rejected by both whites and blacks because she is a Creole, and the indifference of her husband gradually leads her to madness. The fact that she is a victim and that her story is both part of *Jane Eyre* and a response to that authoritative text is symbolic of post-colonial writing. See p. 141

### • V. S. Naipaul

Often caught between two cultures, the protagonists of V. S. Naipaul's novels feel alienated in their own society as well as in the Western world. Naipaul presents a satirical view of both Caribbean life and an imperialist, commercial Western society. (*A House for Mr Biswas*, 1961).

### • Derek Walcott

His poems and plays are about the difficulty of defining one's identity, because of his mixed African and European ancestry[2], but also because of the loss of Caribbean culture after British colonisation.

1. **estrangement:** *la séparation, l'éloignement*
2. **ancestry:** *les ancêtres*

H. Simon is a British silk-painter whose themes are often influenced by Central America.

Hilary SIMON, *Cabbages and Lilies, Solola Region, Guatemala*, 1993 (Coloured inks on silk), Private Collection

**V. S. NAIPAUL, *A Bend in the River*, 1979**

Home was hardly a place I could return to. Home was something in my head. It was something I had lost.

**Derek WALCOTT,**
**'*A Far Cry from Africa*', 1964**

Where shall I turn, divided to the vein?
I who have cursed[1]
The drunken officer of British rule,
  how choose
Between this Africa and the English tongue
  I love?
Betray[2] them both, or give back what they give?
How can I face such slaughter[3] and be cool?
How can I turn from Africa and live?

1. **to curse:** *maudire* 2. **to betray:** *trahir*
3. **a slaughter:** *un massacre*

# South Africa

## From Apartheid to Democracy

South Africa became a dominion in 1910. After the Afrikaner National Party won the elections in 1948, it established Apartheid in South Africa, that is to say a system of racial control and of separation between coloured/blacks and whites. Blacks were exploited and lived in poor townships, mixed marriages were banned, and the regime became increasingly oppressive. It was only in 1994, when Nelson Mandela became president, that the country's Constitution became fully democratic.

The years of Apartheid deeply marked South African writers, whose main themes are:

- the relationship between races,
- confronting violence and violations,
- the right (or not) of white writers to speak on behalf of[1] blacks.

Pemba's paintings depict the lives of poor black people in townships.

George Mnyalaza Milwa PEMBA
*Uhuru-Celebration of independence*, 1992,
Private Collection

## Major writers

### • Nadine Gordimer

Her novels offer a realistic portrait of life under Apartheid in both black and white communities. They deal with discrimination, with attempts to bridge the divide and with love across the colour line, but also explore the world of political movements and activists. (*A World of Strangers*, 1958; *My Son's Story*, 1990).

### • André Brink

In André Brink's novels, the protagonists are often dissidents and rebels who defy the Apartheid state. *A Dry White Season* (1979) is about someone's attempt to discover the truth about the death of a black activist while in detention.

### • J. M. Coetzee

His novels are more allegorical and post-modern and examine themes such as authority and history. *Waiting for the Barbarians* (1980) is the story of an official in an imaginary country who is constantly preparing for an attack from barbarians who may well not exist at all. *Disgrace* (1999) takes place in post-Apartheid South Africa and shows a society which is still full of violence and divisions.

**J. M. COETZEE,**
***Waiting for the Barbarians*, 1980**

One thought alone preoccupies the submerged mind of Empire: how not to end, how not to die, how to prolong its era. By day it pursues its enemies. It is cunning[1] and ruthless[2], it sends its bloodhounds[3] everywhere. By night it feeds on images of disaster: the sack[4] of cities, the rape of populations, pyramids of bones, acres of desolation.

1. **cunning:** *fourbe* 2. **ruthless:** *impitoyable*
3. **a bloodhound:** *un limier* 4. **a sack:** *pillage*

1. **on behalf of:** *au nom de*

# India

India, the first of Britain's colonies to gain full independence in 1947, had often been used as the subject of British novels and poetry, by Kipling and Forster in particular. But it is only recently, in the last three decades, that Indian literature written in English has been universally recognized.

In Indian literature, the recurrent themes are:

› the British influence,

› poverty, injustice, the caste system and the plight[1] of the untouchables,

› Hinduism and Islam and their cultural traditions,

› the violence and religious extremism which accompanied independence and the partition between India and Pakistan,

› the ambiguous position of the English language, reminiscent of colonialism, but also acclimatized to India, appropriated or 'Indianised', and often characterized by liveliness[2] and linguistic creativity.

## Major writers

### • R. K. Narayan

This prolific writer offers a portrait of Indian life between the 1930s and the end of the 20th century. He writes with compassion and humour about everyday events, struggles and psychological crises such as an arranged marriage in *The Bachelor of Arts* (1937).

### • Vikram Seth

He has written both fiction and poetry with great linguistic virtuosity. *The Golden Gate* (1986) is a novel in verse (sonnets written in iambic tetrameters) about the relationships between a group of young professionals in San Francisco. *A Suitable Boy* (1993), a long novel of 'social realism', offers a portrait of India in the 1950s and is about the choice of a husband.

### • Anita Desai

Her novels and stories are about identity: oppressive family relationships, lack of recognition, alienation from society. They examine the inner lives of her characters but also convey a good sense of atmosphere and of the cultural and political background. (*In Custody*, 1984; *Games at Twilight*, short stories, 1978).

### • Arundhati Roy

In *The God of Small Things* (1997), Arundhati Roy tells the complex story of a family, mainly seen from the point of view of children who become the victims of the caste system, of political upheaval and of the family's emotional wounds.

**Vikram Seth, *A Suitable Boy*, 1993**

Lata studies at university and has met a student she likes there. Her mother has just found out. Savita is her sister.

"He has a name, doesn't he? What is he – Kabir Lal, Kabir Mehra – or what? Are you wanting the tea to get cold? Or have you forgotten?"

Lata closed her eyes.

"Kabir Durrani," she said, and waited for the house to come tumbling down[1].

The three deadly syllables had their effect. Mrs Rupa Mehra clutched[2] at her heart, opened her mouth in silent horror, looked unseeingly around the room, and sat down.

Savita rushed to her immediately. Her own heart was beating far too fast.

One last possibility struck Mrs Rupâ Mehra. "Is he a Parsi?" she asked weakly, almost pleadingly[3]. The thought was odious, but not so calamitously horrifying. But a look at Savita's face told her the truth.

"A Muslim!" said Mrs Rupa Mehra, more to herself now than to anyone else. "What did I do in my past life that I have brought this upon my beloved daughter?"

1. **to tumble down:** *s'effondrer* 2. **to clutch:** *saisir*
3. **pleadingly:** *d'un ton suppliant*

1. **the plight:** *la situation épouvantable*
2. **liveliness:** *la vitalité*

# Utopias and dystopias

## Utopias

• There is a long tradition of utopia writing in British literature.

A **utopia** is a work describing a visionary system of political and/or social perfection. The word utopia was first used by Thomas More and comes from the Greek ou-topos (no-where) or *eu-topos* (place of happiness). Indeed, utopias usually take place in imaginary, inaccessible countries, where reason and common sense have led to peace and happiness.

• Utopias tend to be written in periods of political stability, when strong governments make it difficult or dangerous for a writer to criticize the political regime directly. In a utopia, criticism is indirect, giving us a sort of negative of a country and its government at the time.

## Dystopias

In the 20th century, the feeling of anxiety, horror and insecurity which was the result of two world wars and the dissolution of the British empire, led to a shift[1] from utopia to **dystopia**. A dystopia describes a world which is frighteningly evil or absurd. It is no longer a negative of our own world but describes some dangerous tendencies in our own society, the misuse[2] of science for example.

Thomas MORE, from the first edition of *Utopia*, with an engraving by Hans HOLBEIN.

## Early utopias

• The idea of a utopia is a very old one, since it appears in 14th-century poems like *The Land of Cockaygne*, which describes a perfect country reminiscent of the Earthly Paradise, where there is no work but all is "play, joy and mirth." It is clearly the utopia of the hard-working peasants of the Middle Ages.

> Cockaygne offers better fare[1],
> And without worry, work, or care[2];
> The food is good, the drink flows free
> At lunchtime, suppertime, and tea.
> It's true without a doubt, I swear,
> No earthly country could compare;
> Under heaven no land but this
> Has such abundant joy and bliss[3].
>
> From *The Land Of Cockaygne*, Anonymous, 1330s

1. **fare:** la nourriture 2. **care:** l'inquiétude, la responsabilité 3. **bliss:** félicité

## Thomas More

**Thomas More**'s *Utopia* was written in Latin in 1515-1516. He was a politician and humanist who became Henry VIII's Chancellor of the Exchequer[3], but was executed in 1535 for opposing the king's break with Rome. *Utopia* is a condemnation of various aspects of England: the system of justice in which people steal because they have no work; the system of enclosures[4] which only favours[5] the rich; the obsession with property and money.

1. **a shift:** *un changement*
2. **misuse:** *usage abusif, mauvais emploi*
3. **Chancellor of the Exchequer:** *chancelier de l'Échiquier, ministre des Finances*
4. **enclosure:** *le fait de clore, d'entourer par des haies, des espaces autrefois publics*
5. **favour:** *favoriser*

• In *Utopia*. (1)There is no private property, so there is no reason for theft[6] or ambition. Similarly, gold and silver have no value. (2) People elect representatives, who elect rulers, who elect a Prince, who has all political power (like Tudor monarchs), but it is a power based on merit, not inheritance. (3) The family is important, but separation by mutual consent is possible. (4) All children should be taught to read, but should also know about agriculture and sciences. They should be able to choose their profession. The working week is limited to 56 hours. (5) There is religious tolerance.

## Later utopias

• Several utopias followed over the years. **Francis Bacon**'s *New Atlantis* (1622) was based upon the development of science. **Samuel Butler**'s *Erewhon* (1872, the title is an anagram of 'Nowhere') is an attack against machinery and all mechanical materialism. **William Morris**'s *News from Nowhere* (1890) is influenced by Marxism but also shows a longing for[7] an agricultural society where labour[8] is not alienated.

Another vision of nightmare: Francis BACON, *After Velásquez's Portrait of Pope Innocent X*, 1953, coll. William Burden, New York

• As for **Jonathan Swift**'s *Gulliver's Travels* (1726), it is not a real utopia, but comes close to it, since Gulliver's travels lead him to several imaginary countries, some reasonable and some absurd, but all allowing the author to develop his satire against the institutions of his own country.

## Nightmarish utopias

• In the 20th century, dystopias focused not so much on imaginary worlds as on our world in the future – and on a world which is no longer ideal but has become nightmarish[9], as if the possibility of describing an ideal world had become almost indecent in the face of the anguish and terror of the times.

• In **Aldous Huxley**'s *Brave New World* (1932), genetic engineering[10] and conditioning have eradicated pain, old age and emotions. Bred[11] in bottles, babies are predestined to their various functions in society as they are divided into five groups, from alpha pluses down to epsilon minuses. Everyone is controlled through their minds. So every one is "happy" until an outsider comes and disrupts the order of society...

• **George Orwell**'s *1984*, describes a totalitarian country (Oceania) which follows the doctrine of Ingsoc (which evokes English Socialism). Big Brother and the Thought Police control everything with methods reminiscent of Nazism and Stalinism. There is no privacy, history is distorted, language is reduced to simplify people's thoughts, and dissenters are annihilated. Winston Smith, the only man left with emotions and ideas of his own, carries on a forbidden love affair, is arrested and then tortured into betraying[12] his friend and loving Big Brother.

• In 1986, the Canadian writer **Margaret Atwood** also wrote a dystopia, *The Handmaid's Tale*, which examines two favourite themes of hers: women's fate and survival. In the Republic of Gilead, a totalitarian state which has replaced the USA, pollution has caused a high rate of sterility. The women who are fertile are called Handmaids and are forced to couple with men, particularly the rich and influential ones. Any dissent is punished by death.

**6. theft:** *le vol*
**7. a longing for:** *un désir de*
**8. labour:** *le travail*
**9. nightmarish:** *cauchemardesque*
**10. genetic engineering:** *manipulations génétiques*
**11. bred:** *fabriqués* (to breed: *élever*)
**12. to betray:** *trahir*

## TEXT 1 Thomas MORE ~ Utopia, 1515-16 Book II

**Thomas MORE**
(1478-1535)
was Henry VIII's Chancellor of the Exchequer.
His *Utopia* (1515-16) is a condemnation of various aspects of England: the system of justice, the system of enclosures and the obsession with property and money.

IN CHOOSING THEIR WIVES they use a method that would appear to us very absurd and ridiculous, but it is constantly observed among them, and is accounted[1] perfectly consistent with[2] wisdom[3]. Before marriage some grave matron[4] presents the bride naked, whether she is a virgin or a widow, to the bridegroom; and after that some grave man presents the bridegroom naked to the bride. We indeed both laughed at this, and condemned it as very indecent. But they, on the other hand, wondered at the folly of the men of all other nations, who, if they are but to buy a horse of a small value, are so cautious that they will see every part of him, and take off both his saddle[5] and all his other tackle[6], that there may be no secret ulcer hid under any of them; and that yet in the choice of a wife, on which depends the happiness or unhappiness of the rest of his life, a man should venture upon trust[7], and only see about a hand's-breadth of the face, all the rest of the body being covered, under which there may lie hid what may be contagious as well as loathsome[8]. All men are not so wise as to choose a woman only for her good qualities; and even wise men consider the body as that which adds not a little to the mind: and it is certain there may be some such deformity covered with the clothes as may totally alienate[9] a man from his wife when it is too late to part[10] from her. If such a thing is discovered after marriage, a man has no remedy but patience. They therefore think it is reasonable that there should be good provision[11] made against such mischievous[12] frauds.

**1. accounted:** considérée **2. consistent with:** en accord avec **3. wisdom:** la sagesse **4. a matron:** une matrone **5. a saddle:** une selle **6. the tackle:** l'équipement **7. to venture upon trust:** se risquer à faire confiance **8. loathsome:** détestable **9. to alienate:** aliéner **10. to part:** se séparer **11. provision:** précautions, dispositions **12. mischievous:** malveillant

### Zooming in

1. There are three main parts in the text. Sum up what they are about.
   - **a.** (down to 'to the bride', line 5)
   - **b.** (down to 'loathsome', line 14)
   - **c.** (down to the end)
2. Contrast the way a man chooses his wife in the early 16th century and on the island of Utopia.
3. Underline all the words which belong to commercial vocabulary. What is their significance according to you?
4. Does the narrator show his opinion?

# TEXT 2 ALDOUS HUXLEY ~ BRAVE NEW WORLD, 1932 CHAPTER 2

**Aldous HUXLEY**
(1894-1963)
believed in progress through spiritual life rather than through science. This is why *Brave New World* is a dystopia about scientific conditioning.

*The Director is taking a group of students round to show them how the hypnopaedic process works: babies are conditioned into accepting the caste they have been born into through genetic manipulation.*

EIGHTY COTS[1] STOOD IN A ROW against the wall. There was a sound of light regular breathing and a continuous murmur, as of very faint voices remotely whispering.

A nurse rose as they entered and came to attention before the Director.

"What's the lesson this afternoon?" he asked.

"We had Elementary Sex for the first forty minutes," she answered. "But now it's switched over[2] to Elementary Class Consciousness."

The Director walked slowly down the long line of cots. Rosy and relaxed with sleep, eighty little boys and girls lay softly breathing. There was a whisper under every pillow. The D.H.C[3]. halted and, bending over one of the little beds, listened attentively.

"Elementary Class Consciousness, did you say? Let's have it repeated a little louder by the trumpet."

At the end of the room a loud speaker projected from the wall. The Director walked up to it and pressed a switch.

"... all wear green," said a soft but very distinct voice, beginning in the middle of a sentence, "and Delta Children wear khaki. Oh no, I don't want to play with Delta children. And Epsilons are still worse. They're too stupid to be able to read or write. Besides they wear black, which is such a beastly colour. I'm so glad I'm a Beta."

There was a pause; then the voice began again.

"Alpha children wear grey. They work much harder than we do, because they're so frightfully clever. I'm really awfully glad I'm a Beta, because I don't work so hard. And then we are much better than the Gammas and Deltas. Gammas are stupid. They all wear green, and Delta children wear khaki. Oh no, I don't want to play with Delta children. And Epsilons are still worse. They're too stupid to be able ..."

The Director pushed back the switch. The voice was silent. Only its thin ghost continued to mutter[4] from beneath the eighty pillows.

"They'll have that repeated forty or fifty times more before they wake; then again on Thursday, and again on Saturday. A hundred and twenty times three times a week for thirty months. After which they go on to a more advanced lesson."

Roses and electric shocks, the khaki of Deltas and a whiff[5] of asafœtida[6] – wedded[7] indissolubly before the child can speak. But wordless conditioning is crude[8] and wholesale; cannot bring home the finer distinctions, cannot inculcate the more complex courses of behaviour. For that there must be words, but words without reason. In brief, hypnopædia.

**1. a cot:** *un lit d'enfant* **2. to switch over:** *changer de station* **3. D.H.C.:** Director of Hatcheries and Conditioning **4. to mutter:** *marmonner* **5. a whiff:** *une bouffée* **6. asafoetida:** *une odeur fétide.* **7. to wed:** *marier* **8. crude:** *grossier*

## Zooming in

1. Children have been genetically manipulated to belong to 5 castes in *Brave New World*. What are the highest and the lowest? And what caste do the children in the cots belong to?
2. Make a list of all the words which refer to voice and language. What do they show?
3. What are all the forms of conditioning mentioned in the text?
4. Show how the passage reflects the theme of repetition.
5. How does this dystopia compare with that of *1984*?

## TEXT 3 GEORGE ORWELL ~ 1984, 1949 CHAPTER 1 (THE INCIPIT)

**George ORWELL**
(1903-1950)
was the pseudonym of Eric Arthur Blair. He was a committed socialist, who as a novelist, essayist and journalist denounced British imperialism and social problems such as poverty and unemployment. *Animal Farm* and *1984* are warnings against totalitarianism.

IT WAS A BRIGHT COLD DAY IN APRIL, and the clocks were striking thirteen. Winston Smith, his chin nuzzled[1] into his breast in an effort to escape the vile wind, slipped quickly through the glass doors of Victory Mansions, though not quickly enough to prevent a swirl[2] of gritty dust[3] from entering along with him.

The hallway smelt of boiled cabbage[4] and old rag[5] mats[6]. At one end of it a coloured poster, too large for indoor display[7], had been tacked to the wall. It depicted simply an enormous face, more than a metre wide: the face of a man of about forty-five, with a heavy black moustache and ruggedly handsome features. Winston made for the stairs. It was no use trying the lift. Even at the best of times it was seldom working, and at present the electric current was cut off during daylight hours. It was part of the economy drive in preparation for Hate Week. The flat was seven flights up, and Winston, who was thirty-nine and had a varicose ulcer above his right ankle, went slowly, resting several times on the way. On each landing, opposite the lift-shaft, the poster with the enormous face gazed from the wall. It was one of those pictures which are so contrived that the eyes follow you about when you move. BIG BROTHER IS WATCHING YOU, the caption beneath it ran.

Inside the flat a fruity voice was reading out a list of figures which had something to do with the production of pig-iron[8]. The voice came from an oblong metal plaque like a dulled mirror which formed part of the surface of the right-hand wall. Winston turned a switch and the voice sank somewhat, though the words were still distinguishable. The instrument (the telescreen, it was called) could be dimmed[9], but there was no way of shutting it off completely. He moved over to the window: a smallish, frail figure, the meagreness of his body merely emphasized by the blue overalls which were the uniform of the party. His hair was very fair, his face naturally sanguine, his skin roughened by coarse soap and blunt[10] razor blades and the cold of the winter that had just ended.

Outside, even through the shut window-pane, the world looked cold. Down in the street little eddies of wind were whirling dust and torn paper into spirals, and though the sun was shining and the sky a harsh blue, there seemed to be no colour in anything, except the posters that were plastered everywhere. The blackmoustachio'd face gazed down from every commanding corner. There was one on the house-front immediately opposite. BIG BROTHER IS WATCHING YOU, the caption said, while the dark eyes looked deep into Winston's own. Down at streetlevel another poster, torn at one corner, flapped[11] fitfully in the wind, alternately covering and uncovering the single word INGSOC[12]. In the far distance a helicopter skimmed down[13] between the roofs, hovered[14] for an instant like a bluebottle[15], and darted away[16] again with a curving flight. It was the police patrol, snooping[17] into people's windows. The patrols did not matter, however. Only the Thought Police mattered.

Behind Winston's back the voice from the telescreen was still babbling away about pig-iron and the overfulfilment[18] of the Ninth Three-Year Plan. The telescreen received and transmitted simultaneously. Any sound that Winston made, above the level of a very low whisper, would be picked up by it, moreover, so long as he remained within the field of vision which the metal plaque commanded, he could be seen as well as heard. There was of course no way of knowing whether you were being watched at any given moment. How often, or on what system, the Thought Police plugged in[19] on any individual wire was guesswork. It was even conceivable that they watched everybody all the time. But at any rate they could plug in your wire whenever they wanted to. You had to live — did live, from habit that became instinct — in the assumption that every sound you made was overheard, and, except in darkness, every movement scrutinized.

**1. nuzzled:** *enfoui* **2. a swirl:** *un tourbillon* **3. gritty dust:** *poussière mêlée de sable ou de cendres* **4. a cabbage:** *un chou* **5. a rag:** *un chiffon* **6. a mat:** *un paillasson* **7. for indoor display:** *pour être affichée à l'intérieur* **8. pig iron:** *la fonte* **9. to dim:** *réduire la luminosité, mettre en veilleuse* **10. blunt:** *émoussé* **11. to flap:** *battre (au vent)* **12. INGSOC:** English Socialism, the party in power **13. to skim down:** *plonger le long des maisons* **14. to hover:** *planer* **15. a bluebottle:** *une mouche bleue* (in the English slang of the time, the 'bluebottles' were the police) **16. to dart away:** *partir comme une flèche* **17. to snoop:** *espionner* **18. overfulfilment:** *le dépassement des objectifs* **19. to plug in:** *se brancher sur*

## Zooming in

**1** What progression can you find from paragraph 1 to paragraph 5?

**2** The setting
List the elements which show that the setting is between the normal (and dismal[1]) and the strange (and surreal[2]).
Normal / dismal elements
Strange / surreal elements

**3** Control
How are individuals controlled in this society?
Underline all the words which refer to looking or watching.

**4** Contrast Winston Smith and Big Brother:
What do their names evoke?
What about their physical description?
What do they stand for[3]?

**5** What comparisons are used in the text? What is their effect?

**6** Politics
Are any words reminiscent of politics in 1948, when the book was published? What political regimes does Orwell condemn?

1. dismal: *lugubre* 2. surreal: *surréaliste*
3. to stand for: *représenter, incarner*

## MOVING ON

***Read***

- H.G. Wells, *A Modern Utopia* (1905), *The Island of Doctor Moreau* (1896)
- Jack London, *The Iron Heel* (1907)
- Kazuo Ishiguro, *Never Let Me Go* (2005)

***Watch***

- *Lost Horizon*, directed by Frank Capra (1937)
- *Fahrenheit 451*, directed by François Truffaut (1966), adapted from the novel by Ray Bradbury (1951)
- *A Clockwork Orange*, Stanley Kubrick's adaptation of the novel by Anthony Burgess (1962). It is the story of an extremely violent delinquent and his gang. He is finally rehabilitated through controversial Pavlovian conditioning which deprives him of his free will
- *2001: A Space Odyssey*, directed by Stanley Kubrick (1968). The screenplay of this film was the starting point of a novel of the same name by Arthur Clarke in 1968
- *Soylent Green*, directed by Richard Fleisher (1973)
- *1984*, the film by Michael Radford (1984), with John Hurt, Richard Burton and Suzanna Hamilton
- *The Handmaid's Tale* (1990), directed by Volker Schlöndorff

***Look at***

- *Historical Monument of the American Republic*, a painting by Salisbury Field (1888)

# Gothic literature

## Gothic

• Gothic originally describes the architectural excess of Gothic style. When applied to literature the word 'Gothic' refers to horror and terror, to what is fantastic, wild, nightmarish or magical. It is linked to excess and produces excessive emotion rather than a rational response.

• The word Gothic can be used to describe sublime, desolate landscapes (the Alps for example) but mainly refers to events (violence, mystery), atmosphere (gloom[1] and threat[2]), behaviour (cruelty) and values (social and sexual transgression). In literature, it is a typically Anglo-Saxon genre, perhaps as a reaction against the constraints of Puritanism.

## The Gothic novel in the late 18th century...

• The Gothic influence is to be found in many poems, particularly in those of Coleridge, but it is mostly felt in the Gothic novel, a genre which appeared in England towards the end of the 18th century. It shows the influence of sentimentalism and of Rousseau, and is a reaction against the rationality of Locke.

• The numerous novels written in the last two decades of the 18th century centre upon sensitive heroines and their fears amid old castles and abbeys, dark tunnels, labyrinths, ghosts and skeletons, bandits, wicked monks[3] and evil relatives. It was very much a literature **for** women (because the heroines were women, because there were more and more feminine readers) and written **by** women (who needed little knowledge of society to write such books). Indeed, the most popular writer of such novels was **Ann Radcliffe** (*The Mysteries of Udolpho*, 1794).

Take an old castle, half of it ruinous,
A long gallery, with a great many doors,
Some secret ones,
Three murdered bodies, quite fresh,
As many skeletons, in chests and presses
An old woman hanging by the neck,
With her throat cut,
Assassins and desperadoes, quant. suff.[1]
Noises, whispers and groans, threescore[2] at least,
Mix them together, in the form of three volumes,
To be taken at any of the watering-places before going to be
(anomymou

**1. quant. suff.:** in sufficient quantity: *en quantité suffisante* **2. threescore:** three times twenty

• At the very end of the century, because of the influence of German romanticism, Gothic novels became darker, more macabre and violent (**Matthew Gregory Lewis**, *The Monk*, 1796).

## ... and its parody

With *Northanger Abbey* (1818), **Jane Austen** wrote an amusing parody of Gothic novels. Catherine, her heroine, has read too many Gothic novels and interprets the world around her as if she were a character in such a novel.

## The 19th century

Gothic novels remained popular throughout the 19th century, but their nature changed. The villains[4] were no longer wicked uncles; but mad scientists and criminals entered the novel. Dungeons often gave way to the city as a place of terror, and more internalized fears appeared,

**1. gloom:** *la tristesse, la mélancolie*
**2. a threat:** *une menace*
**3. a monk:** *un moine*
**4. the villain:** *le méchant*

with the themes of the double and of alienation for instance.

• In **Mary Shelley**'s *Frankenstein* (1818), a student of natural philosophy decides to create a human being and constructs a monster instead.

• **R. L. Stevenson**'s *Dr Jekyll and Mr Hyde* (1886) is the story of a doctor who finds a drug which allows him to dissociate his good and evil personalities.

• In *The Picture of Dorian Gray* (1891), **Oscar Wilde** shows how a young man keeps his beauty as he grows old, while his portrait becomes hideous and reflects the corruption of his soul.

• **Bram Stoker**'s *Dracula* (1897), an epistolary novel, relates how two young women try to escape from Count Dracula, a vampire.

## The 20th century

The genre remained popular, but took on a variety of forms, for example:

› science fiction,

› horror tales and various kinds of literature of the fantastic,

› magic realism (which combines realism with fantasy).

The genre has become particularly successful in the cinema.

## The United States

There were no old abbeys and haunted castles in the new world, so Gothic fiction became more psychological, threatened from the inside rather than the outside.

The short stories of **Edgar Allan Poe** explore paranormal phenomena as the protagonists doubt the evidence of their own senses and are confronted not so much with vampires and spectres as with their own obsessions, delirium or madness.

In the 20th century, Gothic themes reappeared in the works of Southern writers (**William Faulkner**, **Flannery O'Connor**). Their fiction is full of misfits[5] and grotesque characters, who symbolise the decay[6] of Southern culture.

*A still from House of Usher*, a film directed by Roger Corman, USA, 1960, based on E. A. POE's short story

**5. a misfit:** *un marginal*
**6. the decay:** *la décadence*

## TEXT 1 S. T. COLERIDGE ~ The Rime of the Ancient Mariner, 1798

**Samuel Taylor COLERIDGE**
(1772-1834)
is a Romantic poet, whose works explore the mysterious and supernatural aspects of the universe. *The Rime of the Ancient Mariner* (1798), *Kubla Khan*, *Christabel* (1816).

*In this long poem, a mariner tells how he killed an albatross as he was travelling to the South Pole. He is punished for this killing: the ship stops moving and the crew dies. It is only when he can later bless the ocean creatures that redemption will be possible.*

Alone, alone, all, all alone,
Alone on a wide wide sea!
And never a saint took pity on
My soul in agony[1].

The many men, so beautiful!
And they all dead did lie:
And a thousand thousand slimy[2] things
Lived on; and so did I.

I looked upon the rotting[3] sea,
And drew my eyes away;
I looked upon the rotting deck[4],
And there the dead men lay.

I looked to Heaven, and tried to pray:
But or ever a prayer had gusht[5],
A wicked whisper came, and made
My heart as dry as dust.

I closed my lids, and kept them close,
And the balls[6] like pulses beat;
For the sky and the sea, and the sea and the sky
Lay like a load on my weary eye,
And the dead were at my feet.

*The Rime of the Ancient Mariner*, illustrated by Gustave DORÉ, Dover Publications, 1970

1. **agony:** *la souffrance* 2. **slimy:** *visqueux* 3. **to rot:** *pourrir* 4. **the deck:** *le pont du bateau* 5. **to gush:** *jaillir* 6. **balls:** *les globes oculaires*

### Zooming in

1. What poetic genre does this poem belong to? See p. 146 Why?
2. List all the Gothic elements you can find:
   **a.** concerning the setting and the atmosphere,
   **b.** concerning the mariner himself.
3. List all the repetitions. What is their effect?
4. Find examples of:
   **a.** alliterations,
   **b.** assonance. See p. 148
5. Which rhymes are particularly interesting?
6. What religious message can you find in these stanzas?

# TEXT 2 Jane AUSTEN ~ Northanger Abbey, 1818

**Jane AUSTEN**
(1775-1817)
Her novels are set among the country gentry that she knew. Her heroines are young women who gradually come to a better understanding of themselves and obtain marriage and social status. The absurdities and pretentions of society are denounced with wit and irony. (*Pride and Prejudice*, 1813, *Mansfield Park*, 1814, *Emma*, 1816, *Northanger Abbey*, 1818.)

*Catherine Morland has met Henry Tilney in Bath and been invited to stay at his family home, Northanger Abbey. Catherine has read many Gothic novels and is sure that Northanger Abbey contains secrets and mysteries. During her first night at the Abbey, she believes she has discovered an old manuscript in her room.*

The dimness[1] of the light her candle emitted made her turn to it with alarm; but there was no danger of its sudden extinction; it had yet some hours to burn; and that she might not have any greater difficulty in distinguishing the writing than what its ancient date might occasion, she hastily snuffed[2] it. Alas! It was snuffed and cxtinguished in one. A lamp could not have expired with more awful effect. Catherine, for a few moments, was motionless with horror. It was done completely; not a remnant of light in the wick[3] could give hope to the rekindling[4] breath. Darkness impenetrable and immovable filled the room. A violent gust of wind, rising with sudden fury, added fresh horror to the moment. Catherine trembled from head to foot. In the pause which succeeded, a sound like receding[5] footsteps and the closing of a distant door struck on her affrighted ear. Human nature could support no more. A cold sweat stood on her forehead, the manuscript fell from her hand, and groping[6] her way to the bed, she jumped hastily in, and sought some suspension of agony by creeping far underneath the clothes. To close her eyes in sleep that night, she felt must be entirely out of the question. With a curiosity so justly awakened, and feelings in every way so agitated, repose must be absolutely impossible. The storm too abroad[7] so dreadful! She had not been used to feel alarm from wind, but now every blast[8] seemed fraught with[9] awful intelligence. The manuscript so wonderfully found, so wonderfully accomplishing the morning's prediction, how was it to be accounted for? What could it contain? To whom could it relate? By what means could it have been so long concealed? And how singularly strange that it should fall to her lot[10] to discover it! Till she had made herself mistress of its contents, however, she could have neither repose nor comfort; and with the sun's first rays she was determined to peruse[11] it. But many were the tedious hours which must yet intervene. She shuddered, tossed about in her bed, and envied every quiet sleeper. The storm still raged, and various were the noises, more terrific even than the wind, which struck at intervals on her startled ear.

**1. dimness:** *faiblesse (de la lumière)* **2. to snuff a candle:** *moucher une bougie* **3. the wick:** *la mèche* **4. to rekindle:** *rallumer, raviver* **5. to recede:** *s'éloigner* **6. to grope:** *avancer à tâtons* **7. abroad:** outside **8. a blast of wind:** *une rafale* **9. fraught with:** *plein de* **10. to fall to someone's lot:** *le sort veut que quelqu'un...* **11. to peruse:** *lire*

## Zooming in

**1** A Gothic novel?
List all the elements which are typical of Gothic novels:
- the setting (inside and outside): ...
- the noises: ...
- suspense: ...
- the heroine's feelings: ...

**2** The parody of a Gothic novel
With *Northanger Abbey* Jane Austen wrote a parody of Gothic novels. Read the passage carefully again and list all the elements which point to parody.

**3** Whose point of view do we have in this passage? The narrator's? Catherine? What effect is thus created?

**4** To what extent is this passage a reflection upon reading?

# TEXT 3 Mary SHELLEY ~ FRANKENSTEIN, 1816

**Mary SHELLEY**
(1797-1851)
was the daughter of the political philosopher William Godwin and of the feminist writer Mary Wollstonecraft; she married the Romantic poet Shelley. She is best-known for her Gothic novel *Frankenstein: or, The New Prometheus* (1816).

*Frankenstein has succeeded in giving life to a human being, but he looks revolting and feels different and miserable. The monster hates his creator, and has vowed[1] to be revenged on Frankenstein. This passage takes place on Frankenstein's wedding day.*

IT WAS EIGHT O'CLOCK WHEN WE LANDED; we walked for a short time on the shore, enjoying the transitory light, and then retired to the inn and contemplated the lovely scene of waters, woods, and mountains, obscured in darkness, yet still displaying[2] their black outlines.

The wind, which had fallen in the south, now rose with great violence in the west. The moon had reached her summit in the heavens and was beginning to descend; the clouds swept[3] across it swifter than the flight of the vulture[4] and dimmed[5] her rays, while the lake reflected the scene of the busy heavens, rendered still busier by the restless waves that were beginning to rise. Suddenly a heavy storm of rain descended.

I had been calm during the day, but so soon as night obscured the shapes of objects, a thousand fears arose in my mind. I was anxious and watchful, while my right hand grasped a pistol which was hidden in my bosom[6]; every sound terrified me, but I resolved that I would sell my life dearly and not shrink from[7] the conflict until my own life or that of my adversary was extinguished.

Elizabeth observed my agitation for some time in timid and fearful silence, but there was something in my glance which communicated terror to her, and trembling, she asked, 'What is it that agitates you, my dear Victor? What is it you fear?'

'Oh! Peace, peace, my love,' replied I; 'this night, and all will be safe; but this night is dreadful, very dreadful.'

I passed an hour in this state of mind, when suddenly I reflected how fearful the combat which I momentarily expected would be to my wife, and I earnestly entreated[8] her to retire, resolving not to join her until I had obtained some knowledge as to the situation of my enemy.

She left me, and I continued some time walking up and down the passages of the house and inspecting every corner that might afford a retreat to my adversary. But I discovered no trace of him and was beginning to conjecture that some fortunate chance had intervened to prevent the execution of his menaces when suddenly I heard a shrill and dreadful scream. It came from the room into which Elizabeth had retired. As I heard it, the whole truth rushed into my mind, my arms dropped, the motion of every muscle and fibre was suspended; I could feel the blood trickling[9] in my veins and tingling[10] in the extremities of my limbs. This state lasted but for an instant; the scream was repeated, and I rushed into the room.

Great God! Why did I not then expire! Why am I here to relate the destruction of the best hope and the purest creature of earth? She was there, lifeless and inanimate, thrown across the bed, her head hanging down and her pale and distorted features half covered by her hair. Everywhere I turn I see the same figure - her bloodless arms and relaxed form flung by the murderer on its bridal[11] bier[12]. Could I behold this and live? Alas! Life is obstinate and clings[13] closest where it is most hated. For a moment only did I lose recollection; I fell senseless on the ground.

When I recovered I found myself surrounded by the people of the inn; their countenances[14] expressed a breathless terror, but the horror of others appeared only as a mockery, a shadow of the feelings that oppressed me. I escaped from them to the room where lay the body of Elizabeth, my love, my wife, so lately living, so dear, so worthy[15]. She had been moved from the posture in which I had first beheld her, and now, as she lay, her head upon her arm and a handkerchief thrown across her face and neck, I might have supposed her asleep. I rushed towards her and embraced her with ardour, but the deadly languor and coldness of the limbs told me that what I now held in my arms had ceased to be the Elizabeth whom I had loved and cherished. The murderous mark of the fiend's grasp was on her neck, and the breath had ceased to issue from her lips.

J. H. Füssli, *The Nightmare*, 1781, Goethe Museum, Francfort

While I still hung over her in the agony of despair, I happened to look up. The windows of the room had before been darkened, and I felt a kind of panic on seeing the pale yellow light of the moon illuminate the chamber. The shutters had been thrown back, and with a sensation of horror not to be described, I saw at the open window a figure the most hideous and abhorred. A grin was on the face of the monster; he seemed to jeer[16], as with his fiendish[17] finger he pointed towards the corpse of my wife. I rushed towards the window, and drawing a pistol from my bosom, fired; but he eluded[18] me, leaped from his station, and running with the swiftness of lightning, plunged into the lake.

**1. to vow:** *faire le serment de* **2. to display:** *montrer* **3. to sweep:** *passer, balayer* **4. a vulture:** *un vautour* **5. to dim:** *assombrir* **6. the bosom:** *la poitrine* **7. to shrink from:** *reculer devant* **8. to entreat:** *supplier* **9. to trickle:** *tomber goutte à goutte* **10. to tingle:** *piquer* **11. bridal:** *nuptial* **12. the bier:** *la bière (pour mettre un corps)* **13. to cling:** *s'accrocher, se cramponner* **14. the countenance:** *l'expression du visage* **15. worthy:** *digne de louanges* **16. to jeer:** *se moquer de* **17. fiendish:** from a fiend: a demon: *diabolique* **18. to elude:** *échapper à*

## Zooming in

**1** What does Victor mean when he says: "the whole truth rushed into my mind" (line 30)?

**2** Study the way terror is expressed in the passage:

**a.** through the progression from anxiety to horror,

**b.** through the setting (compare the beginning, and the end of the passage).

**3** This is Victor's wedding night. List all the elements which show that what we find here is the inversion of a traditional wedding-night scene.

**4** Everyone watches or is watched.

**a.** List all the examples of watching.

**b.** What is their significance?

# EDGAR ALLAN POE ~ 'THE TELL-TALE HEART', 1843

**Edgar Allan POE**
(1809-1849)
wrote poems, short stories and a novel. His stories explore psychological terror (*Tales of the Grotesque and Arabesque*, 1840) as well as the powers of reasoning and deduction. He is considered as the inventor of the detective story (*The Murders in the Rue Morgue*, 1841)

*In this short story, the narrator explains that he has come to hate an old man, mainly because he has "a pale blue eye", "the eye of a vulture[1]". He decides to kill him and carefully plans the murder. For some time after the man has been killed, the narrator hears the beating of his heart. This is the end of the story.*

IF STILL YOU THINK ME MAD, you will think so no longer when I describe the wise precautions I took for the concealment[2] of the body. The night waned[3], and I worked hastily, but in silence.

I took up three planks[4] from the flooring of the chamber, and deposited all between the scantlings[5]. I then replaced the boards so cleverly so cunningly[6], that no human eye — not even his — could have detected anything wrong. There was nothing to wash out — no stain of any kind — no blood-spot whatever. I had been too wary[7] for that.

When I had made an end of these labours, it was four o'clock — still dark as midnight. As the bell sounded the hour, there came a knocking at the street door. I went down to open it with a light heart, — for what had I *now* to fear? There entered three men, who introduced themselves, with perfect suavity, as officers of the police. A shriek had been heard by a neighbour during the night; suspicion of foul play[8] had been aroused; information had been lodged at the police office, and they (the officers) had been deputed to search the premises[9].

I smiled, — for *what* had I to fear? I bade[10] the gentlemen welcome. The shriek, I said, was my own in a dream. The old man, I mentioned, was absent in the country. I took my visitors all over the house. I bade them search — search *well*. I led them, at length, to his chamber. I showed them his treasures, secure, undisturbed. In the enthusiasm of my confidence, I brought chairs into the room, and desired them *here* to rest from their fatigues, while I myself, in the wild audacity of my perfect triumph, placed my own seat upon the very spot beneath which reposed the corpse of the victim.

Illustration by Harry CLARKE for 'The Tell-Tale Heart', in *Tales of Mystery and Imagination*, c. 1919

The officers were satisfied. My *manner* had convinced them. I was singularly at ease. They sat and while I answered cheerily, they chatted[11] of familiar things. But, ere[12] long, I felt myself getting pale and wished them gone. My head ached, and I fancied a ringing in my ears; but still they sat, and still chatted. The ringing became more distinct: I talked more freely to get rid of the feeling: but it continued and gained definitiveness — until, at length, I found that the noise was *not* within my ears.

No doubt I now grew *very* pale; but I talked more fluently, and with a heightened[13] voice. Yet the sound increased — and what could I do? It was *a low, dull, quick sound — much such a sound as a watch makes when enveloped in cotton.* I gasped for breath, and yet the officers heard it not. I talked more quickly, more vehemently but the noise steadily increased. I arose and argued about trifles[14], in a high key and with violent gesticulations; but the noise steadily increased. Why *would* they not be gone? I paced the floor to and fro with heavy strides, as if excited to fury by the observations of the men, but the noise steadily increased. O God! what *could* I do? I foamed[15]— I raved[16]— I swore[17]! I swung the chair upon which I had been sitting, and grated[18] it upon the boards, but the noise arose over all and continually increased. It grew louder — louder — *louder*! And still the men chatted pleasantly, and smiled. Was it possible they heard not? Almighty God! — no, no? They heard! — they suspected! — they *knew*! — they were making a mockery of my horror! — this I thought, and this I think. But anything was better than this agony[19]! Anything was more tolerable than this derision! I could bear those hypocritical smiles no longer! I felt that I must scream or die! — and now — again — hark[20]! louder! louder! louder! *louder*!

"Villains!" I shrieked, "dissemble[21] no more! I admit the deed[22]! — tear up the planks! — here, here! — it is the beating of his hideous heart!"

In *Tales of Mystery and Imagination*, 1843

**1. a vulture:** *un vautour* **2. the concealment:** *la dissimulation* **3. the night wanes:** *la nuit se passe, touche à sa fin* **4. a plank:** *une planche* **5. the scantlings:** *les traverses* **6. cunningly:** *astucieusement* **7. wary:** *prudent* **8. foul play:** *un acte criminel* **9. the premises:** *le lieu* **10. bade:** *préterit de 'bid': dire, inviter, convier* **11. to chat:** *bavarder* **12. ere:** before **13. heightened:** *plus forte* **14. trifles:** *des choses sans importance* **15. to foam:** *écumer* **16. to rave:** *divaguer* **17. swore:** *prétérit de 'swear', jurer* **18. to grate:** *râcler, faire grincer* **19. agony:** *la torture* **20. to hark:** *écouter* **21. to dissemble:** *feindre* **22. the deed:** *l'acte, le crime*

## Zooming in

1. Explain the double meaning of the title Poe gave his story.
2. At the end of the text, the narrator accuses the police of being "villains" who "dissemble". What does he mean? Why is it an indirect recognition of his own guilt?
3. The growth of terror: quoting as many words as possible, show the evolution of the text, from the beginning to the end, in terms of:
   - **a.** the narrator's attitude,
   - **b.** sounds,
   - **c.** style (sentence length, dashes...).
4. Whom do you think the speaker is addressing in the story? Why does he need to talk?

## TEXT 5 A. CARTER ~ "The Werewolf[1]", in The Bloody Chamber, 1979

**Angela CARTER**
(1940-1992)
Her novels and stories are post-modern. They use parody, pastiche and magic realism to question conventional representations of reality in fiction and to explore subjects such as transgression and tyranny.

*This is the whole short story.*

IT IS A NORTHERN COUNTRY; they have cold weather, they have cold hearts. Cold; tempest; wild beasts in the forest. It is a hard life. Their houses are built of logs[2], dark and smoky within. There will be a crude[3] icon of the virgin behind a guttering[4] candle, the leg of a pig hung up to cure, a string of drying mushrooms. A bed, a stool, a table. Harsh[5], brief, poor lives.

To these upland[6] woodsmen, the Devil is as real as you or I. More so; they have not seen us nor even know that we exist, but the Devil they glimpse often in the graveyards[7], those bleak and touching townships of the dead where the graves are marked with portraits of the deceased[8] in the naif style and there are no flowers to put in front of them, no flowers grow there, so they put out small votive offerings, little loaves, sometimes a cake that the bears come lumbering[9] from the margins of the forests to snatch away. At midnight, especially on Walpurgisnacht, the Devil holds picnics in the graveyards and invites the witches; then they dig up fresh corpses, and eat them. Anyone will tell you that.

Wreaths[10] of garlic[11] on the doors keep out the vampires. A blue-eyed child born feet first on the night of St. John's Eve will have second sight. When they discover a witch – some old woman whose cheeses ripen[12] when her neighbours' do not, another old woman whose black cat, oh, sinister! follows her about all the time, they strip[13] the crone[14], search for her marks, for the supernumerary[15] nipple[16] her familiar[17] sucks[18]. They soon find it. Then they stone her to death.

Winter and cold weather.

Go and visit grandmother, who has been sick. Take her the oatcakes I've baked for her on the hearthstone[19] and a little pot of butter.

The good child does as her mother bids – five miles' trudge[20] through the forest; do not leave the path because of the bears, the wild boar, the starving wolves. Here, take your father's hunting knife; you know how to use it.

The child had a scabbby[21] coat of sheepskin to keep out the cold, she knew the forest too well to fear it but she must always be on her guard. When she heard that freezing howl of a wolf, she dropped her gifts, seized her knife, and turned on the beast.

It was a huge one, with red eyes and running, grizzled[22] chops[23]; any but a mountaineer's child would have died of fright at the sight of it. It went for her throat, as wolves do, but she made a great swipe[24] at it with her father's knife and slashed off[25] its right forepaw[26].

The wolf let out a gulp[27], almost a sob, when it saw what had happened to it; wolves are less brave than they seem. It went lolloping off[28] disconsolately between the trees as well as it could on three legs, leaving a trail of blood behind it. The child wiped the blade of her knife clean on her apron, wrapped up the wolf's paw in the cloth in which her mother had packed the oatcakes and went on towards her grandmother's house. Soon it came on to snow so thickly that the path and any footsteps, track or spoor[29] that might have been upon it were obscured.

She found her grandmother was so sick she had taken to her bed and fallen into a fretful[30] sleep, moaning and shaking so that the child guessed she had a fever. She felt the forehead, it burned. She shook out the cloth from her basket, to use it to make the old woman a cold compress, and the wolf's paw fell to the floor.

But it was no longer a wolf's paw. It was a hand, chopped off[31] at the wrist, a hand toughened[32] with work and freckled[33] with old age. There was a wedding ring on the third finger and a wart[34] in the index finger. By the wart, she knew it for her grandmother's hand.

She pulled back the sheet but the old woman woke up, at that, and began to struggle, squawking[35] and shrieking like a thing possessed. But the child was strong, and armed with her father's hunting knife; she managed to hold her grandmother down long enough to see the cause of her fever. There was a bloody stump[36] where her right hand should have been, festering[37] already.

The child crossed herself and cried out so loud the neighbours heard her and came rushing in. They knew the wart on the hand at once for a witch's nipple; they drove the old woman, in her shift[38] as she was, out into the snow with sticks, beating her old carcass as far as the edge of the forest, and pelted[39] her with stones until she fell dead.

Now the child lived in her grandmother's house; she prospered.

**1. a werewolf:** *un loup-garou* **2. logs:** *des rondins* **3. crude:** *grossier, rudimentaire* **4. guttering:** *qui coule, qui brûle mal* **5. harsh:** *dur* **6. an upland:** *un plateau* **7. a graveyard:** *un cimetière* **8. the deceased:** *les morts* **9. to lumber:** *marcher lourdement* **10. a wreath:** *une guirlande* **11. garlic:** *l'ail* **12. to ripen:** *mûrir, affiner* **13. to strip:** *devêtir* **14. the crone:** *la vieille (péjoratif)* **15. supernumerary:** *supplémentaire, en trop* **16. the nipple:** *le mamelon, le bout du sein* **17. her familiar:** *son démon familier* **18. to suck:** *sucer* **19. the hearthstone:** *la cheminée (pierre de)* **20. a trudge:** *une marche pénible* **21. scabby:** *galeux* **22. grizzled:** *grisonnant* **23. chops:** *les mâchoires* **24. a swipe:** *un grand coup* **25. to slash off:** *couper* **26. the forepaw:** *la patte de devant* **27. a gulp:** *un cri étouffé, la gorge serrée* **28. to lollop off:** *partir à grandes enjambées maladroites* **29. the track, the spoor:** *la trace* **30. fretful:** *agité* **31. to chop off:** *couper* **32. to toughen:** *durcir* **33. freckled:** *couvert de taches de rousseur* **34. a wart:** *une verrue* **35. to squawk:** *pousser des cris rauques* **36. a stump:** *un moignon* **37. to fester:** *suppurer* **38. her shift:** *sa chemise* **39. to pelt:** *bombarder de*

## Zooming in

1. What traditional tale is this a rewriting of?
2. Show the differences between the traditional tale and Angela Carter's story:
   - **a.** the atmosphere & the setting,
   - **b.** the girl,
   - **c.** the wolf,
   - **d.** the grandmother,
   - **e.** the moral.
3. There are two very different parts in the story. What are they?
4. What is the narrator's attitude towards the Gothic background of the setting? Do we readers accept the moral? Do we feel superior to these "northern people"? Is the world in which we live less cruel? To what extent is this a "tale for our times"?

## MOVING ON

***Read***

- Washington Irving, "Rip Van Winkle" (1819)
- Henry James, *The Turn of the Screw* (1898)
- Stephen King, *Misery* (1987)
- Doris Lessing, *The Fifth Child* (1988)

***Watch***

- *The Night of the Hunter* (1955), directed by Charles Laughton
- *Psycho* (1960), directed by Hitchcock
- *The Fearless Vampire Killers* (1967), directed by Roman Polanski
- Roman Polanski's *Rosemary's Baby* (1968), from the novel by Ira Levin
- The musical *The Rocky Horror Show* (1975) directed by Jim Sharman
- Francis Ford Coppola's *Dracula* (1993)
- Neil Jordan's *Interview with the Vampire* (1994), from the novels by Anne Rice

***Look at***

- Fuseli's paintings (such as *The Nightmare*)
- Piranesi's *Prisons*

# Political and social statements

With the Glorious Revolution leading to a constitutional monarchy in 1688, Britain reached political stability early in its history, so there was never any need for violent political opposition. However, that very system encouraged a tradition of free expression which is reflected in literature, particularly when it comes to denouncing social suffering. As for the United States, the revolution which led to the birth of the nation was accompanied by a sense of enormous pride, and it was only later that critical voices were heard condemning social, economic and political evils.

## A few periods which best lent themselves to political writings

• The Elizabethan age, with its celebration of a divinely ordained monarchy, but also with much questioning about what a good king should be like (*King Lear*, *Macbeth* or *Richard III*) or about whether a weak king could rightly be deposed (*Richard II*).

• The political and religious upheavals[1] in the 17th century, which led to the beheading of Charles I and to the Commonwealth (**Milton**'s pamphlets).

> 'as good almost kill a man as kill a good book; who kills a man kills a reasonable creature, God's image, but he who destroys a good book, kills reason itself'.
>
> JOHN MILTON, *AREOPAGITICA, A DEFENCE OF FREEDOM OF PRINTING*, 1644

• The Romantic age, with its idealism and rebellion against conventions.

• The Victorian era, in particular with the 'Condition of England' novels showing the gap between the rich and the poor (**Charles Dickens**'s *Oliver Twist* or *Hard Times*; **Mrs Gaskell**'s *North and South*).

• The harsh conditions of life created by the consequences of industrialisation towards the end of the 19th century, which inspired the naturalistic novel (**Thomas Hardy**'s *Tess of the d'Urbervilles*, **Theodore Dreiser**'s *Sister Carrie*).

• War, its violence and absurdity: the American Civil War (**Stephen Crane**'s *The Red Badge of Courage*), the two world wars, the Vietnam war (war poetry in British literature, **Norman Mailer**'s *The Naked and the Dead*).

• The Great Depression and its consequences (the poetry of **Auden** in Britain, **Dos Passos**'s *USA*, **Steinbeck**'s *The Grapes of Wrath*).

• McCarthyism (**Miller**'s *The Crucible*, the Beat Generation).

• The political rights and social conditions of minorities See p. 100.

• The Troubles in Northern Ireland.

## A few favourite modes of expression

Reflections upon politics and society can be expressed:

› through a genre such as pastiche or utopia See p. 52,

› directly in a variety of tones: laudatory[2], serious, bitter... See p. 163,

› more or less indirectly through irony, wit, humour or symbolism.

1. **upheavals:** *les bouleversements*
2. **laudatory:** *élogieux*

# TEXT 1 William BLAKE ~ London, 1794

**William BLAKE**
(1757-1827)
was a visionary poet and an engraver. He was a radical, who opposed materialism, rationalism and conventional morality which cut men off from their original unity with the divine. Only through imagination and the instincts could this divine be regained. (*Songs of Innocence*, 1789, *Songs of Experience*, 1794)

I wander thro' each charter'd[1] street,
Near where the charter'd Thames does flow,
And mark[2] in every face I meet
Marks of weakness, marks of woe[3].

In every cry of every Man,
In every Infant's cry of fear,
In every voice, in every ban[4],
The mind-forg'd[5] manacles[6] I hear.

How the Chimney-sweeper[7]'s cry
Every black'ning Church appalls[8];
And the hapless[9] Soldier's sigh
Runs in blood down Palace walls.

But most thro' midnight streets I hear
How the youthful Harlot[10]'s curse[11]
Blasts[12] the new born Infant's tear,
And blights[13] with plagues[14] the Marriage hearse[15].

**1. charter'd:** *qui a été fondé grâce à une charte royale ; répertorié* **2. to mark:** *remarquer* **3. woe:** *la tristesse, le malheur* **4. a ban:** *une interdiction* **5. mind-forg'd:** *forgé par l'esprit* **6. manacles:** *des menottes* **7. a chimney-sweeper:** *un ramoneur* **8. to appal:** *épouvanter* **9. hapless:** *malheureux* **10. a harlot:** *une prostituée* **11. a curse:** *une malédiction* **12. to blast:** *détruire* **13. to blight:** *anéantir* **14. a plague:** *un fléau* **15. a hearse:** *un corbillard*

## Zooming in

1. Show what the progression in the poem is.
2. The poem denounces many of the evils of the time. What are they according to Blake?
3. What tense is used in the poem? Why?
4. Listen to the poem read out. Note that two types of rhythms alternate. Why?
5. What is the rhyme pattern? Can you notice any interesting rhymes?
6. What is the role of the poet in this poem?

William BLAKE, *London*, 1794

# TEXT 2 PERCY BYSSHE SHELLEY ~ OZYMANDIAS, 1818

**Percy Bysshe SHELLEY**
(1792-1822)
was passionately involved in politics and fought against all forms of oppression. His idealism and rejection of conventional morality and religion caused a scandal in England and led him to live abroad. (*Prometheus Unbound*, *Ode to the West Wind*, 1820)

I met a traveller from an antique land
Who said: "Two vast and trunkless[1] legs of stone
Stand in the desert. Near them on the sand,
Half sunk[2], a shattered[3] visage lies, whose frown[4]
And wrinkled[5] lip and sneer[6] of cold command"
Tell that its sculptor well those passions read[7]
Which yet survive[8], stamped[9] on these lifeless things,
The hand that mocked them and the heart that fed[10].
And on the pedestal these words appear:
"My name is Ozymandias, King of Kings:
Look on my works, ye Mighty[11], and despair!"
Nothing beside remains. Round the decay[12]
Of that colossal wreck[13], boundless[14] and bare,
The lone and level sands stretch far away.

1. **trunkless legs:** *des jambes sans tronc* 2. **sunk:** *participe passé de 'sink' : enfoncé* 3. **shattered:** *brisé, en morceaux* 4. **a frown:** *un froncement de sourcils* 5. **wrinkled:** *plissé, froncé* 6. **a sneer:** *un ricanement* 7. **well those passions read:** read those passions well 8. *la structure est :* 'which yet survive... the hand' *(les fragments de la statue ont survécu après la mort du sculpteur* (hand) *et celle d'Ozymandias* (heart) 9. **stamped:** *marqué* 10. **fed:** *participe passé de 'feed' : nourrir. C'est le cœur qui nourrit les passions* 11. **ye Mighty:** *vous qui êtes puissants* 12. **the decay:** *le délabrement* 13. **a wreck:** *une épave* 14. **boundless:** *sans limite (qualifie les sables)*

## Zooming in

1. Although its rhyme pattern is not very regular, this poem is a sonnet. Sum up the main idea of each of its parts.
   › The octave (lines 1-8).
   › The sestet: first triplet (lines 9-11),
   second triplet (lines 12-14).
2. There are three embedded[1] stories in the poem. What are they?
   1... → 2... → 3...
   What message is conveyed?
3. Find several ironic juxtapositions in the poem. What message do they point to?
4. What does the poem tell us about the work of the sculptor and that of an artist more generally?

1. **embedded:** *enchâssées, imbriquées*

# TEXT 3 CHARLES DICKENS ~ GREAT EXPECTATIONS, 1861

*This is the incipit of the novel.*

**Charles DICKENS**
(1812-1870)
started working very young when his father was imprisoned for debt and that experience partly explains his concern for all kinds of social injustice: poverty, child labour, corruption, the prison system. He also had a gift for caricature and the theatrical presentation of a scene. (*Oliver Twist*, 1838, *David Copperfield*, 1850, *Great Expectations*, 1861).

MY FATHER'S FAMILY NAME BEING PIRRIP, and my Christian name Philip, my infant tongue could make of both names nothing longer or more explicit than Pip. So, I called myself Pip, and came to be called Pip.

I give Pirrip as my father's family name, on the authority of his tombstone and my sister – Mrs Joe Gargery, who married the blacksmith[1]. As I never saw my father or my mother, and never saw any likeness[2] of either of them (for their days were long before the days of photographs), my first fancies[3] regarding what they were like, were unreasonably derived from their tombstones. The shape of the letters on my father's, gave me an odd idea that he was a square, stout[4], dark man, with curly[5] black hair. From the character and turn of the inscription, "Also Georgiana Wife of the Above," I drew a childish conclusion that my mother was freckled[6] and sickly. To five little stone lozenges[7], each about a foot and a half long which were arranged in a neat row beside their grave, and were sacred to the memory of five little brothers of mine – who gave up trying to get a living, exceedingly early in that universal struggle – I am indebted for a belief I religiously entertained[8] that they had all been born on their backs with their hands in their trousers-pockets, and had never taken them out in this state of existence.

An illustration for the Household Edition of Dickens's *Great Expectations*, by F. A. Fraser, 1877

Ours was the marsh[9] country, down by the river, within, as the river wound[10], twenty miles of the sea. My first most vivid and broad impression of the identity of things, seems to me to have been gained on a memorable raw[11] afternoon towards evening. At such a time I found out for certain, that this bleak[12] place overgrown with nettles[13] was the churchyard; and that Philip Pirrip, late of this parish[14], and also Georgiana wife of the above, were dead and buried; and that Alexander, Bartholomew, Abraham, Tobias, and Roger, infant children of the aforesaid[15], were also dead and buried; and that the dark flat wilderness beyond the churchyard, intersected with dykes[16] and mounds and gates, with scattered[17] cattle feeding on it, was the marshes; and that the low leaden[18] line beyond, was the river; and that the distant savage lair[19] from which the wind was rushing was the sea; and that the small bundle of[20] shivers[21] growing afraid of it all and beginning to cry, was Pip.

"Hold your noise[22]!" cried a terrible voice, as a man started up from among the graves at the side of the church porch. "Keep still, you little devil, or I'll cut your throat!"

A fearful man, all in coarse[23] grey, with a great iron on his leg. A man with no hat, and with broken shoes, and with an old rag[24] tied round his head. A man who had been soaked[25] in water, and smothered[26] in mud, and lamed[27] by stones, and cut by flints[28], and stung by nettles, and torn by briars[29]; who limped[30], and shivered, and glared[31] and growled[32]; and whose teeth chattered in his head as he seized me by the chin.

"O! Don't cut my throat, sir," I pleaded in terror. "Pray don't do it, sir."

"Tell us your name!" said the man. "Quick!"

"Pip, sir."

"Once more," said the man, staring at me. "Give it mouth!"

"Pip. Pip, sir."

"Show us where you live," said the man. "Pint out[33] the place!"

I pointed to where our village lay, on the flat in-shore among the alder-trees and pollards[34], a mile or more from the church.

The man, after looking at me for a moment, turned me upside down, and emptied my pockets. There was nothing in them but a piece of bread. When the church came to itself — for he was so sudden and strong that he made it go head over heels before me, and I saw the steeple under my feet — when the church came to itself, I say, I was seated on a high tombstone, trembling, while he ate the bread ravenously[35].

**1. the blacksmith:** *le forgeron* **2. the likeness:** the picture **3. fancy:** *idée, imagination* **4. stout:** *corpulent, robuste* **5. curly:** *bouclé* **6. freckled:** *qui a des taches de rousseur* **7. a lozenge:** *un losange* **8. to entertain a belief:** *croire quelque chose* **9. a marsh:** *un marécage* **10. wound:** *participe passé de 'to wind': serpenter* **11. raw:** *glacial* **12. bleak:** *morne, désolé* **13. nettles:** *des orties* **14. late of this parish:** *autrefois domicilié dans cette paroisse* **15. aforesaid:** *précité, déjà mentionné* **16. a dyke:** *une digue* **17. scattered:** *dispersé, éparpillé* **18. leaden:** *de plomb* **19. a lair:** *une tanière, un repaire* **20. a bundle of:** *un paquet de* **21. a shiver:** *un frisson* **22. hold your noise:** *tais-toi* **23. coarse:** *grossier* **24. a rag:** *un chiffon* **25. soaked:** *trempé* **26. smothered:** *étouffé* **27. lamed:** *estropié* **28. flint:** *le silex* **29. briars:** *des ronces* **30. to limp:** *boiter* **31. to glare:** *lancer un regard furieux* **32. to growl:** *grogner, gronder* **33. to pint out:** point out: *montrer* **34. alder trees and pollards:** *aulnes et arbres écimés* **35. ravenously:** *avec voracité*

## Zooming in

**1** On what line does the passage move from generalities to a specific day?
Sum up the information given in each of the two parts:
Part 1: ...
Part 2: ...

**2** What elements contribute to a Gothic and melodramatic atmosphere?
- in the setting,
- in the child's situation,
- in the meeting with the man,
- in some contrasts.

**3** As is usual in an incipit, we are told about the identity of the hero. What do all the elements given us show?
- his name: ...
- his parents: ...

**4** What is the 'universal struggle' (line 26) a reference to? What does it mean for Pip?

**5** Who do you think the man could be?

**6** Can you find some humour in the text?

**7** What rhetorical effects can you find in paragraph 5 (line 46 to 51)?

# TEXT 4 JOHN STEINBECK ~ The Grapes of Wrath, 1939

**John STEINBECK**
(1902-1968)
wrote about ordinary working men during the Great Depression. *Of Mice and Men* (1937) is about the relationship between two migrant workers whose dream of owning a little bit of land fails. *The Grapes of Wrath* (1939) is about the exodus of the Okies (migrant agricultural workers from Oklahoma) from Oklahoma to California.

*In 1937, a bad drought[1] in Oklahoma turned it into a 'Dust Bowl' and made it impossible to work on the land, which was repossessed by the banks. Farmers and labourers left for California, in the hope of finding work there. But they often ended up in government camps, where they half starved[2]. The novel follows the Joad family in their journey west and criticizes government policies and capitalism. Only love and friendship can help people survive. This passage is taken from one of the 'interchapters' in which Steinbeck gives background information about the social and historical background.*

THE SQUATTING[3] MEN looked down again. What do you want us to do? We can't take less share[4] of the crop[5] — we're half starved now. The kids are hungry all the time. We got no clothes, torn an' ragged[6]. If all the neighbors weren't the same, we'd be ashamed to go to meeting[7].

And at last the owner men came to the point. The tenant[8] system won't work any more. One man on a tractor can take the place of twelve or fourteen families. Pay him a wage[9] and take all the crop.

We have to do it. We don't like to do it. But the monster's sick. Something's happened to the monster.

But you'll kill the land with cotton.

We know. We've got to take cotton quick before the land dies. Then we'll sell the land. Lots of families in the East would like to own a piece of land.

The tenant men looked up alarmed. But what'll happen to us? How'll we eat?

You'll have to get off the land. The plows[10]' 'll go through the dooryard.

And now the squatting men stood up angrily. Grampa took up the land, and he had to kill the Indians and drive them away. And Pa was born here, and he killed weeds and snakes. Then a bad year came and he had to borrow[11] a little money. An' we was born here. There in the door — our children born here. And Pa had to borrow money. The bank owned the land then, but we stayed and we got a little bit of what we raised.

We know that — all that. It's not us, it's the bank. A bank isn't like a man. Or an owner with fifty thousand acres, he isn't like a man either. That's the monster.

Sure, cried the tenant men, but it's our land. We measured it and broke it up. We were born on it, and we got killed on it, died on it. Even if it's no good, it's still ours. That's what makes it ours — being born on it, working it, dying on it. That makes ownership, not a paper with numbers on it.

We're sorry. It's not us. It's the monster. The bank isn't like a man.

Yes, but the bank is only made of men.

No, you're wrong there – quite wrong there. The bank is something else than men. It happens that every man in a bank hates what the bank does, and yet the bank does it. The bank is something more than men, I tell you. It's the monster. Men made it, but they can't control it.

The tenants cried, Grampa killed Indians, Pa killed snakes for the land. Maybe we can kill banks — they're worse than Indians and snakes. Maybe we got to fight to keep our land, like Pa and Grampa did.

And now the owner men grew angry. You'll have to go.

But it's ours, the tenant men cried. We –

No. The bank, the monster owns it. You'll have to go.

We'll get our guns, like Grampa when the Indians came. What then?

Well – first the sheriff, and then the troops. You'll be stealing if you try to stay, you'll be murderers if you kill to stay. The monster isn't men, but it can make men do what it wants.

But if we go, where'll we go? How'll we go? We got no money.

We're sorry, said the owner men. The bank, the fifty-thousand-acre owner can't be responsible. You're on land that isn't yours. Once over the line[12] maybe you can pick cotton in the fall. Maybe you can go on relief[13]. Why don't you go on west to California? There's work there, and it never gets cold. Why, you can reach out anywhere and pick an orange. Why, there's always some kind of crop to work in. Why don't you go there? And the owner men started their cars and rolled away.

The tenant men squatted down on their hams[14] again to mark the dust with a stick, to figure, to wonder. Their sunburned faces were dark, and their

**Dorothea LANGE, *Tractored out***
This photograph is part of the Farm Security Administration photographic project. Created by Roosevelt in 1935, the FSA's aim was to improve the conditions of life of America's farm population, particularly that of sharecroppers and of California migrant workers.

sun-whipped[15] eyes were light. The women moved cautiously out of the doorways toward their men, and the children crept behind the women, cautiously, ready to run. The bigger boys squatted beside their fathers, because that made them men. After a time the women asked, What did he want?

And the men looked up for a second, and the smolder[16] of pain was in their eyes. We got to get off. A tractor and a superintendent. Like factories.

Where'll we go? the women asked.

We don't know. We don't know.

And the women went quickly, quietly back into the houses and herded[17] the children ahead of them. They knew that a man so hurt and so perplexed may turn in anger, even on people he loves. They left the men alone to figure and to wonder in the dust.

After a time perhaps the tenant man looked about – at the pump put in ten years ago, with a goose-neck[18] handle and iron flowers on the spout[19], at the chopping block[20] where a thousand chickens had been killed, at the hand plow lying in the shed, and the patent crib[21] hanging in the rafters[22] over it.

The children crowded about the women in the houses. What we going to do, Ma? Where we going to go?

The women said, We don't know, yet. Go out and play. But don't go near your father. He might whale[23] you if you go near him. And the women went on with the work, but all the time they watched the men squatting in the dust – perplexed and figuring.

**1. a drought:** *une sécheresse* **2. to starve:** *mourir de faim* **3. to squat:** *être accroupi* **4. a share:** *une part* **5. the crop:** *la récolte* **6. ragged:** *en haillons* **7. to go to meeting:** *aller à l'église* **8. a tenant (farmer):** *un métayer* **9. a wage:** *un salaire* **10. plows:** *les charrues (tracteurs)* **11. to borrow:** *emprunter* **12. the line:** *la frontière (entre deux états)* **13. to go on relief:** *bénéficier d'aides sociales* **14. their hams:** *leurs cuisses* **15. sun whipped:** *mot à mot : yeux fouettés par le soleil* **16. the smolder:** *vient de* 'to smolder'*: couver (feu, émotion)* **17. to herd:** *mener* **18. goose neck:** *en forme de cou d'oie* **19. the spout:** *le dégorgeoir (de la pompe)* **20. the chopping block:** *le billot* **21. the patent crib:** *le berceau de leur fabrication* **22. the rafters:** *les poutres* **23. to whale:** *frapper (familier)*

## Zooming in

1. There are two main parts in this text. What are they?
2. What are the participants in the dialogue called? What is the effect?
3. Study the confrontation between the tenants and the owners and the arguments they give:
   - in relation to the land,
   - in relation to what is driving them away,
   - regarding the future of the men.
4. What characterizes the men and their families – in terms of their movements – in the second part of the text?
5. How does the style underline the tension in the scene?

# TEXT 5 W. H. AUDEN ~ The Unknown Citizen, 1940

**W. H. AUDEN**
(1907-1973)
is best known as a committed poet who supported Communism and the Spanish Republican cause, and warned against the rise of Fascism. He wanted his poetry to be accessible and used a variety of traditional poetic forms.

*The Unknown Citizen*
*(To JS 07/378 This Marble Monument Is Erected by the State)*

He was found by the Bureau of Statistics to be
One against whom there was no official complaint,
And all the reports on his conduct agree
That, in the modern sense of an old-fashioned word, he was a saint,
For in everything he did he served the Greater Community.
Except for the War till the day he retired
He worked in a factory and never got fired[1],
But satisfied his employers, Fudge Motors Inc.
Yet he wasn't a scab[2] or odd in his views,
For his Union reports that he paid his dues[3],
(Our report on his Union shows it was sound[4])
And our Social Psychology workers found
That he was popular with his mates and liked a drink.
The Press are convinced that he bought a paper every day
And that his reactions to advertisements were normal in every way.
Policies taken out in his name prove that he was fully insured,
And his Health-card shows he was once in hospital but left it cured.
Both Producers Research and High-Grade Living declare
He was fully sensible to the advantages of the Instalment Plan[5]
And had everything necessary to the Modern Man,
A phonograph, a radio, a car and a frigidaire.
Our researchers into Public Opinion are content
That he held the proper opinions for the time of year;
When there was peace, he was for peace; when there was war, he went.
He was married and added five children to the population,
Which our Eugenist says was the right number for a parent of his generation,
And our teachers report that he never interfered with their education.
Was he free? Was he happy? The question is absurd:
Had anything been wrong, we should certainly have heard.

**1. to be fired:** *être renvoyé* **2. a scab:** *un briseur de grève* **3. his dues:** *sa cotisation* **4. sound:** *fiable, sûr* **5. the instalment plan:** *le paiement en plusieurs versements*

## Zooming in

**1** What does the expression 'Unknown Citizen' remind you of? What is the difference here? Who is being described in the poem? Why is the person described as 'unknown'?

What sort of life did this citizen lead?

**2** What trends in modern society or what political or social tendencies are satirized in the poem?

**3** The satire in the poem is mainly conveyed through irony. Underline all the words and expressions you find ironic.

**4** Imagine conveying the same ideas without using irony. Rewrite two or three lines of the poem, expressing the ideas directly instead of ironically. What difference does it make?
What is the main reason for using irony, in this poem and in literature more generally?
When does one first become conscious that this poem is ironic? What is the effect thus created?

**5** How would you describe the tone of the poem?

**6** What do you think of the rhyme pattern of the poem?

# TEXT 6 ARTHUR MILLER ~ THE CRUCIBLE, 1953

**Arthur MILLER**
(1915–2005)
believed that the theatre had a social function. His plays are about the relationship between public and private lives and explore such themes as social duty and conscience. (*Death of a Salesman*, 1949, *The Crucible*, 1953)

*The Crucible*[1] *was written in 1953, during McCarthyism, when many Americans, including Arthur Miller, were accused of pro-Communist beliefs and asked to denounce some of their friends. The Crucible is set in 17th-century Salem, during a period of witch-hunts.*

*Led by Abigail (Reverend Parris's niece), several girls including Tituba, Reverend Parris's black servant from Barbados*[2]*, and Betty (Parris's daughter) have been dancing in the forest. In fact Abigail wanted Tituba to prepare a potion to kill Proctor's wife (Abigail wants to seduce her husband). Parris catches the girls and Betty faints and remains unconscious. There is of course rumour of witchcraft. Abigail accuses Tituba of being a witch and Reverend Hale, a specialist of occult phenomena is sent for. Tituba is terrified of being hanged but understands that she might be saved if she accuses others, even though they are innocent.*

**HALE:** When the Devil comes to you does he ever come – with another person?
*(She stares up into his face.)*
Perhaps another person in the village? Someone you know.
**PARRIS:** Who came with him?
**PUTNAM:** Sarah Good? Did you ever see Sarah Good with him? Or Osburn?
**PARRIS:** Was it man or woman came with him?
**TITUBA:** Man or woman. Was – was woman.
**PARRIS:** What woman? A woman, you said. What woman?
**TITUBA:** It was black dark, and I –
**PARRIS:** You could see him, why could you not see her?
**TITUBA:** Well, they was always talking; they was always runnin' round and carryin' on –
**PARRIS:** You mean out of Salem? Salem witches?
**TITUBA:** I believe so, yes, sir.
*(Now Hale takes her hand. She is surprised.)*

**HALE:** Tituba. You must have no fear to tell us who they are, do you understand? We will protect you. The Devil can never overcome a minister[3]. You know that, do you not?
**TITUBA** *(kisses Hale's hand)*: Aye, sir, oh, I do.
**HALE:** You have confessed yourself to witchcraft, and that speaks a wish to come to Heaven's side. And we will bless[4] you, Tituba.
**TITUBA** *(deeply relieved)*: Oh, God bless you, Mr Hale!
**HALE:** *(with rising exaltation)*: You are God's instrument put in our hands to discover the Devil's agents among us. You are selected, Tituba, you are chosen to help us cleanse[5] our village. So speak utterly, Tituba, turn your back on

him and face God – face God, Tituba, and God will protect you.

**TITUBA** *(joining with him)*: Oh, God, protect Tituba!

**HALE** *(kindly)*: Who came to you with the Devil? Two? Three? Four? How many?

*(Tituba pants, and begins rocking back and forth again, staring ahead.)*

**TITUBA**: There was four. There was four.

**PARRIS** *(pressing in on her)*: Who? Who? Their names, their names!

**TITUBA** *(suddenly bursting out*[6]*)*: Oh, how many times he bid[7] me kill you, Mr Parris!

**PARRIS**: Kill me!

**TITUBA** *(in a fury)*: He say Mr Parris must be kill! Mr Parris no goodly man, Mr Parris mean man and no gentle man, and he bid me rise out of my bed and cut your throat! *(They gasp.)* But I tell him 'No! I don't hate that man. I don't want kill that man.' But he say, 'You work for me, Tituba, and I make you free! I give you pretty dress to wear, and put you way high up in the air, and you gone fly back to Barbados!' And I say, 'You lie, Devil, you lie!' And then he come one stormy night to me, and he say, ' Look! I have *white* people belong to me.' And I look – and there was Goody[8] Good.

From *The Crucible*, 1996 directed by Nicholas Hytner

**PARRIS**: Sarah Good !

**TITUBA** *(rocking and weeping)*: Aye, sir, and Goody Osburn.

**MRS PUTNAM**: I knew it! Goody Osburn were midwife[9] to me three times. I begged you, Thomas, did I not? I begged him not to call Osburn because I feared her. My babies always shrivelled[10] in her hands!

**HALE**: Take courage, you must give us all their names. How can you bear to see this child suffering? Look at her, Tituba. *(He is indicating Betty on the bed.)* Look at her God-given innocence; her soul is so tender; we must protect her, Tituba; the Devil is out and preying[11] on her like a beast upon the flesh of the pure lamb. God will bless you for your help.

*(Abigail rises, staring as though inspired, and cries out.)*

**ABIGAIL**: I want to open myself!

*(They turn to her, startled. She is enraptured*[12]*, as though in a pearly light.)* I want the light of God, I want the sweet love of Jesus! I danced for the Devil; I saw him; I wrote in his book; I go back to Jesus; I kiss His hand. I saw Sarah Good with the Devil: I saw Goody Osburn with the Devil! I saw Bridget Bishop with the Devil!

*(As she is speaking, Betty is rising from the bed, a fever in her eyes, and picks up the chant.)*

**BETTY** *(staring too)*: I saw George Jacobs with the Devil! I saw Goody Howe with the Devil!

**PARRIS:** She speaks ! *(He rushes to embrace Betty.)* She speaks!

**HALE:** Glory to God! It is broken, they are free!

**BETTY** *(calling out hysterically and with great relief)*: I saw Martha Bellows with the Devil!

**ABIGAIL:** I saw Goody Sibber with the Devil! *(It is rising to a great glee[13].)*

**PUTNAM:** The marshal[14], I'll call the marshal!

*(Parris is shouting a prayer of thanksgiving.)*

**BETTY:** I saw Alice Barrow with the Devil!

*(The curtain begins to fall.)*

**HALE** *(as Putnam goes out)*: Let the marshal bring irons!

**ABIGAIL:** I saw Goody Hawkins with the Devil!

**BETTY:** I saw Goody Bibber with the Devil!

**ABIGAIL:** I saw Goody Booth with the Devil!

*(On their ecstatic cries)*

THE CURTAIN FALLS

**1. a crucible:** *un creuset* **2. Barbados:** *la Barbade* **3. a minister:** *un pasteur* **4. to bless:** *bénir* **5. to cleanse:** *purifier* **6. to burst out:** *éclater* **7. to bid:** *ordonner* **8. Goody** (short for goodwife) was the name given to women **9. a midwife:** *une sage-femme* **10. to shrivel:** *se flétrir* **11. to prey on so:** *s'attaquer à quelqu'un* **12. enraptured:** *sous un enchantement* **13. glee:** *la jubilation* **14. a marshal:** *un homme de loi*

## Zooming in

1. The structure of the scene.
   - What are the two main parts of the scene?
   - What are the different steps of Tituba's confession?
2. Study the development of hysteria, which affects both the ministers and the girls, in:
   - stage directions,
   - repetitions.
3. What means do the accusers use to get an answer, whether it be true or untrue?
4. What is the relevance of this scene for the time it was written?
5. Show that this scene is a perversion of true Christianity.

# TEXT 7 Seamus HEANEY ~ 'Digging', in *Death of a Naturalist*, 1966

**Seamus HEANEY**
(born 1939)
an Irish poet, writes about the land and the rural world, which become the starting points of a reflection upon identity and history.

## Digging

Between my finger and my thumb
The squat pen rests; as snug as a gun.

Under my window a clean rasping sound
When the spade sinks into gravelly ground:
My father, digging. I look down

Till his straining rump among the flowerbeds
Bends low, comes up twenty years away
Stooping in rhythm through potato drills
Where he was digging.

The coarse boot nestled on the lug, the shaft
Against the inside knee was levered firmly.
He rooted out tall tops, buried the bright edge deep
To scatter new potatoes that we picked
Loving their cool hardness in our hands.

By God, the old man could handle a spade,
Just like his old man.

My grandfather could cut more turf in a day
Than any other man on Toner's bog.
Once I carried him milk in a bottle
Corked sloppily with paper. He straightened up
To drink it, then fell to right away
Nicking and slicing neatly, heaving sods
Over his shoulder, digging down and down
For the good turf. Digging.

The cold smell of potato mold, the squelch and slap
Of soggy peat, the curt cuts of an edge

## Creuser

*Entre mon stylo et mon pouce*
*Le stylo trapu repose ; comme un pistolet.*

*Sous ma fenêtre, le crissement net*
*De la bêche qui plonge dans le sol caillouteux :*
*Mon père qui creuse. Je le regarde*

*Jusqu'à ce que ses reins tendus parmi les plates-bandes*
*Se courbent à terre, remontent vingt ans après*
*Se voûtent en rythme dans les sillons de pommes de terre*
*Où il creusait.*

*La grosse botte blottie contre le fer, le manche*
*Contre l'intérieur du genou était facile à manier.*
*Il déterrait de hautes tiges, enfonçait loin la lame brillante*
*Éparpillait les pommes de terre nouvelles que nous ramassions.*
*Comme nous aimions leur fermeté fraîche dans nos mains !*

*Pardi, le vieux savait manier la bêche*
*Juste comme son vieux avant lui.*

*Mon grand-père coupait plus de tourbe en un jour*
*Qu'aucun autre homme de la tourbière de Toner !*
*Une fois, je lui ai porté du lait dans une bouteille*
*Mal bouchée avec du papier. Il se redressa*
*Pour boire, puis s'y remis aussitôt,*
*Il taillait net tranchait nettement, balançant les mottes*
*Par dessus l'épaule, il descendait de plus en plus bas*
*Vers la bonne tourbe. Il creusait.*

TEXT **7** SEAMUS HEANEY ~ 'DIGGING', IN DEATH OF A NATURALIST, 1966

Through living roots awaken in my
head.
But I've no spade to follow men like
them.

Between my finger and my thumb
The squat pen rests.
I'll dig with it.

From *Death of a Naturalist*, 1966

*L'odeur froide de la terre remuée, le*
*gargouillis*
*De la tourbe détrempée, les courtes*
*entailles d'une lame*
*Au travers de racines vivantes*
*s'éveillent dans ma tête.*
*Mais je n'ai plus de pelle pour suivre*
*de tels hommes.*

*Entre mon doigt et mon pouce*
*Le stylo trapu repose.*
*Je creuserai avec.*

Traduction Paul Bensimon, dans
*Anthologie bilingue de la poésie anglaise*,
coll. « La Pléïade », Gallimard, 2005

## Zooming in

**1** The structure of the poem.

**a.** How many generations of the poet's family are mentioned here? Show which lines they correspond to.

**b.** What main activity is linked to each generation?

**c.** What tenses are used in the poem? Why?

**2** What objects are symbolic of:

- political violence: ...
- traditional Ireland: ...
- the poet's own choice: ...

**3** Think of at least two things the activity of digging is symbolic of in the poem.
Are there any other metaphors/similes in the poem?

**4** What differences are there between the first and last stanzas? What do they mean?

**5** How does the poet succeed in evoking closeness to the land?

- onomatopoeia: ...
- alliteration: ...
- technical words: ...

**6** To what extent is this poem a reflection upon Irish society?

## MOVING ON

**Watch**

– Different versions of some of Shakespeare's plays such as *Macbeth*, *Richard III* or *Henry V*.
– The BBC film from Mrs Gaskell's *North and South*, which gives a very good idea of the divisions between North and South in Victorian England
– John Ford's film *The Grapes of Wrath* (1940).
– Orson Welles's *Citizen Kane* (1941) or *The Magnificent Ambersons* (1942)
– Elia Kazan's *On the Waterfront* (1954).
– Compare Jean-Paul Sartre's *Les Sorcières de Salem* (1957) and Miller's film *The Crucible* (1996), with Paul Scofield and Daniel Day-Lewis
– Dennis Hopper's *Easy Rider* (1969)
– Roman Polanski's *Tess of the d'Urbervilles* (1979)

**Read**

– *Gulliver's Travels* (1726), by Jonathan Swift
– *Jude the Obscure* (1895), by Thomas Hardy
– *The Great Gatsby* (1925), by Scott Fitzgerald
– *Of Mice and Men* (1937), by John Steinbeck
– The poetry of the Beats (Ginsberg, Ferlinghetti See p. 44)
– *On the Road*, by Jack Kerouac (1951)

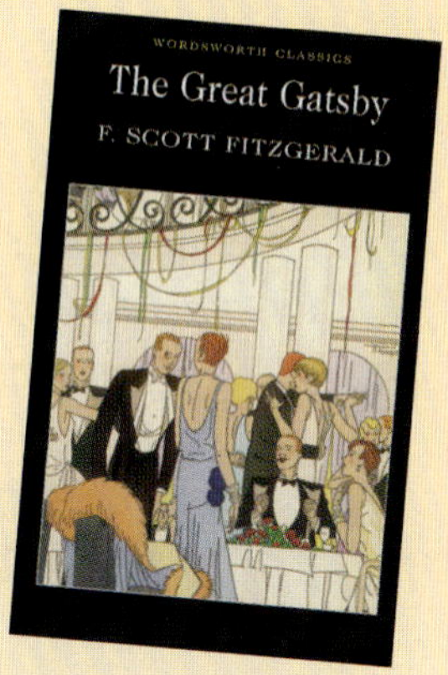


**Listen to**

On the internet, you will find readings of Auden's poetry – some of it by Auden himself – as well as recordings of Ginsberg's first reading of 'Howl'.

# Humour and nonsense

## What is humour?

• It is a way of perceiving and describing what is strange or ridiculous, but not in a critical way. The humorist does not denounce. Humour implies gentleness, sympathy, sentimentality and a benevolent[1] vision of others. It is not corrective and is therefore different from irony, which is often an attack. See p. 163

› For example: *I like work; it fascinates me. I can sit and look at it for hours. I love to keep it by me: the idea of getting rid of it nearly breaks my heart.* (J. K. Jerome, *Three Men in a Boat*, 1889)

• **Black humour** uses what is morbid for humour.

› For example: *Yes, I'd like a bulletproof vest.* (James Rodgers, the murderer, on his final request before the firing squad, 1960).

## Wit

• **Wit** is different from humour; it is the use of brilliant, inventive language, and is often based on paradox.

› For example: *Always forgive your enemies; nothing annoys them so much.* (Oscar Wilde)

• **Repartee** is a clever, witty reply to what was already witty, each person trying to outdo[2] the other.

› For example: *Lady Astor: "Winston, if you were my husband, I'd put poison in your coffee."*
*Churchill: "Nancy, if you were my wife, I'd drink it."*

Wit is verbal only, whereas humour can be non-verbal (situation, gestures, or in cartoons[3]).

## Why is humour so typically Anglo-Saxon?

Can it be related to British eccentricity? Or to the British temperament, since the British are said to be phlegmatic, to keep their self-control, not to express emotions in public? Humour would then be a form of distantiation. Or does it come from the fear of being pedantic, of taking oneself too seriously?

## What is nonsense?

A nonsense text is a text which has no logical meaning. But nonsense is also a literary genre, used in limericks See p. 151 and by some writers such as **Lewis Carroll**. The world of nonsense is a world which is without emotions and without a didactic purpose. It may partly be explained by the fact that children learn nursery rhymes[4], which are usually nonsensical. It is also certainly related to the creative quality of the English language.

› For example:

Hey diddle diddle, the cat and the fiddle[1],
The cow jumped over the moon;
The little dog laughed to see such sport,
And the dish ran away with the spoon.

(A traditional nursery rhyme)

1. a fiddle: *un violon*

## Humour in literature

Humour can be found in much of Anglo-Saxon literature, and in particular in several of **Shakespeare**'s plays, even in tragedies, in Restoration comedy, in the novels of **Fielding** and those of **Laurence Sterne**, in **Byron**'s *Don Juan*, in **Charles Dickens**'s novels, as well as in those of **Mark Twain** and in much postmodern fiction.

But humour and nonsense can also hide wisdom or a reflection on the human condition, as in much of the theatre of the absurd See p. 124.

1. **benevolent:** *bienveillant*
2. **to outdo someone:** *l'emporter sur quelqu'un*
3. **a cartoon:** *un dessin humoristique*
4. **a nursery rhyme:** *une comptine*

TEXT 1 **LEWIS CARROLL ~ THROUGH THE LOOKING-GLASS, 1871**

*In* Through the Looking-Glass, *Alice climbs through a mirror and finds herself in a world where everything is illogical or upside down*[1]. *In this passage, she has just met a knight*[2].

**Lewis CARROLL**
(1832-1898)
was a professor of mathematics and an eccentric. His books were written to amuse children, but also reflect aspects of Victorian society. (*Alice in Wonderland*, 1865, *Through the Looking-Glass*, 1871)

SHE THOUGHT SHE HAD NEVER SEEN such a strange-looking soldier in all her life. He was dressed in tin[3] armour, which seemed to fit him very badly, and he had a queer little deal box[4] fastened[5] across his shoulders upside-down, and with the lid[6] hanging open. Alice looked at it with great curiosity.

Illustration by John Tenniel, *Alice through the Mirror*, 1870

"I see you're admiring my little box," the Knight said in a friendly tone. "It's my own invention — to keep clothes and sandwiches in. You see I carry it upside-down, so that the rain can't get in."

"But the things can get out," Alice gently remarked. "Do you know the lid's open?"

"I didn't know it," the Knight said, a shade of vexation passing over his face. "Then all the things must have fallen out! And the box is no use without them." He unfastened it as he spoke, and was just going to throw it into the bushes, when a sudden thought seemed to strike, and he hung it carefully on a tree. "Can you guess why I did that? " he said to Alice.

Alice shook her head. "In hopes some bees[7] may make a nest in it — then I should get the honey."

"But you've got a bee-hive[8] — or something like one — fastened to the saddle[9]," said Alice.

"Yes, it's a very good bee-hive," the Knight said in a discontented tone, "one of the best kind. But not a single bee has come near it yet. And the other thing is a mouse-trap. I suppose the mice keep the bees out — or the bees keep the mice out, I don't know which."

"I was wondering what the mouse-trap was for," said Alice. "It isn't very likely there would be any mice on the horse's back."

"Not very likely, perhaps," said the Knight; "but if they do come, I don't choose to have them running all about."

"You see," he went on after a pause, "it's as well to be provided for everything. That's the reason the horse has anklets[10] round his feet."

"But what are they for?" Alice asked in a tone of great curiosity.

"To guard against the bites of sharks[11]," the Knight replied. "It's an invention of my own. And now help me on. I'll go with you to the end of the wood. — What's that dish for?"

"It's meant for plum-cake," said Alice.

"We'd better take it with us," the Knight said. It'll come in handy if we find any plum-cake. Help me to get it into this bag."

This took a long time to manage, though Alice held the bag open very carefully, because the Knight was so very awkward in putting in the dish: the first two or three times that he tried he fell in himself instead. "It's rather a tight fit[12], you see," he said, as they got it in at last; "there are so many candlesticks[13] in the bag." And he hung it to the saddle, which was already loaded with bunches of carrots, and fire-irons, and many other things.

"I hope you've got your hair well fastened on?" he continued, as they set off.

"Only in the usual way," Alice said, smiling.

"That's hardly enough," he said, anxiously. "You see the wind is so very strong here. It's as strong as soup."

"Have you invented a plan for keeping one's hair from being blown off?" Alice enquired.

"Not yet," said the Knight. "But I've got a plan for keeping it from falling off."

(From chapter VIII)

**1. upside down:** *à l'envers* **2. a knight:** *un chevalier* **3. tin:** *l'étain, le fer-blanc* **4. a deal box:** *une boîte en bois* **5. to fasten:** *attacher* **6. the lid:** *le couvercle* **7. a bee:** *une abeille* **8. a bee-hive:** *une ruche* **9. the saddle:** *la selle (de cheval)* **10. anklets:** *des anneaux de cheville* **11. a shark:** *un requin* **12. it is a tight fit:** *c'est un peu juste* **13. a candlestick:** *un bougeoir*

## Zooming in

1. List all the objects carried by the knight and the reasons why they are absurd.
2. Despite this absurdity, show that the dialogue remains quite logical.
3. Why is this adventure with the knight similar to a child's dream?
4. Could the knight have a symbolic meaning?

# TEXT 2 MARK TWAIN ~ THE ADVENTURES OF TOM SAWYER, 1876

**Mark TWAIN**
(1835-1910)
His stories and novels reflect Southwestern American humour. In his novels of initiation, his main characters are children who discover America, and through whose innocent eyes we see a satire of Southern society.

*Tom Sawyer is a poor 13-year-old boy. Tom's Aunt Polly has ordered him to whitewash[1] her fence[2] as a punishment. Tom hates the work and decides to try and get some of his friends to do it for him. As Tom is working, Ben, one of his friends, arrives, holding an apple.*

Tom surveyed his last touch with the eye of an artist, then he gave his brush[3] another gentle sweep[4] and surveyed the result, as before. Ben ranged up alongside of him. Tom's mouth watered for the apple, but he stuck to his work[5]. Ben said:

"Hello, old chap, you got to work, hey?"

Tom wheeled[6] suddenly and said:

"Why, it's you, Ben! I warn't[7] noticing."

"Say — I'm going in a-swimming, I am. Don't you wish you could? But of course you'd druther[8] WORK — wouldn't you? Course you would!"

Tom contemplated the boy a bit, and said:

"What do you call work?"

"Why, ain't THAT work?"

Tom resumed[9] his whitewashing, and answered carelessly:

"Well, maybe it is, and maybe it ain't. All I know, is, it suits Tom Sawyer."

"Oh come, now, you don't mean to let on that you LIKE it?"

The brush continued to move.

"Like it? Well, I don't see why I oughtn't to like it. Does a boy get a chance to whitewash a fence every day?"

That put the thing in a new light. Ben stopped nibbling[10] his apple. Tom swept his brush daintily[11] back and forth — stepped back to note the effect — added a touch here and there — criticised the effect again — Ben watching every move and getting more and more interested, more and more absorbed. Presently he said:

"Say, Tom, let ME whitewash a little."

Tom considered, was about to consent; but he altered his mind[12]:

"No — no — I reckon it wouldn't hardly do, Ben. You see, Aunt Polly's awful particular about this fence — right here on the street, you know — but if it was the back fence I wouldn't mind and SHE wouldn't. Yes, she's awful particular about this fence; it's got to be done very careful; I reckon there ain't one boy in a thousand, maybe two thousand, that can do it the way it's got to be done."

"No — is that so? Oh come, now — lemme[13] just try. Only just a little — I'd let YOU, if you was me, Tom."

"Ben, I'd like to, honest injun[14]; but Aunt Polly — well, Jim wanted to do it, but she wouldn't let him; Sid wanted to do it, and she wouldn't let Sid. Now don't you see how I'm fixed? If you was to tackle[15] this fence and anything was to happen to it —"

"Oh, shucks, I'll be just as careful. Now lemme try. Say — I'll give you the core[16] of my apple."

"Well, here — No, Ben, now don't. I'm afeard —"

"I'll give you ALL of it!"

Tom gave up the brush with reluctance[17] in his face, but alacrity[18] in his heart. And while the late steamer[19] Big Missouri worked and sweated in the sun, the retired[20] artist sat on a barrel[21] in the shade[22] close by, dangled[23] his legs, munched his apple, and planned the slaughter[24] of more innocents. There was no lack[25] of material; boys happened along every little while; they came to jeer[26], but remained to whitewash. By the time Ben was fagged out[27], Tom had traded the next chance to Billy Fisher for a kite[28], in good repair; and when he played out[29], Johnny Miller bought in for a dead rat and a string to swing it with — and so on, and so on, hour after hour.

**1. to whitewash:** *blanchir à la chaux* **2. a fence:** *une barrière* **3. a brush:** *un pinceau* **4. a sweep:** *un coup (de pinceau)* **5. he stuck to his work:** *il continua à travailler* **6. to wheel around:** *se retourner* **7. warn't:** wasn't (dialectal) **8. you'd druther:** you'd rather **9. to resume:** *reprendre* **10. to nibble:** *grignoter* **11. daintily:** *délicatement* **12. altered his mind:** *changea d'avis* **13. lemme:** let me (familiar) **14. honest injun:** *parole d'honneur* **15. to tackle:** *s'attaquer à, se mettre à faire quelque chose* **16. an apple core:** *un trognon de pomme* **17. with reluctance:** *à contrecoeur* **18. alacrity:** *empressement* **19. a steamer:** *un bateau à vapeur* **20. retired:** *à la retraite* **21. a barrel:** *un tonneau* **22. in the shade:** *à l'ombre* **23. to dangle:** *laisser pendre* **24. the slaughter:** *le massacre* **25. the lack of:** *le manque de* **26. to jeer:** *se moquer* **27. fagged out:** *épuisé* **28. a kite:** *un cerf-volant* **29. to play out:** *être éreinté*

## Zooming in

**1** What method is used by Tom to get his friends to do his work for him? In what order do the following "arguments" appear in the text?

**a.** It's very important work.

**b.** Tom likes doing it.

**c.** It's artistic work.

**d.** Aunt Polly does not want anyone but Tom to do it.

**e.** Tom is so interested in his work that he does not notice Ben.

› Tom's progression: ...
› Ben's progression: ...

Show that this progression is paralleled by another progression in Ben's reactions.

**2** Humour here is based on the playing of a trick on someone. Why do we smile or laugh and not disapprove?

**3** Tom keeps trading, exchanging things with his friends. What does this symbolize in American society?

# TEXT 3 O. WILDE ~ The Importance of Being Earnest, 1895

**Oscar WILDE**
(1854-1900)
wrote plays (*The Importance of Being Earnest*, *An Ideal Husband*, 1895), poems, and a novel (*The Picture of Dorian Gray* (1890) – all influenced by aestheticism and criticizing the conventional values and hypocrisy of Victorian society.

*This scene takes place in Algernon's London flat very soon after the beginning of the play. Lane is the manservant.*

ALGERNON: Why is it that at a bachelor[1]'s establishment the servants invariably drink the champagne? I ask merely for information.

LANE: I attribute it to the superior quality of the wine, sir. I have often observed that in married households the champagne is rarely of a first-rate brand.

ALGERNON: Good heavens! Is marriage so demoralising as that?

LANE: I believe it IS a very pleasant state, sir. I have had very little experience of it myself up to the present. I have only been married once. That was in consequence of a misunderstanding between myself and a young person.

ALGERNON: *(Languidly.)* I don't know that I am much interested in your family life, Lane.

LANE: No, sir; it is not a very interesting subject. I never think of it myself.

ALGERNON: Very natural, I am sure. That will do, Lane, thank you.

LANE: Thank you, sir. *(Lane goes out.)*

ALGERNON: Lane's views on marriage seem somewhat lax[2]. Really, if the lower orders don't set us a good example, what on earth is the use of them? They seem, as a class, to have absolutely no sense of moral responsibility.

*(Enter Lane.)*

LANE: Mr Ernest Worthing.

*(Enter Jack.) (Lane goes out.)*

ALGERNON: How are you, my dear Ernest? What brings you up to town?

JACK: Oh, pleasure, pleasure! What else should bring one anywhere? Eating as usual, I see, Algy!

ALGERNON: *(Stiffly.)* I believe it is customary in good society to take some slight refreshment at five o'clock. Where have you been since last Thursday?

JACK: *(Sitting down on the sofa.)* In the country.

*The Importance of Being Earnest*, directed by Peter GILL, London, 2008

**ALGERNON:** What on earth do you do there?

**JACK:** *(Pulling off his gloves.)* When one is in town one amuses oneself. When one is in the country one amuses other people. It is excessively boring.

**ALGERNON:** And who are the people you amuse?

**JACK:** *(Airily.)* Oh, neighbours, neighbours.

**ALGERNON:** Got nice neighbours in your part of Shropshire?

**JACK:** Perfectly horrid! Never speak to one of them.

**ALGERNON:** How immensely you must amuse them! *(Goes over and takes sandwich.)* By the way, Shropshire is your county, is it not?

**JACK:** Eh? Shropshire? Yes, of course. Hallo! Why all these cups? Why cucumber sandwiches? Why such reckless[3] extravagance in one so young? Who is coming to tea?

**ALGERNON:** Oh! merely Aunt Augusta and Gwendolen.

**JACK:** How perfectly delightful!

**ALGERNON:** Yes, that is all very well; but I am afraid Aunt Augusta won't quite approve of your being here.

**JACK:** May I ask why?

**ALGERNON:** My dear fellow, the way you flirt with Gwendolen is perfectly disgraceful. It is almost as bad as the way Gwendolen flirts with you.

**JACK:** I am in love with Gwendolen. I have come up to town expressly to propose[4] to her.

**ALGERNON:** I thought you had come up for pleasure?... I call that business.

**JACK:** How utterly unromantic you are!

**ALGERNON:** I really don't see anything romantic in proposing. It is very romantic to be in love. But there is nothing romantic about a definite proposal. Why, one may be accepted. One usually is, I believe. Then the excitement is all over. The very essence of romance is uncertainty. If ever I get married, I'll certainly try to forget the fact.

**JACK:** I have no doubt about that, dear Algy. The Divorce Court was specially invented for people whose memories are so curiously constituted.

**ALGERNON:** Oh! there is no use speculating on that subject. Divorces are made in Heaven—*(Jack puts out his hand to take a sandwich. Algernon at once interferes.)* Please don't touch the cucumber sandwiches. They are ordered specially for Aunt Augusta. *(Takes one and eats it.)*

**JACK:** Well, you have been eating them all the time.

**ALGERNON:** That is quite a different matter. She is my aunt.

**1. a bachelor:** *un célibataire* **2. lax:** *relâché* **3. reckless:** *imprudent, irresponsable*
**4. to propose:** *demander en mariage*

## Zooming in

1. Find examples of wit / paradox / cynicism / false logic, creating a comic effect.
2. Can you call this scene realistic? Can it be taken in "earnest"?
3. What aspects of Victorian society are criticized here? (Think in terms of marriage, hypocrisy, appearances and social class.)

# TEXT 4 C. RAINE ~ A Martian Sends a Postcard Home, 1979

**Craig RAINE**
(born 1944)

belonged to the movement called "Martian poetry" in the late 1970s. Their aim was to de-familiarize reality – as if it was seen through the eyes of a Martian. The result may look, at first sight, close to nonsense.

### A Martian Sends A Postcard Home

Caxtons[1] are mechanical birds with many wings
and some are treasured[2] for their markings—

they cause the eyes to melt[3]
or the body to shriek without pain.

I have never seen one fly, but
sometimes they perch on the hand.

Mist[4] is when the sky is tired of flight
and rests its soft machine on ground:

then the world is dim[5] and bookish
like engravings[6] under tissue paper.

Rain is when the earth is television.
It has the property of making colours darker.

Model T[7] is a room with the lock inside—
a key is turned to free the world

for movement, so quick there is a film
to watch for anything missed.

But time is tied to the wrist
or kept in a box, ticking with impatience.

In homes, a haunted apparatus[8] sleeps,
that snores[9] when you pick it up.

If the ghost cries, they carry it
to their lips and soothe[10] it to sleep

with sounds. And yet, they wake it up
deliberately, by tickling[11] with a finger.

Only the young are allowed to suffer
openly. Adults go to a punishment room

with water but nothing to eat.
They lock the door and suffer the noises

alone. No one is exempt
and everyone's pain has a different smell.

At night, when all the colours die,
they hide in pairs

and read about themselves –
in colour, with their eyelids shut.

Craig Raine, © Craig Raine, 1979, O.U.P.

1. **Caxton** (1422-1491) was the first Englishman to print books 2. **to treasure:** *chérir*
3. **to melt:** *fondre* 4. **mist:** *la brume* 5. **dim:** *sombre* 6. **an engraving:** *une gravure*
7. **Model T** was the first car mass-produced by the Ford company in the 1920s
8. **an apparatus:** *un appareil* 9. **to snore:** *ronfler* 10. **to soothe:** *calmer* 11. **to tickle:** *chatouiller*

## Zooming in

1. What are the different things described by the Martian? Show what the details correspond to. A first example is given.
   Stanzas 1-2:
   Thing described: books
   Details
   - The wings = the pages;
   - their markings = words on the pages;
   - the eyes melting = tears;
   - shrieking without pain = fear
2. List the different ways in which this poem de-familiarizes.
3. Classify the metaphors used: which are poetic, which humorous, which strange?
4. Write one or two additional stanzas to the poem.

## MOVING ON

**Watch**
- Different versions of William Shakespeare's *Twelfth Night* or *As You Like It*
- Television comedy, such as Monty Python's *Flying Circus* or Tony Hancock's *Half Hour*
- Oscar Wilde's plays, most of which are available on DVD
- Robert Hamer's *Kind Hearts and Coronets* (1949)
- Stanley Kubrick's *Dr Strangelove* (1963)
- Blake Edwards's *The Party* (1969)
- Woody Allen's *Take the Money and Run* (1969)
- Norman Wisdom films

**Read**
- Sheridan's *The School for Scandal* (1777)
- Charles Dickens, *The Pickwick Papers* (1836-37)
- Jerome K. Jerome, *Three Men in a Boat* (1889)
- James Thurber, *Fables for Our Time* (1961)
- Edward Lear's limericks

**Listen to**
The reading of *Alice in Wonderland* as you turn the pages of the book on the site of the British Library (Virtual Books).

# Feminine voices

Even though there were a few women writers in the 17th and 18th centuries (**Aphra Behn**, **Fanny Burney**, **Mrs Radcliffe** See p. 58), it was mainly at the beginning of the 19th century that women appeared on the literary scene.

## 19th century women writers

• **Jane Austen** studied the confined world that she knew (the country gentry), satirizing hypocrisy, stupidity and self-importance; she gave women such as Elizabeth in *Pride and Prejudice* an independent voice, yet always defended traditional values.

All through the 19th century the fiction written by women relates similar stories of women who often challenged the patriarchal system and their position in society. The novels of **Charlotte Brontë** or **Mrs Gaskell** or **George Eliot**'s *Middlemarch*, are examples of this. Jane Austen's heroines nevertheless ended up conforming since the economic and legal systems made them entirely dependent on men, being little better than objects. These social and material limitations made it difficult for a woman to write, when she had to devote most of her time to family and household tasks.

• Some women writers still succeeded in observing the society of their time, for instance **George Eliot**, whose real name was Mary Anne Evans, hid behind a man's identity. Her novels examined the influence of the social environment upon people (*The Mill on the Floss*, 1860; *Middlemarch*, 1872)

## The 20th century

• In her seminal essay *A Room of One's Own* (1929), **Virginia Woolf** explained that a woman in the past could not produce major works as she was deprived of the freedom to write, since "to have a room of her own was out of the question, unless her parents were exceptionally rich". This manifesto, written the year after women obtained full voting rights in Britain, helped to make people aware of the problem.

• Several major women writers made their voices heard in the second half of the century, for instance **Iris Murdoch**, **Muriel Spark** or **Doris Lessing**. They are particularly well represented in post-modern fiction (**Jeanette Winterson**, for example, or **Angela Carter** See p. 66) and in post colonial writings See p. 134 since they have often compared their alienation to that of colonized countries.

## The United States

• Even more so than in Britain, literature chiefly remained the prerogative of men in the 19th century apart from a few exceptions (the poetry of **Anne Bradstreet** in colonial times, or the poetry of **Emily Dickinson** in the late 19th century). The first voice that was raised to speak about women's need for an identity of their own was that of **Kate Chopin** who, with *The Awakening* (1899) shocked the country with references to female sexuality.

• **Edith Wharton** wrote novels of manners which satirize the fashionable cosmopolitan society of her time, with its pretentions and corruption.

• It was mainly after World War II and with the rise of feminist movements that women were more widely heard:

– poets such as **Marianne Moore**, **Adrienne Rich** or **Sylvia Plath**,

– southern novelists (**Eudora Welty**, **Carson McCullers**, **Flannery O'Connor**), who wrote about alienated, often grotesque characters in the Deep South,

– short story writers like **Grace Paley**,

– and many 'ethnic voices' from the Black, Latino or Asian communities See p. 100.

# TEXT 1 JANE AUSTEN ~ PRIDE AND PREJUDICE, 1813

**Jane AUSTEN**
(1775-1817)

Her novels are set among the country gentry that she knew. Her heroines are young women who gradually come to a better understanding of themselves and obtain marriage and social status. The absurdities and pretentions of society are denounced with wit and irony. (*Pride and Prejudice*, 1813, *Mansfield Park*, 1814, *Emma*, 1816, *Northanger Abbey*, 1818.)

*This is the incipit of the novel.*

IT IS A TRUTH UNIVERSALLY ACKNOWLEDGED[1], that a single man in possession of a good fortune must be in want of a wife.

However little known the feelings or views of such a man may be on his first entering a neighbourhood, this truth is so well fixed in the minds of the surrounding families, that he is considered as the rightful[2] property of some one or other of their daughters.

"My dear Mr Bennet," said his lady to him one day, "have you heard that Netherfield Park is let at last?"

Mr Bennet replied that he had not.

"But it is," returned she; "for Mrs Long has just been here, and she told me all about it."

Mr Bennet made no answer.

"Do not you want to know who has taken it?" cried his wife impatiently.

"You want to tell me, and I have no objection to hearing it.''

This was invitation enough.

"Why, my dear, you must know, Mrs Long says that Netherfield is taken by a young man of large fortune from the north of England; that he came down on Monday in a chaise and four[3] to see the place, and was so much delighted with it that he agreed with Mr. Morris immediately; that he is to take possession before Michaelmas[4], and some of his servants are to be in the house by the end of next week."

"What is his name?"

"Bingley."

"Is he married or single?"

"Oh! single, my dear, to be sure! A single man of large fortune; four or five thousand a year. What a fine thing for our girls!"

"How so? how can it affect them?"

"My dear Mr Bennet,' replied his wife, "how can you be so tiresome[5]! You must know that I am thinking of his marrying one of them."

"Is that his design[6] in settling here?"

"Design! nonsense, how can you talk so! But it is very likely that he may fall in love with one of them, and therefore you must visit him as soon as he comes."

"I see no occasion for that. You and the girls may go, or

you may send them by themselves, which perhaps will be still better; for, as you are as handsome as any of them, Mr. Bingley might like you the best of the party."

"My dear, you flatter me. I certainly have had my share of beauty, but I do not pretend to be any thing extraordinary now. When a woman has five grown up daughters, she ought to give over thinking of her own beauty."

**1. to acknowledge:** *reconnaître* **2. rightful:** *légitime* **3. a chaise and four:** *un cabriolet tiré par quatre chevaux* **4. Michaelmas:** *29 septembre, date de début de trimestre pour le loyer* **5. tiresome:** *pénible* **6. his design:** *son intention*

## Zooming in

**1** How good an incipit is this text? What do we learn?
- about the Bennet family: ...
- about Mr Bingley: ...
- about the main subject of the novel: ...
- about the social background: ...

**2** Irony
The very first sentence of the novel is very famous, largely because of its irony. Explain why it is ironic.

**3** Characterization through contrast: contrast the way Mr and Mrs Bennet speak. What does it reveal about their characters?
- Who talks more? Why?
- Is direct speech used for both of them to report the dialogue?
- Give examples of irony. Who uses it? How is it received?

# TEXT 2 KATE CHOPIN ~ THE STORY OF AN HOUR, 1894

*This is the complete short story.*

**Kate CHOPIN**
(1851-1904)
wrote short stories and a novel, *The Awakening* (1899). She mainly addresses the problem of women's repressed lives in a society dominated by men.

KNOWING THAT MRS MALLARD was afflicted with a heart trouble, great care was taken to break to her as gently as possible the news of her husband's death. It was her sister Josephine who told her, in broken sentences; veiled hints[1] that revealed in half concealing. Her husband's friend Richards was there, too, near her. It was he who had been in the newspaper office when intelligence[2] of the railroad disaster was received, with Brently Mallard's name leading the list of "killed." He had only taken the time to assure himself of its truth by a second telegram, and had hastened[3] to forestall[4] any less careful, less tender friend in bearing the sad message.

She did not hear the story as many women have heard the same, with a paralyzed inability to accept its significance. She wept[5] at once, with sudden, wild abandonment, in her sister's arms. When the storm of grief[6] had spent itself she went away to her room alone. She would have no one follow her.

There stood, facing the open window, a comfortable, roomy[7] armchair. Into this she sank[8], pressed down by a physical exhaustion that haunted her body and seemed to reach into her soul.

J. W. WATERHOUSE, 'I am half sick of shadows', 1915, Illustration for *The Lady of Shalott*, by Alfred Tennyson, Art Gallery of Ontario, Toronto

She could see in the open square before her house the tops of trees that were all aquiver[9] with the new spring life. The delicious breath of rain was in the air. In the street below a peddler[10] was crying his wares[11]. The notes of a distant song which some one was singing reached her faintly, and countless sparrows[12] were twittering in the eaves[13].

There were patches of blue sky showing here and there through the clouds that had met and piled one above the other in the west facing her window.

She sat with her head thrown back upon the cushion of the chair, quite motionless, except when a sob[14] came up into her throat and shook her, as a child who has cried itself to sleep continues to sob in its dreams.

She was young, with a fair, calm face, whose lines bespoke[15] repression and even a certain strength. But now there was a dull stare in her eyes, whose gaze was fixed away off yonder[16] on one of those patches of blue sky. It was not a glance of reflection, but rather indicated a suspension of intelligent thought.

There was something coming to her and she was waiting for it, fearfully. What was it? She did not know; it was too subtle and elusive[17] to name. But she felt it, creeping[18] out of the sky, reaching toward her through the sounds, the scents, the color that filled the air.

Now her bosom[19] rose and fell tumultuously. She was beginning to recognize this thing that was approaching to possess her, and she was striving[20] to beat it back with her will — as powerless as her two white slender hands would have been.

When she abandoned herself a little whispered word escaped her slightly parted[21] lips. She said it over and over under her breath: "free, free, free!" The vacant stare and the look of terror that had followed it went from her eyes. They stayed keen and bright. Her pulses beat fast, and the coursing blood warmed and relaxed every inch of her body.

She did not stop to ask if it were or were not a monstrous joy that held her. A clear and exalted perception enabled her to dismiss the suggestion as trivial.

She knew that she would weep again when she saw the kind, tender hands folded in death; the face that had never looked save with love upon her, fixed and gray and dead. But she saw beyond that bitter moment a long procession of years to come that would belong to her absolutely. And she opened and spread her arms out to them in welcome.

There would be no one to live for during those coming years; she would live for herself. There would be no powerful will bending hers in that blind persistence with which men and women believe they have a right to impose a private will upon a fellow-creature. A kind intention or a cruel intention made the act seem no less a crime as she looked upon it in that brief moment of illumination.

And yet she had loved him — sometimes. Often she had not. What did it matter! What could love, the unsolved mystery, count for in the face of this possession of self-assertion[22] which she suddenly recognized as the strongest impulse of her being!

"Free! Body and soul free!" she kept whispering.

Josephine was kneeling before the closed door with her lips to the keyhole, imploring for admission. "Louise, open the door! I beg, open the door – you will make yourself ill. What are you doing Louise? For heaven's sake open the door."

"Go away. I am not making myself ill." No; she was drinking in a very elixir of life through that open window.

Her fancy[23] was running riot[24] along those days ahead of her. Spring days, and summer days, and all sorts of days that would be her own. She breathed a quick prayer that life might be long. It was only yesterday she had thought with a shudder that life might be long.

She arose at length and opened the door to her sister's importunities. There was a feverish triumph in her eyes, and she carried herself unwittingly[25] like a goddess of Victory. She clasped[26] her sister's waist[27], and together they descended the stairs. Richards stood waiting for them at the bottom.

Some one was opening the front door with a latchkey. It was Brently Mallard who entered, a little travel-stained, composedly carrying his grip-sack and umbrella. He had been far from the scene of accident, and did not even know there had been one. He stood amazed at Josephine's piercing cry; at Richards' quick motion to screen him from the view of his wife.

But Richards was too late.

When the doctors came they said she had died of heart disease – of joy that kills.

**1. a hint:** *une allusion* **2. intelligence:** *information* **3. to hasten:** *se hâter* **4. to forestall:** *devancer* **5. to weep:** *pleurer* **6. grief:** *le chagrin* **7. roomy:** *ample* **8. sank:** *preterit de 'sink' couler, s'enfoncer* **9. aquiver:** *frémissant* **10. a peddler:** *un colporteur* **11. his wares:** *sa marchandise* **12. a sparrow:** *un moineau* **13. the eaves:** *l'avant-toit* **14. a sob:** *un sanglot* **15. to bespeak:** *indiquer* **16. yonder:** *là-bas, au loin* **17. elusive:** *insaisissable* **18. to creep:** *se faufiler* **19. her bosom:** *sa poitrine* **20. to strive:** *s'efforcer* **21. parted:** *entrouvert* **22. self-assertion:** *affirmation de soi* **23. fancy:** *l'imagination* **24. to run riot:** *être déchaîné.* **25. unwittingly:** *involontairement* **26. to clasp:** *étreindre* **27. the waist:** *la taille*

## Zooming in

**1** The structure
There are two main turning points in the story. What are they?

**2** Is it joy that kills Mrs Mallard?

**3** What outside elements bring about the change in Mrs Mallard? What are they symbolic of?

**4** In the paragraph which precedes the first turning point ('She was young...' line 42), find four words which characterize her life as a married woman. What do they have in common?

**5** Mrs Mallard does not immediately feel free. What are the different steps in her new awareness?

**6** Show that the story is built around a number of oppositions.
- Inside / outside: ...
- Up and down: .. .
- Stiffness / movement: ...

**7** What is the double meaning of Mrs Mallard's 'heart trouble'?

**8** Why is the story deeply ironic? What is Kate Chopin's message in this short story?

**9** Match the following expressions and the corresponding figures of speech:
**a.** the storm of grief **b.** a monstrous joy **c.** joy that kills **d.** a breath of rain
paradox – hyperbole – metaphor - oxymoron

# TEXT 3 Edith WHARTON ~ The House of Mirth[1], 1905

**Edith WHARTON**
(1862-1937)
Her novels analyse the rich New York society of the early 20th century. She particularly addresses the situation of women who could not discover their individuality amid conventions and superficiality. She was the first woman to be awarded a Pulitzer Prize in 1921, for *The Age of Innocence*.

*Beautiful, intelligent, well-educated, but poor, Lily Bart lives with her aunt and gets invited to the homes of the rich. She is constantly torn between her desire for love and respect and her need for money and social status. In this passage she is staying at Bellomont, the home of Gus and Judy Trenor.*

SHE HAD BEEN BORED all the afternoon by Percy Gryce — the mere[2] thought seemed to waken an echo of his droning[3] voice — but she could not ignore him on the morrow, she must follow up her success, must submit to more boredom, must be ready with fresh compliances[4] and adaptabilities, and all on the bare[5] chance that he might ultimately decide to do her the honour of boring her for life.

It was a hateful fate — but how escape from it? What choice had she? To be herself, or a Gerty Farish[6]. As she entered her bedroom, with its softly-shaded lights, her lace[7] dressing-gown lying across the silken bedspread, her little embroidered slippers[8] before the fire, a vase of carnations[9] filling the air with perfume, and the last novels and magazines lying uncut on a table beside the reading-lamp, she had a vision of Miss Farish's cramped[10] flat, with its cheap conveniences and hideous wall-papers. No; she was not made for mean[11] and shabby[12] surroundings, for the squalid[13] compromises of poverty. Her whole being dilated in an atmosphere of luxury; it was the background she required, the only climate she could breathe in. But the luxury of others was not what she wanted. A few years ago it had sufficed her: she had taken her daily meed[14] of pleasure without caring who provided it. Now she was beginning to chafe at[15] the obligations it imposed, to feel herself a mere pensioner on the splendour which had once seemed to belong to her. There were even moments when she was conscious of having to pay her way. [...]

For in the last year she had found that her hostesses expected her to take a place at the card-table. It was one of the taxes she had to pay for their prolonged hospitality, and for the dresses and trinkets[16] which occasionally replenished[17] her insufficient wardrobe. And since she had played regularly the passion had grown on her. [...]

But of course she had lost — she who needed every penny, while Bertha Dorset, whose husband showered money on her, must have pocketed at least five hundred, and Judy Trenor, who could have afforded to lose a thousand a night, had left the table clutching such a heap of bills that she had been unable to shake hands with her guests when they bade her good night.

A world in which such things could be seemed a miserable place to Lily Bart; but then she had never been able to understand the laws of a universe which was so ready to leave her out of its calculations.

She began to undress without ringing for her maid, whom she had sent to bed. She had been long enough in bondage[18] to other people's pleasure to be considerate of those who depended on hers, and in her bitter moods it sometimes struck her that she and her maid were in the same position, except that the latter received her wages more regularly.

As she sat before the mirror brushing her hair, her face looked hollow[19] and pale, and she was frightened by two little lines near her mouth, faint flaws[20] in the smooth curve of the cheek.

"Oh, I must stop worrying!" she exclaimed. "Unless it's the electric light —" she reflected, springing up from her seat and lighting the candles on the dressing-table. [...]

Lily rose and undressed in haste.

"It is only because I am tired and have such odious things to think about," she kept repeating; and it seemed an added injustice that petty cares should leave a trace on the beauty which was her only defence against them.

But the odious things were there, and remained with her. She returned wearily to the thought of Percy Gryce, as a wayfarer[21] picks up a heavy load and toils on[22] after a brief rest. She was almost sure she had "landed"[23] him: a few days' work and she would win her reward. But the reward itself seemed unpalatable[24] just then: she could get no zest[25] from the thought of victory. It would be a rest from worry, no more — and how little that would have seemed to her a few years earlier! Her ambitions had shrunk gradually in the desiccating[26] air of failure. But why had she failed? Was it her own fault or that of destiny?

She remembered how her mother, after they had lost their money, used to say to her with a kind of fierce vindictiveness[27]: "But you'll get it all back — you'll get it all back, with your face." [...] The remembrance roused a whole train of association, and she lay in the darkness reconstructing the past out of which her present had grown.

**1. mirth:** *la gaieté* **2. mere:** *simple (la simple pensée)* **3. droning:** *monotone* **4. compliance:** *la servilité.* **5. the bare chance:** *la simple possibilité* **6. Gerty Farish:** her only real friend **7. lace:** *la dentelle* **8. embroidered slippers:** *pantoufles brodées* **9. carnations:** *oeillets* **10. cramped:** *où l'on est à l'étroit* **11. mean:** *misérable.* **12. shabby:** *miteux* **13. squalid:** *sordide* **14. meed (mead):** *l'hydromel* **15. to chafe at:** *s'irriter de* **16. a trinket:** *une babiole, un colifichet* **17. to replenish:** *remplir de nouveau* **18. in bondage to:** *esclave de* **19. hollow:** *creux* **20. a flaw:** *une imperfection* **21. a wayfarer:** *un voyageur* **22. to toil on:** *continuer à avancer péniblement* **23. to land something:** *décrocher quelquechose (familier)* **24. unpalatable:** *désagréable* **25. zest:** *le plaisir, l'entrain* **26. desiccating:** *desséchant* **27. vindictiveness:** *le caractère vindicatif*

## Zooming in

**1** Whose point of view do we have in the text?

**2** A circular structure

Sum up the main movements of the text and find which lines they correspond to. What does such a structure reflect?

**a.** A possibility of escape:

lines ... and lines ...

What's wrong with it?

**b.** Lily Bart gives three reasons why that possibility of escape might be necessary:

› lines ...
› lines ...
› lines ...

**3** List the main elements which show that society (and Lily) is obsessed with ...

money: ... clothes:... appearances: ...

**4** What two semantic fields are contrasted in the second paragraph?

**5** What does Lily mean when she uses the word 'bondage'?

**6** The title of the novel comes from the Bible (Ecclesiastes 7:4 "The heart of the wise is in the house of mourning; but the heart of fools is in the house of mirth.") Why is it appropriate to this passage?

**7** What aspect of American society is shown here?

# TEXT 4 C. McCULLERS ~ The Heart is a Lonely Hunter, 1940

**Carson McCULLERS**
(1917-1967)
represents the Southern Gothic trend in literature (p. 59). Her characters are often misfits and outsiders, adolescents as well, who cannot communicate and whose love remains unfulfilled. (*The Heart is a Lonely Hunter*, 1940, *The Ballad of the Sad Café*, 1943, *The Member of the Wedding*, 1943).

*This is the incipit of the novel.*

IN THE TOWN THERE WERE TWO MUTES[1], and they were always together. Early every morning they would come out from the house where they lived and walk arm in arm down the street to work. The two friends were very different. The one who always steered the way[2] was an obese and dreamy Greek. In the summer he would come out wearing a yellow or green polo shirt stuffed sloppily[3] into his trousers in front and hanging loose behind. When it was colder he wore over this a shapeless grey sweater. His face was round and oily, with half-closed eyelids and lips that curved in a gentle, stupid smile. The other mute was tall. His eyes had a quick, intelligent expression. He was always immaculate and very soberly dressed.

Every morning the two friends walked silently together until they reached the main street of the town. Then when they came to a certain fruit and candy store they paused for a moment on the sidewalk outside. The Greek, Spiros Antonapoulos, worked for his cousin, who owned this fruit store. His job was to make candies and sweets, uncrate[4] the fruits, and to keep the place clean. The thin mute, John Singer, nearly always put his hand on his friend's arm and looked for a second into his face before leaving him. Then after this good-bye Singer crossed the street and walked on alone to the jewellery store where he worked as a silverware engraver[5].

In the late afternoon the friends would meet again. Singer came back to the fruit store and waited until Antonapoulos was ready to go home. The Greek would be lazily unpacking a case of peaches or melons, or perhaps looking at the funny paper[6] in the kitchen behind the store where he cooked. Before their departure Antonapoulos always opened a paper sack he kept hidden during the day on one of the kitchen shelves. Inside were stored various bits of food he had collected – a piece of fruit, samples[7] of candy, or the butt-end of liverwurst[8]. Usually before leaving Antonapoulos waddled[9] gently to the glassed case in the front of the store where some meats and cheeses were kept. He glided[10] open the back of the case and his fat hand groped lovingly for some particular dainty[11] inside which he had wanted. Sometimes his cousin who owned the place did not see him. But if he noticed he stared at his cousin with a warning in his tight, pale face. Sadly Antonapoulos would shuffle[12] the morsel from one corner of the case to the other. During these times Singer stood very straight with his hands in his pockets and looked in another direction. He did not like to watch this little scene between the two Greeks. For, excepting drinking and a certain solitary pleasure, Antonapoulos loved to eat more than anything else in the world.

In the dusk[13] the two mutes walked slowly home together. At home Singer was always talking to Antonapoulos. His hands shaped the words in a swift series of designs. His face was eager and his grey-

green eyes sparkled brightly. With his thin, strong hands he told Antonapoulos all that had happened during the day.

Antonapoulos sat back lazily and looked at Singer. It was seldom that he ever moved his hands to speak at all – and then it was to say that he wanted to eat or to sleep or to drink. These three things he always said with the same vague, fumbling[14] signs. At night, if he were not too drunk, he would kneel down before his bed and pray awhile. Then his plump hands shaped the words 'Holy Jesus', or 'God', or 'Darling Mary'. These were the only words Antonapoulos ever said. Singer never knew just how much his friend understood of all the things he told him. But it did not matter.

**1. a mute:** *un muet* **2. to steer the way:** *montrer le chemin* **3. sloppily:** *n'importe comment* **4. to uncrate:** *sortir (les fruits) des cageots* **5. an engraver:** *un graveur* **6. the funny paper:** *les bandes dessinées du journal* **7. a sample:** *un échantillon* **8. the butt-end of liverwurst:** *le bout d'une saucisse* **9. to waddle:** *se dandiner* **10. to glide:** *faire glisser* **11. a dainty:** *un mets délicat* **12. to shuffle:** *pousser* **13. dusk:** *la nuit tombante, le crépuscule* **14. fumbling:** *tâtonnant*

## Zooming in

1. Show the structure of the text by looking at the beginning of each paragraph.
2. The narrator says 'The two friends were very different.' Show the main differences between Singer and Antonapoulos:
   - appearance: ...
   - character: ...
   - main interest: ...

   How is this difference conveyed by the structure of the text?
3. What kind of narrator do we have here? How are the habits of the two men reported? What is the tone of the passage?
4. What does the form of the first sentence remind you of? Are the men, the place, the time clearly defined? What effect is produced?
5. Can you give a religious interpretation of the passage?
6. In *The Ballad of the Sad Café*, Carson McCullers wrote: "Love is a joint experience between two persons – but the fact that it is a joint experience does not mean that it is a similar experience to the two people involved. There are the lover and the beloved, but these come from different countries. Often the beloved is only a stimulus for all the stored-up love which has lain quiet within the lover for a long time hitherto... The most outlandish people can be the stimulus for love"

   How does this help you understand the meaning of the incipit?

## MOVING ON

**Watch**

– Joe Wright's *Pride and Prejudice* and the BBC version of Jane Austen's novel. The BBC has made films of all six of Jane Austen's novels, but also of Mrs Gaskell's *North and South* and of George Eliot's *Middlemarch* – all available on DVD

– Terence Davies' s adaptation of Edith Wharton's *The House of Mirth*

– Fred Zinnemann's *Julia*, adapted from the novel by Lillian Hellman

– Stephen Daldry's *The Hours* (2002), adapted from a novel by Michael Cunningham in which the plot focuses on three women of different generations whose lives are interconnected by Virginia Woolf's *Mrs Dalloway*

**Read**

– *My Antonia* (1918), by Willa Cather

– *Mrs Dalloway* (1925), by Virginia Woolf

– *The Bell Jar* (1963), by Sylvia Plath

– *The Golden Notebook* (1964), by Doris Lessing

– Angela Carter's *The Bloody Chamber* See p. 66

– some of Grace Paley's short stories

– Jeanette Winterson's *Oranges are not the Only Fruit* (1985)

**Listen to**

Recordings of Emily Dickinson's poems (on the internet).

# A diversity of voices

Bringing people of different cultures together has been the cornerstone[1] of the American nation. In Britain, it is the more recent immigration waves (mainly post World War II), often from the Commonwealth or from African countries, which have changed the social and cultural landscape of the country.
In both the United States and Britain, therefore, the themes of integration, alienation and identity have been central to literature.

## Black voices

• During the long years of slavery in the United States, black people were not given a voice. Lack of education and, for the few who could write, fear of being punished made writing an almost impossible gesture of defiance and independence. There were a few exceptions, however, such as **Frederick Douglass**'s *Narrative of the Life of Frederick Douglass* (1845).

**Strange Fruit**

Southern trees bear strange fruit,
Blood on the leaves and blood at the root,
Black body swinging in the Southern breeze,
Strange fruit hanging from the poplar trees.
Pastoral scene of the gallant South,
The bulging eyes[1] and the twisted mouth,
Scent of magnolia sweet and fresh,
Then the sudden smell of burning flesh!
Here is fruit for the crows[2] to pluck[3],
For the rain to gather, for the wind to suck,
For the sun to rot, for the trees to drop,
Here is a strange and bitter crop.

*This well-known song was performed by Billie Holiday in 1939, to protest against the lynching of Black people.*

**1. bulging eyes:** *des yeux exorbités* **2. crows:** *corbeaux*
**3. to pluck:** *cueillir*

• Several black writers, such as **Paul Laurence Dunbar** or **W.E.B. Du Bois**, appeared after the Civil War and the abolition of slavery, mainly to express their frustrations and anxiety at being excluded from the national mainstream[2]. But it was with the Harlem Renaissance in the 1920s and 1930s – a movement that brought together writers and artists in Harlem – that a new pride in the black race appeared. It replaced the former sense of humiliation with confidence, a search for one's roots and linguistic creativity. This is reflected in the poetry of **Claude McKay**, **Countee Cullen** and **Langston Hughes**. *See p. 41*

• During the Depression years, social tension and unemployment led to a more radical literature of protest. One if its representatives is **Richard Wright**, whose novels are about racial violence (*Uncle Tom's Children*, 1938) and rebellion (*Native Son*, 1940).

• After WWII and during the years that led to the Civil Rights movements of the 1960s, two opposing movements appeared: some Black writers wanted to be integrated into mainstream American literary life, while others believed that they could not protest against their condition and be 'in' at the same time. A novel such as **Ralph Ellison**'s *Invisible Man* (1952) reconciled both of these views: it is a protest novel with universal appeal. *See p. 45*

• **James Baldwin** (*Go Tell It on the Mountain*, 1953) went beyond the protest novel to explore the problems of identity, understanding and love, which are not those of Black people alone.

• Modern African American writers examine the themes of identity and self expression – often linked to feminism. Some prominent names are **Maya Angelou**, **Alice Walker** (*The Color Purple*, 1982) and **Toni Morrison** (*The Bluest Eye*, 1970; *Beloved*, 1987.)

Soraïda MARTINEZ, *Interracial Family*, 1992, *Private collection*

• Black writing often has the rhythm of black speech and shows the influence of African American oral culture, as well as that of Jazz, Negro Spirituals and Blues.

## From Melting Pot to Mosaic

For years, immigrants to the United States aimed at losing their national identities and becoming Americans; America would be a 'melting pot', with different cultures becoming one homogeneous nation. In the 1960s and 1970s, however, this idea began to be challenged and was replaced by the notion of a 'mosaic', where each community would keep its cultural differences. Instead of being just Americans, they were hyphenated[3] Americans: Chinese-Americans, Hispano-Americans, Afro-Americans. As a result, and because Ethnic Studies programmes appeared in most universities, voices so far unheard were raised, expressing the problems of their communities in a language often influenced by various oral traditions.

• **Native Americans**. One talks of a Native American Renaissance after 1970 with many novels addressing themes such as the influence of legends, and the ambiguous relationship to the land and to the materialism of white culture: **N. Scott Momaday** (*House Made of Dawn*, 1969), **Louise Erdrich** (*Love Medicine*, 1984).

• **Asian American literature** has focused on the gap between Asian traditions, particularly family traditions, and American ones: **Amy Tan** (*The Joy Luck Club*, 1989), **Ha Jin** (*Waiting*, 1999).

• **Latino literature** has not only written about the influence of myths and legends, but also about contemporary problems such as migration and social protest: **Sandra Cisneros**, *The House on Mango Street*, 1984.

## Stronger voices

Although they had already been heard before, some groups asserted their identity more forcefully after World War II.

• Jewish American literature has often addressed the themes of assimilation within American society as well as the marks left by the Holocaust: **Saul Bellow** (*Herzog*, 1964), **Bernard Malamud**, **Philip Roth** (*Portnoy's Complaint*, 1969).

• Women had for long tried to assert their rights and identity in America, for instance **Kate Chopin** (*The Awakening*, 1899), but many new voices were raised in the last decades of the 20th century: **Toni Morrison** (see above), **Joyce Carol Oates**, (*We Were the Mulvaneys*, 1996); **Grace Paley** (*The Little Disturbances of Man*, 1959). See p. 93.

## Multiculturalism in Britain

Britain has always prided itself on its multiculturalism, based on diversity and tolerance. But, with the rising number of immigrants, such a policy has encouraged the new immigrants to remain together and keep their identities instead of gradually assimilating into British culture.

• Several writers – first or second generation immigrants – have dealt with these themes in their works: **Hanif Kureishi**, *The Buddha of Suburbia* (1990), **Monica Ali**, *Brick Lane* (2003), **Zadie Smith**, *White Teeth* (2000), *On Beauty* (2005).

1. **the cornerstone:** *la pierre angulaire*
2. **the mainstream:** *le courant dominant*
3. **hyphenated:** *de 'hyphen', un trait d'union*

**Frederick DOUGLASS**
(1818-1895)
spent over twenty years as a slave before he succeeded in escaping to the north. The Boston Anti-Slavery Society asked him to speak at meetings, which led him to write his *Narrative*. It made him quite famous.

*This is the incipit of the book.*

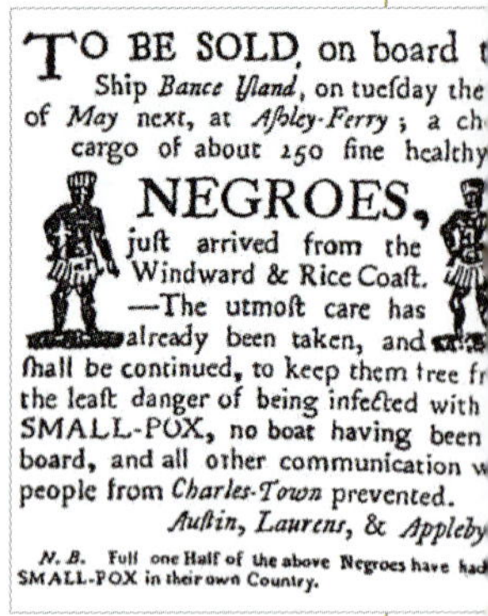


I was born in Tuckahoe, near Hillsborough, and about twelve miles from Easton, in Talbot county, Maryland. I have no accurate[1] knowledge of my age, never having seen any authentic record[2] containing it. By far the larger part of the slaves know as little of their ages as horses know of theirs, and it is the wish of most masters within my knowledge to keep their slaves thus ignorant. I do not remember to have ever met a slave who could tell of his birthday. They seldom come nearer to it than planting-time, harvest-time, cherry-time, spring-time, or fall-time. A want of information concerning my own was a source of unhappiness to me even during childhood. The white children could tell their ages. I could not tell why I ought to be deprived of[3] the same privilege. I was not allowed to make any inquiries of my master concerning it. He deemed[4] all such inquiries on the part of a slave improper and impertinent, and evidence of a restless spirit. The nearest estimate I can give makes me now between twenty-seven and twenty-eight years of age. I come to this, from hearing my master say, some time during 1835, I was about seventeen years old.

My mother was named Harriet Bailey. She was the daughter of Isaac and Betsey Bailey, both colored, and quite dark. My mother was of a darker complexion than either my grandmother or grandfather.

My father was a white man. He was admitted to be such by all I ever heard speak of my parentage. The opinion was also whispered that my master was my father; but of the correctness of this opinion, I know nothing; the means of knowing was withheld[5] from me. My mother and I were separated when I was but an infant—before I knew her as my mother. It is a common custom, in the part of Maryland from which I ran away, to part[6] children from their mothers at a very early age. Frequently, before the child has reached its twelfth month, its mother is taken from it, and hired out[7] on some farm a considerable distance off, and the child is placed under the care of an old woman, too old for field labor. For what this separation is done, I do not know, unless it be to hinder[8] the development of the child's affection toward its mother, and to blunt[9] and destroy the natural affection of the mother for the child. This is the inevitable result.

I never saw my mother, to know her as such, more than four or five times in my life; and each of these times was very short in duration, and at night. She was hired by a Mr. Stewart, who lived about twelve miles from my home. She made her journeys to see me in the night, travelling the whole distance on foot, after the performance of her day's work. She was a field hand, and a whipping[10] is the penalty of not being in the field at sunrise, unless a slave has special permission from his or her master to the contrary—a permission which they seldom get, and one that gives to him that gives it the proud name of being a kind master. I do not recollect of ever seeing my mother by the light of day. She was with me in the night. She would lie down with me, and get me to sleep, but long before I waked she was gone. Very little communication ever took place between us. Death soon ended what little we could have while she lived, and with it her hardships and suffering. She died when I was about seven years old, on one of my master's farms, near Lee's Mill. I was not allowed to be present during her illness, at her death, or burial. She was gone long before I knew any thing about it. Never having enjoyed, to any considerable extent, her soothing[11] presence, her tender and watchful care, I received the tidings[12] of her death with much the same emotions I should have probably felt at the death of a stranger.

Called thus suddenly away, she left me without the slightest intimation[13] of who my father was. The whisper that my master was my father, may or may not be true; and, true or false, it is of but little consequence to my purpose whilst the fact remains, in all its glaring[14] odiousness, that slaveholders have ordained[15], and by law established, that the children of slave women shall in all cases follow the condition of their mothers; and this is done too obviously to administer to their own lusts[16], and make a gratification of their wicked desires profitable as well as pleasurable; for by this cunning[17] arrangement, the slaveholder, in cases not a few, sustains to his slaves the double relation of master and father.

I know of such cases; and it is worthy of remark that such slaves invariably suffer greater hardships, and have more to contend with[18], than others. They are, in the first place, a constant offence to their mistress. She is ever disposed to find fault with them; they can seldom do any thing to please her; she is never better pleased than when she sees them under the lash[19], especially when she suspects her husband of showing to his mulatto children favors which he withholds from his black slaves. The master is frequently compelled[20] to sell this class of his slaves, out of deference to the feelings of his white wife; and, cruel as the deed[21] may strike any one to be, for a man to sell his own children to human flesh-mongers[22], it is often the dictate of humanity for him to do so; for, unless he does this, he must not only whip them himself, but must stand by and see one white son tie up his brother, of but few shades darker complexion than himself, and ply[23] the gory[24] lash to his naked back; and if he lisp one word of disapproval, it is set down to his parental partiality[25], and only makes a bad matter worse, both for himself and the slave whom he would protect and defend.

**1. accurate:** *précis* **2. a record:** *un document, des archives* **3. deprived of:** *privé de* **4. to deem:** *considérer* **5. to withhold:** *retirer, taire, cacher* **6. to part:** *séparer* **7. to hire out:** *louer* **8. to hinder:** *empêcher* **9. to blunt:** *émousser, atténuer* **10. a whipping:** to whip: *fouetter* **11. soothing:** *apaisante* **12. the tidings:** *la nouvelle* **13. intimation:** *suggestion* **14. glaring:** *aveuglant, flagrant* **15. to ordain:** *décréter* **16. lust:** *le désir sexuel* **17. cunning:** *rusé, fourbe* **18. to contend with:** *faire face à* **19. the lash:** *le fouet* **20. to compel:** *obliger* **21. the deed:** *cette action* **22. a flesh-monger:** *un marchand de chair* **23. to ply:** *manier* **24. gory:** *sanglant* **25. partiality:** *favoritisme*

## Zooming in

**1** A well-built text. Sum up the subject of each paragraph in a few words:
- paragraph 1: ...
- paragraph 2: ...
- paragraph 3: ...
- paragraphs 3 & 4: ...
- paragraphs 5 & 6: ...

**2** A justification. Douglass wrote his *Narrative* to justify himself as many believed that a Black man who spoke intelligently could not possibly have been a slave. How does Douglass prove the veracity of his story here?

**3** Two types of narrative alternate here. Give examples of each:
- his story: ...
- complementary background information: ...

**4** Give examples of the different ways in which the narrator was denied an identity. What was the point of such denial?
- words linked to lack: ...
- verbs about withholding: ...
- comparisons: ...

**5** Rhetoric. Find examples of:
- binary and ternary rhythms: ...
- chiasmus: ...
- sentimentalism: ...

## TEXT 2 G. BROOKS ~ "WE REAL COOL", *Selected Poems*, 1959

**Gwendolyn BROOKS** (1917-2000) is a Black American poetess who wrote about the black urban poor of Chicago (*Selected Poems* (1963).

THE POOL[1] PLAYERS.
SEVEN AT THE GOLDEN SHOVEL.

We real cool. We
Left school. We

Lurk[2] late. We
Strike straight. We

Sing sin. We
Thin gin. We

Jazz June. We
Die soon.

You can listen to Gwendolyn Brooks reading the poem and commenting on it at poets.org.

1. **pool:** *le billard* 2. **to lurk:** *se cacher, rôder*

### Zooming in

1. Who speaks in the poem? How old can they be?
2. What is the most striking feature of the poem?
   What is its effect?
   Rewrite the poem, beginning each line with 'We'.
3. Contrast what the 'we' say about themselves and what Gwendolyn Brooks said about the poem in the following interview.
   "They're a little uncertain of the strength of their identity [...] The 'We'— you're supposed to stop after the 'We' and think about their validity, and of course there's no way for you to tell whether it should be said softly or not, I suppose, but I say it rather softly because I want to represent their basic uncertainty, which they don't bother to question every day, of course."
   From "An Interview with Gwendolyn BROOKS" in *Contemporary Literature*, Winter 1970
4. What about the rhythm of the poem?
   What contributes to its particular cadence?

V. F. STEPANOVA, ***Billiard players***, 1920, Museo Thyssen-Bornemisza, Madrid

## TEXT 3 N. Scott MOMADAY ~ House Made of Dawn, 1968

**N. Scott MOMADAY**
(born 1934)
grew up on a Kiowa reservation in Arizona. In 1969, he was awarded the Pulitzer Prize for *House Made of Dawn*. He also wrote *The Way to Rainy Mountain* and *The Names* (1976).

*Abel has been fighting in WWII and returns to his reservation in New Mexico drunk and psychologically traumatized. His grandfather has come to meet him.*

HE WAS ALONE on the wagon road. The pavement lay on a higher parallel at the base of the hills to the east. The trucks of the town — and those of the lumber[1] camps at Paliza and Vallecitos — made an endless parade on the highway, but the wagon road was used now only by the herdsmen[2] and planters whose fields lay to the south and west. When he came to the place called Seytokwa, Francisco remembered the race for good hunting and harvests[3]. Once he had played a part; he had rubbed himself with[4] soot[5], and he ran on the wagon road at dawn. He ran so hard that he could feel the sweat fly from his head and arms, though it was winter and the air was filled with snow. He ran until his breath burned in his throat and his feet rose and fell in a strange repetition that seemed apart from all his effort. At last he had overtaken[6] Mariano, who was everywhere supposed to be the best of the long-race runners. For a long way Mariano kept just beyond his reach; then, as they drew near the corrals on the edge of the town, Francisco picked up the pace. He drew even[7] and saw for an instant Mariano's face, wet and contorted in defeat... *"Se diopor venddo"*... and he struck it with the back of his hand, leaving a black smear[8] across the mouth and jaw. And Mariano fell and was exhausted. Francisco held his stride[9] all the way to the Middle, and even then he could have gone on running, for no reason, for only the sake of running on. And that year he killed seven bucks[10] and seven does[11]. Some years afterward, when he was no longer young and his leg had been stiffened by disease, he made a pencil drawing on the first page of a ledger[12] book which he kept with his store of prayer feathers in the rafters[13] of his room. It was the likeness of a straight black man running in the snow. Beneath it was the legend "1889."

Navajo sand painting

He crossed the river below the bridge at San Ysidro. The roan mares strained as they brought the wagon up the embankment and onto the pavement. It was almost noon. The doors of the houses were closed against the heat, and even the usual naked children who sometimes shouted and made fun of him had gone inside. Here and there a dog, content to have found a little shade, raised its head to look but remained outstretched and quiet. Well before he came to the junction, he could hear the slow whine of the tires on the Cuba and Bloomfield road. It was a strange sound; it began at a high and descending pitch, passed, and rose again to become at last inaudible, lost in the near clatter[14] of the rig[15] and hoofs[16] — lost even in the slow, directionless motion of the flies. But it was recurrent: another, and another; and he turned into the intersection and drove on to the trading post[17]. He had come about seven miles.

## TEXT 3 N. Scott MOMADAY ~ House Made of Dawn, 1968

At a few minutes past one, the bus came over a rise far down in the plain and its windows caught for a moment the light of the sun. It grew in the old man's vision until he looked away and limped around in a vague circle and smoothed the front of his new shirt with his hands. "Abelito, Abelito," he repeated under his breath, and he glanced at the wagon and the mares to be sure that everything was in order. He could feel the beat of his heart, and instinctively he drew himself up in the dignity of his age. He heard the sharp wheeze[18] of the brakes[19] as the big bus rolled to a stop in front of the gas pump, and only then did he give attention to it, as if it had taken him by surprise. The door swung open and Abel stepped heavily to the ground and reeled[20]. He was drunk, and he fell against his grandfather and did not know him. His wet lips hung loose and his eyes were half closed and rolling. Francisco's crippled[21] leg nearly gave way. His good straw hat fell off and he braced himself[22] against the weight of his grandson. Tears came to his eyes, and he knew only that he must laugh and turn away from the faces in the windows of the bus. He held Abel upright and led him to the wagon, listening as the bus moved away at last and its tires began to sing upon the road. On the way back to the town, Abel lay ill in the bed of the wagon and Francisco sat bent to the lines. The mares went a little faster on the way home, and near the bridge a yellow dog came out to challenge them.

1. **lumber:** *du bois de charpente* 2. **a herdsman:** *un berger, un gardien de troupeau* 3. **the harvest:** *la récolte* 4. **to rub oneself with:** *se couvrir de, s'enduire de* 5. **soot:** *la suie* 6. **to overtake:** *dépasser* 7. **to draw even:** *arriver à son niveau* 8. **smear:** *une trace, une traînée* 9. **held his stride:** *garda son rythme* 10. **a buck:** *le mâle de la biche* 11. **a doe:** *un chevreuil* 12. **a ledger:** *un grand livre, un registre* 13. **a rafter:** *une poutre* 14. **the clatter:** *le fracas* 15. **a rig:** *une semi-remorque* 16. **a hoof:** *un sabot* 17. **a trading post:** *un comptoir* 18. **the wheeze:** *le souffle, le sifflement* 19. **the brakes:** *les freins* 20. **to reel:** *tituber* 21. **crippled:** *handicapé, abîmé* 22. **to brace oneself:** *s'arc-bouter*

## Zooming in

**1** The structure
› What are the two main parts of the text?
› The passage refers to two different times. What are they?
- Where in the text? ...
- Date? ...
- What happened? ...

**2** The race
What was the reason for the race? Was its aim achieved?
List all the natural elements associated with the race. Why are they important?

**3** List all the words and expressions which show the grandfather's eagerness to see Abel.
Why do they make the end of the text more poignant?
What words underline the contrast between expectations and reality?

**4** What is the symbolic meaning of the passage concerning the Indian community?

# TEXT 4 ALICE WALKER ~ THE COLOR PURPLE, 1982

**Alice WALKER**
(born 1944)
was born into a family of farmers in the Deep South. She was active in the civil rights movement in the 1960s. *The Color Purple* was much acclaimed but also criticized within the black community for focusing on sexism and black stereotypes. Alice Walker has also written short stories: *Short Stories of Black Women* (1973) and *You Can't Keep a Good Woman Down* (1981).

*Celie is fourteen, has been raped by her father and has seen her mother die. Celie had two children by him: one dies, he sells the other. A widower*[1]*, Mr ___ wants to marry Nettie, the younger sister Celie is very fond of. But their father refuses. Celie offers to marry him instead, so as to leave her father's house and help Nettie afterwards.*

Dear God,

It took him[2] the whole spring, from March to June, to make up his mind to take me. All I thought about was Nettie. How she could come to me if I marry him and he be so love struck with her I could figure out a way for us to run away. Us both be hitting Nettie's schoolbooks pretty hard, cause us know we got to be smart to git away. I know I'm not as pretty or as smart as Nettie, but she say I ain't dumb[3].

The way you know who discover America, Nettie say, is think bout cucumbers. That what Columbus sound like. I learned all about Columbus in first grade, but look like he the first thing I forgot. She say Columbus come here in boats call the Neater, the Peter, and the Santomareater[4]. Indians so nice to him he force a bunch of 'em back home with him to wait on the queen.

But it hard to think with gitting married to Mr__ hanging over my head.

The first time I got big[5] Pa took me out of school. He never care that I love it. Nettie stood there at the gate holding tight to my hand. I was all dress for first day. You too dumb to keep going to school. Pa say. Nettie the clever one in this bunch.

But Pa, Nettie say, crying, Celie smart too. Even Miss Beasley say so. Nettie dote on[6] Miss Beasley. Think nobody like her in the world.

Pa say. Whoever listen to anything Addie Beasley have to say. She run off at the mouth[7] so much no man would have her. That how come she have to teach school. He never look up from cleaning his gun. Pretty soon a bunch of white mens come walking cross the yard. They have guns too.

Pa git up and follow 'em. The rest of the week I vomit and dress wild game[8].

But Nettie never give up. Next thing I know Miss Beasley at our house trying to talk to Pa. She say long as she been a teacher she never know nobody want to learn bad as Nettie and me. But when Pa call me out and she see how tight[9] my dress is, she stop talking and go.

Nettie still don't understand. I don't neither. All us notice is I'm all the time sick and fat.

I feel bad sometime Nettie done pass me[10] in learnin. But look like nothing she say can git in my brain and stay. She try to tell me something bout the ground not being flat. I just say. Yeah, like I know it. I never tell her how flat it look to me.

Mr__ come finally one day looking all drug out[11]. The woman he had helping him done quit[12]. His mammy done said No More.

He say. Let me see her again.

Pa call me. Celie, he say. Like it wasn't nothing. Mr__ want another look at you.

I go stand in the door. The sun shine in my eyes. He's still up on his horse. He look me up and down.

Pa rattle his newspaper. Move up, he won't bite[13], he say.

I go closer to the steps, but not too close cause I'm a little scared of his horse.

Turn round. Pa say.

I turn round. One of my little brothers come up. I think it was Lucious. He fat and playful, all the time munching[14] on something.

He say. What you doing that for?

Pa say. Your sister thinking bout marriage.

Didn't mean nothing to him. He pull my dresstail and ast[15] can he have some blackberry jam out the safe.

I say. Yeah.

She good with children. Pa say, rattling his paper open more. Never heard her say a hard word to nary one of them. Just give 'em everything they ast for, is the only problem.

Mr_ say. That cow still coming?

He say. Her cow[16].

Dear God,

I spend my wedding day running from the oldest boy[17]. He twelve. His mama died in his arms and he don't want to hear nothing bout no new one. He pick up a rock and laid my head open. The blood run all down tween my breasts. His daddy say Don't do that! But that's all he say. He got four children, instead of three, two boys and two girls. The girls hair ain't been comb since their mammy died. I tell him I'll just have to shave it off[18]. Start fresh. He say bad luck to cut a woman hair. So after I bandage my head best I can and cook dinner – they have a spring, not a well, and a wood stove[19] look like a truck – I start trying to untangle hair. They only six and eight and they cry. They scream. They cuse[20] me of murder. By ten o'clock I'm done. They cry theirselves to sleep. But I don't cry. I lay there thinking bout Nettie while he on top of me, wonder if she safe. And then I think bout Shug Avery[21]. I know what he doing to me he done to Shug Avery and maybe she like it. I put my arm around him.

**1. a widower:** *un veuf* **2. him:** Mr_ **3. dumb:** *stupide* **4.** the Niña, the Pinta, and the Santa Maria **5. big:** *grosse, enceinte* **6. to dote on:** *adorer* **7. to run off at the mouth:** *parler sans cesse* **8. dress wild game:** *prépare du gibier* **9. tight:** *serrée, tendue* **10. pass me:** *me dépasse* **11. drug out:** *déprimé* **12. done quit:** *est partie* **13. to bite:** *mordre* **14. to munch:** *mâchonner* **15. ast:** *asked* **16. her cow:** Celie has a cow that belongs to her **17. the oldest boy:** Mr_ already has four children **18. shave off:** *raser* **19. a wood stove:** *un poêle à bois* **20. cuse:** *accuse* **21. Shug Avery:** a woman Mr_ had an affair with

## Zooming in

**1** The language
Celie speaks poor, non-standard English. Find examples and explain what the correct usage would be.
- Phonetic spelling: ...
- Omission of the auxiliary be: ...
- Omission of the third-person 's': ...
- Omission of the subject: ...
- Double negations: ...
- Tenses: ...
- Punctuation marks: ...

**2** There are two embedded time sequences in these two letters. What are they?

**3** In the middle sequence, what details show that Celie is pregnant?

**4** Reading between the lines
Explain what these sentences mean:
- 'Nettie still don't understand. I don't neither.'?
- 'His mammy done said No More'.

**5** Whose words are reported in direct speech in these two letters?
- What about Celie's words?
- What does this show?

**6** *The Color Purple* is an epistolary novel. Why does Celie write to God?

**7** Show that the text is a mix of humour and pathos.

# TEXT 5 Wole SOYINKA ~ 'Telephone Conversation', 1980

**Wole SOYINKA**
(born 1934)
is a West Nigerian playwright, novelist and poet, who believes that literature can encourage social change. His language is marked by wit and inventiveness. He was awarded the Nobel Prize in 1986. (*The Lion and the Jewel*, a play, 1963).

The price seemed reasonable, location[1]
Indifferent. The landlady swore[2] she lived
Off premises[3]. Nothing remained
But[4] self-confession. "Madam," I warned,
"I hate a wasted[5] journey — I am — African."
Silence. Silenced transmission of
Pressurised good breeding. Voice, when it came,
Lipstick-coated, long gold-rolled
Cigarette-holder pipped[6]. Caught I was, foully[7].
"HOW DARK?"... I had not misheard... "ARE YOU LIGHT
OR VERY DARK?" Button B. Button A. Stench[8]
Of rancid[9] breath of public-hide-and-speak.
Red booth. Red pillar box. Red double-tiered
Omnibus squelching tar[10]. It was real! Shamed
By ill-mannered silence, surrender
Pushed dumbfoundment[11] to beg simplification.
Considerate she was, varying the emphasis —
"ARE YOU DARK? OR VERY LIGHT?" Revelation came.
"You mean — like plain or milk chocolate?"
Her assent was clinical, crushing[12] in its light
Impersonality. Rapidly, wave-length adjusted,
I chose. "West African sepia"— and as an afterthought,
"Down in my passport". Silence for spectroscopic[13]
Flight of fancy, till truthfulness clanged[14] her accent
Hard on the mouthpiece. "WHAT'S THAT?" conceding
"DON'T KNOW WHAT THAT IS". – "Like brunette. "
"THAT'S DARK, ISN'T IT?" — "Not altogether.
Facially, I am a brunette, but, Madam, you should see
The rest of me. Palm of my hand, soles of my feet
Are a peroxide blond. Friction, caused —
Foolishly, Madam — by sitting down, has turned
My bottom raven black — one moment, Madam!" — sensing
Her receiver rearing[15] on the thunder clap[16]
About my ears — "Madam," I pleaded, "wouldn't you rather
See for yourself?"

**1. location:** *le lieu* **2. swore:** *prétérit de 'swear', jurer* **3. off premises:** *pas sur place* **4. but:** *sauf* **5. wasted:** *perdu* **6. pipped:** *évoque à la fois une voix guindée et une réaction un peu choquée* **7. foully:** *épouvantablement* **8. stench:** *puanteur* **9. rancid:** *rance* **10. squelching tar:** *écrasant le goudron* **11. dumbfoundment:** *la stupéfaction* **12. crushing:** *écrasant* **13. spectroscopic:** *allusion au spectre des couleurs* **14. to clang:** *émettre un bruit métallique* **15. to rear:** *se cabrer, se dresser* **16. the thunder clap:** *le coup de tonnerre*

## Zooming in

**1** The situation
Who are the two characters and what is the purpose of the conversation?
What should they normally discuss? Where and how is this mentioned in the poem?

**2** Why is the word 'self-confession' ironic? What other word is used ironically on the same line? Why?

**3** How would you describe the landlady's reaction? What are the different steps in the speaker's reaction?

**4** What is the function of the description in lines 12 to 14. Why is the adjective 'red' repeated?

**5** What does this conversation tell us about each of the two characters? Look at the vocabulary used by the speaker.
- The landlady: ...
- The speaker: ...

**6** What is the meaning of 'Button B. Button A.'(line 11)? Comment on the expression 'hide and speak' (line 12)

**7** Why are the landlady's words capitalized?

**8** There are several 'silences'. Why?

**Wole Soyinka, 'Nobel lecture', 1986, in *Literature 1981-1990*, 1993**

*This is the very end of Wole Soyinka's Nobel lecture, which he delivered in 1986.*

On that testing ground[1] which, for us, is Southern Africa, that medieval camp of biblical terrors, primitive suspicions, a choice must be made by all lovers of peace: either to bring it into the modern world, into a rational state of being within that spirit of human partnership, a capacity for which has been so amply demonstrated by every liberated black nation on our continent, or – to bring it abjectly to its knees by ejecting it, in every aspect, from humane recognition, so that it caves in[2] internally, through the strategies of its embattled[3] majority. Whatever the choice, this inhuman affront cannot be allowed to pursue our twentieth century conscience into the twenty-first, that symbolic coming-of-age which peoples of all cultures appear to celebrate with rites of passage. That calendar, we know, is not universal, but time is, and so are the imperatives of time. And of those imperatives that challenge our being, our presence, and humane definition at this time, none can be considered more pervasive[4] than the end of racism, the eradication[5] of human inequality, and the dismantling[6] of all their structures. The Prize is the consequent enthronement[7] of its complement: universal suffrage, and peace.

From 'Nobel Lectures', in *Literature 1981-1990*,
World Scientific Publishing Co., Singapore, 1993 © The Nobel Foundation 1986

1. **a testing ground:** *un banc d'essai* 2. **to cave in:** *s'effondrer* 3. **embattled:** *assiégé*
4. **pervasive:** *omniprésent* 5. **the eradication:** *la suppression* 6. **the dismantling:** *le démantèlement*
7. **the enthronement:** *le couronnement*

# TEXT 6 ZADIE SMITH ~ WHITE TEETH, 2000

**Zadie SMITH**
born 1975
was born in London; her father was English, her mother Jamaican. Her novels (*White Teeth*, 2000, *On Beauty*, 2005) explore multiculturalism in contemporary Britain and America.

*THE NOVEL portrays several immigrant families in London. Archie Jones is a working-class Englishman whose wife, Clara is a black Jamaican. Irie is their daughter.*

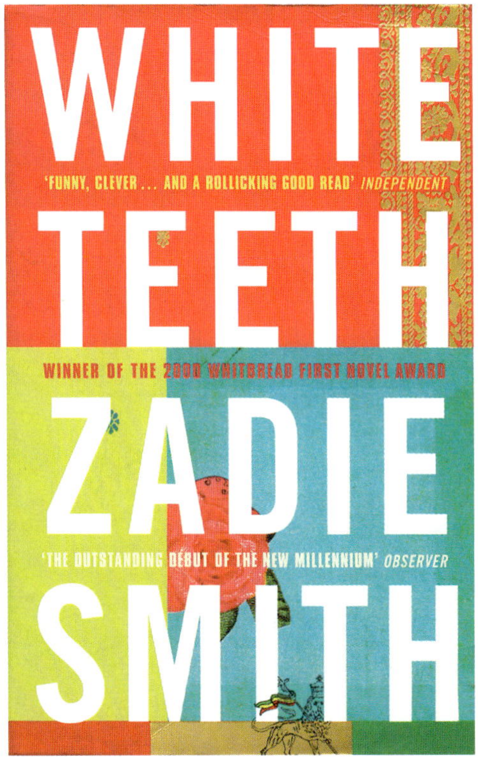


THERE WAS TROUBLE at the Joneses. Irie was about to become the first Bowden or Jones (possibly, maybe, all things willing, by the grace of God, fingers crossed) to enter a university. Her A-levels were chemistry, biology and religious studies. She wanted to study dentistry (white collar! £20k+[1] !), which everyone was very pleased about, but she also wanted to take a 'year off' in the subcontinent and Africa (Malaria! Poverty! Tapeworm[2]!), which led to three months of open warfare between her and Clara. One side wanted finance and permission, the other side was resolved to concede neither. The conflict was protracted[3] and bitter, and all mediators were sent home empty-handed (She has made up her mind, there are no arguments to be had with the woman – Samad[4]) or else embroiled[5] in the war of words (Why can't she go to Bangladesh if she wants to? Are you saying my country is not good enough for your daughter? – Alsana).

The stalemate[6] was so pronounced that land had been divided and allocated; Irie claimed her bedroom and the attic, Archie, a conscientious objector, asked only for the spare room, a television and a satellite (state) dish, and Clara took everything else, with the bathroom acting as shared territory. Doors were slammed. The time for talking was over.

On the 25th of October 1991, 01.00 hours, Irie embarked upon a late-night attack. She knew from experience that her mother was most vulnerable when in bed; late at night she spoke softly like a child, her fatigue gave her a pronounced lisp[7]; it was at this point that you were most likely to get whatever it was you'd been pining for: pocket money, a new bike, a later curfew[8]. It was such a well-worn tactic that until now Irie had not considered it worthy of this, her fiercest and longest dispute with her mother. But she hadn't any better ideas.

"Irie? Wha –? Iss sa middle of sa nice… Go back koo bed…"

Irie opened the door further, letting yet more hall light flood the bedroom.

Archie submerged his head in a pillow. "Bloody hell, love, it's one in the morning! Some of us have got work tomorrow."

"I want to talk to Mum," said Irie firmly, walking to the end of the bed. "She won't talk to me during the day, so I'm reduced to this."

"Irie, pleaze … I'm exhaushed… I'm shrying koo gesh shome shleep."

"I don't just want to have a year off, I need one. It's essential – I'm young, I want some experiences. I've lived in this bloody suburb all my life. Everyone's the same here. I want to go and see the people of the world... that's what Joshua's doing and his parents support him!"

"Well, we can't bloody afford it," grumbled Archie, emerging from the eider-down[9]. "We haven't all got posh[10] jobs in science, now have we?"

"I don't care about the money - I'll get a job, somehow or something, but I do want your permission! Both of you. I don't want to spend six months away and spend every day thinking you're angry."

"Well, it's not up to me, love, is it? It's your mother, really, I..."

"Yes, Dad. Thanks for stating the bloody obvious."

"Oh, right," said Archie huffily[11], turning to the wall. "I'll keep my comments to meself, then ..."

"Oh, Dad, I didn't mean... Mum? Can you please sit up and speak properly? I'm trying to talk to you? It seems like I'm talking to myself here?" said Irie with absurd intonations, for this was the year Antipodean soap operas were teaching a generation of English kids to phrase everything as a question. "Look, I want your permission, yeah?"

Even in the darkness, Irie could see Clara scowl[12]. "Permishon for what? Koo go and share and ogle[13] at poor black folk? Dr Livingshone, I prejume? Iz dat what you leant from da Shalfenz? Because if thash what you want, you can do dat here. Jush sit and look at me for shix munfe!"

Jamaican girls, Notting Hill Carnival inLondon, 1997

"It's nothing to do with that! I just want to see how other people live!"

"An' gek youshelf killed in da proshess! Why don' you go necksh door, dere are uwer people dere. Go shee how dey live!"

Infuriated, Irie grabbed the bed knob[14] and marched round Clara's side of the bed. "Why can't you just sit up properly and talk to me properly and drop the ridiculous little girl voi -"

In the darkness Irie kicked over a glass and sucked in[15] a sharp breath as the cold water seeped[16] between her toes and into the carpet. Then, as the last of the water ran away, Irie had the strange and horrid sensation that she was being bitten.

"Ow!"

"Oh, for God's sake," said Archie, reaching over to the side lamp and switching it on. "What now?"

Irie looked down to where the pain was. In any war, this was too low a blow. The front set of some false teeth, with no mouth attached to them, were bearing down upon[17] her right foot.

"Fucking hell! What the fuck are they?"

But the question was unnecessary; even as the words formed in her mouth, Irie had already put two and two together. The midnight voice. The perfect daytime straightness and whiteness.

**1. 20K+:** *£20,000 a year* **2. tapeworm:** *le ver solitaire* **3. protracted:** *prolongé*
**4.** Samad and Alsana are good friends of the family – their marriage was an arranged one
**5. to be embroiled in:** *être mêlé à* **6. a stalemate:** *une impasse* **7. a lisp:** *un zézaiement*
**8. a curfew:** *un couvre-feu* **9. the eiderdown:** *l'édredon* **10. posh:** *chic, de riches* **11. huffily:** *d'un ton froissé* **12. to scowl:** *se renfrogner* **13. to ogle:** *lorgner* **14. a knob:** *un bouton (de porte par exemple)* **15. to suck in:** *aspirer* **16. to seep:** *suinter* **17. to bear down upon:** *foncer sur*

## Zooming in

1. What are the three main parts of the text? Give each a title.
2. Why doesn't Clara 'speak properly'. Show that your explanation changes as you read the text.
3. Rewrite the following sentences:
   - 'I'm shrying koo gesh shome shleep': ...
   - 'Jush sit and look at me for shix munfe!': ...
   - 'An' gek youshelf killed in da proshess! Why don' you go necksh door, dere are uwer people dere. Go shee how dey live!': ...
4. What running metaphor is used throughout the text? Give as many examples as you can.
5. There are different types of humour in this passage. Explain what they are in each part of the text.
   - 1. ...
   - 2. ...
   - 3. ...
6. What does the text tell us about multiculturalism in Britain?
7. There is mention of dentistry and of white teeth (the false teeth) in the text. Is it significant?

## MOVING ON

**Watch**

- Stephen Spielberg's film *The Color Purple*, based on Alice Walker's novel
- *Little Big Man* (1970), Arthur Penn's adaptation of the novel by Thomas Berger (1964)
- Richardson Morse's adaptation of *House Made of Dawn* (1972)
- Peter Weir's *The Last Wave* (1977), about an Australian lawyer who takes on the case of Aborigines in Australia
- Jerrold Freedman's adaptation of Richard Wright's *Native Son* (1986)

**Read**

- *To Kill a Mockingbird* (1960), by Harper Lee
- *A Lesson Before Dying* (1988), by Ernest J. Gaines

**Listen to**

- Jazz, blues and Negro Spirituals
- Recordings of Langston Hughes' poetry on the internet
- Interviews with Toni Morrison on the internet
- Recordings of Maya Angelou's poems on the internet

# Literary experimentation

There is a rich tradition of literary experimentation in Britain and the United States, perhaps because the flexibility of the English language lends itself to innovation and inventiveness.

Experimentation is not something new. Parts of **Shakespeare**'s plays must have seemed daring[1] at the time and a novel such as **Sterne**'s *Tristram Shandy* could easily be called post-modern, with

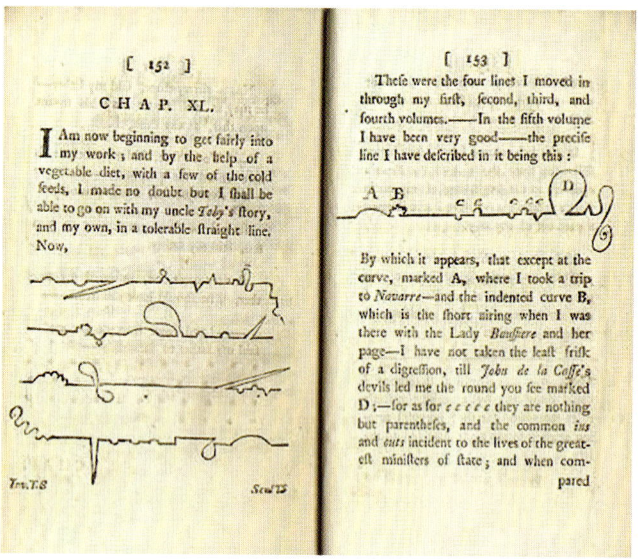
[ 152 ]

CHAP. XL.

I Am now beginning to get fairly into my work; and by the help of a vegetable diet, with a few of the cold ſeeds, I made no doubt but I ſhall be able to go on with my uncle *Toby's* ſtory, and my own, in a tolerable ſtraight line. Now,

[ 153 ]

Theſe were the four lines I moved in through my firſt, ſecond, third, and fourth volumes.——In the fifth volume I have been very good——the preciſe line I have deſcribed in it being this:

A B c c c c c D

By which it appears, that except at the curve, marked A, where I took a trip to *Navarre*,—and the indented curve B, which is the ſhort airing when I was there with the Lady *Bauſſiere* and her page,—I have not taken the leaſt friſk of a digreſſion, till *John de la Caſſe's* devils led me the round you ſee marked D;—for as for *c c c c c* they are nothing but parentheſes, and the common *ins* and *outs* incident to the lives of the greateſt miniſters of ſtate; and when compared

*Tristram Shandy*: a summary by the narrator of the structure of each part of his book.

its lack of plot or chronology, its metatextuality, and even its drawings. However, it was mainly in the 20th century that literary and artistic experimentation reached a climax.

## Modernism (1910-1930)

The origins of modernism are to be found in:

- a reaction against 19th realism in the arts (cubism, futurism) as well as in literature: the mere representation of reality was no longer enough,
- a new emphasis on the unconscious with the works of Freud and others in which there is a focus on inner states of consciousness.
- the social, industrial and economic upheavals at the end of the 19th century,
- the doubts and scars which followed World War I.

Modernism is not limited to Britain and the US but is international.

## Modernist Experimentation

- With stream of consciousness: what matters is not so much the outside world itself as the way it is perceived in someone's mind, hence the interest in the chaos of ideas, memories, perceptions that go through a mind at one given moment (**Joyce**'s *Ulysses*).
- With structure: time is no longer linear but can be fragmented (in **Faulkner**'s *As I Lay Dying*), cyclical, or can obey a certain rhythm rather than a chronology (**Woolf**'s *Mrs Dalloway*.) The novel can even be a collage of different types of sections, as is the case in **Dos Passos**'s trilogy *USA*.
- With point of view: the reliable and omniscient Victorian narrator often disappears to give way to far more unstable narrators or to multiplicity of points of view as in Faulkner's *The Sound and the Fury*.
- Literature becomes increasingly inspired by the cinema and by other arts, borrowing techniques such as close-ups and collage (**T. S. Eliot**'s *The Waste Land*).

## Postmodernism (1950-1990)

- Postmodernism came as a reaction against modernism, against the horrors of World War II, and is linked to the rise of post-colonialism.

1. **daring:** *osé*

Gerald MURPHY, *Watch*, 1925, Museum of Art, Dallas

• The modernists looked for meaning in a fragmented world. The postmodernists deny the possibility of a single authoritative meaning or undermine[2] it through the use of pastiche, black humour or absurdity. The chaos of the world is irremediable, so that you can either accept the idea and make do with[3] it (The Theatre of the Absurd) or distance yourself from chaos and play with it.

• Fiction becomes a reflection upon language rather than upon reality. It is constantly metafictional – fiction concerned with the writing of fiction (**Fowles**'s *The French Lieutenant's Woman*) – in order to sabotage the writer's authority. Language itself becomes unreliable[4].

**2. to undermine:** *saper, miner*
**3. to make do with:** *faire avec*
**4. unreliable:** *non fiable*

• The traditional distinctions between genres often disappear with parody, burlesque, pastiche and intertextuality. Many post-modern works thus play with the conventions of fairy-tales (**Angela Carter**'s *The Bloody Chamber*, See p. 66), of detective fiction, or of science-fiction.

## A few postmodern trends

- The Theatre of the Absurd. See p. 124
- The Beat Generation.
- Magic Realism (which breaks down the barriers between the supernatural and the real).

**John FOWLES, *The French Lieutenant's Woman*, the beginning of chapter 13, 1969**

*For the drift of the Maker is dark,*
*an Isis hid by the veil...*
Tennyson, *Maud* (1855)

I do not know. This story I am telling is all imagination. These characters I create never existed outside my own mind. If I have pretended until now to know my characters' minds and innermost thoughts, it is because I am writing in (just as I have assumed some of the vocabulary and 'voice' of) a convention universally accepted at the time of my story: that the novelist stands next to God. He may not know all, yet he tries to pretend that he does. But I live in the age of Alain Robbe-Grillet and Roland Barthes; if this is a novel, it cannot be a novel in the modern sense of the word.

So perhaps I am writing a transposed autobiography; perhaps I now live in one of the houses I have brought into the fiction; perhaps Charles is myself disguised. Perhaps it is only a game. Modern women like Sarah exist, and I have never understood them. Or perhaps I am trying to pass off[1] a concealed[2] book of essays on you.(...)

Perhaps you suppose that a novelist has only to pull the right strings[3] and his puppets[4] will behave in a lifelike manner; and produce on request a thorough[5] analysis of their motives and intentions.

1. **to pass off:** *faire passer (pour)* 2. **concealed:** *caché*
3. **to pull the strings:** *tirer les ficelles* 4. **a puppet:** *une marionette*
5. **thorough:** *complète*

# TEXT 1 Virginia WOOLF ~ "A Haunted House", 1921

*The story is based on a real place, Asheham House, situated in Sussex where Virginia Woolf and her husband Leonard lived in 1912.*

**Virginia WOOLF**
(1882-1941)
Very little happens in her novels and stories. Everything takes place in the minds of the protagonists. The writing attempts to convey the 'myriad impressions' (memories, perceptions...) which are present at any given moment in someone's mind. (*Mrs Dalloway*, 1925; *To the Lighthouse*, 1927; *The Years*, 1937).

WHATEVER HOUR YOU WOKE there was a door shutting. From room to room they went, hand in hand, lifting here, opening there, making sure – a ghostly couple.

"Here we left it," she said. And he added, "Oh, but here too!" "It's upstairs," she murmured, "And in the garden," he whispered. "Quietly," they said, "or we shall wake them."

But it wasn't that you woke us. Oh, no. "They're looking for it; they're drawing the curtain," one might say, and so read on a page or two. "Now they've found it," one would be certain, stopping the pencil on the margin. And then, tired of reading, one might rise and see for oneself, the house all empty, the doors standing open, only the wood pigeons[1] bubbling with content and the hum[2] of the threshing[3] machine sounding from the farm. "What did I come here for? What did I want to find?" My hands were empty. "Perhaps it's upstairs then?" The apples were in the loft. And so down again, the garden still as ever, only the book had slipped into the grass.

But they had found it in the drawing room. Not that one could ever see them. The window-panes reflected apples, reflected roses; all the leaves were green in the glass. If they moved in the drawing-room, the apple only turned its yellow side. Yet, the moment after, if the door was opened, spread about the floor, hung upon the walls, pendant from ceiling – what? My hands were empty. The shadow of a thrush[4] crossed the carpet; from the deepest wells of silence the wood pigeon drew its bubble of sound. "Safe, safe, safe," the pulse[5] of the house beat softly. "The treasure buried; the room..." the pulse stopped short. Oh was that the buried treasure?

A moment later the light had faded. Out in the garden then? But the tree spun[6] darkness for a wandering beam of sun. So fine, so rare, coolly sunk beneath the surface the beam I sought always burnt behind the glass. Death was the glass; death was between us; coming to the woman first, hundreds of years ago, leaving the house, sealing[7] all the windows; the rooms were darkened. He left it, left her, went North, went East, saw the stars turned in the Southern sky; sought the house, found it dropped beneath the Downs[8]. "Safe, safe, safe," the pulse of the house beat gladly, "The treasure yours."

This is a 1943 edition of *A Haunted House*. Published by the Hogarth Press (the publishing House founded by Leonard Woolf in 1917), it has a jacket designed by Vanessa Bell, Virginia Woolf's sister.

TEXT **1** **Virginia WOOLF ~ "A Haunted House", 1921**

The wind roars up the avenue. Trees stoop and bend this way and that. Moonbeams splash and spill wildly in the rain. But the beam of the lamp falls straight from the window. The candle burns stiff and still. Wandering through the house, opening the windows, whispering not to wake us, the ghostly couple seek their joy.

"Here we slept," she says. And he adds, "Kisses without number" "Waking in the morning–" "Silver between the trees–" "Upstairs–" "In the garden–" "When summer came–" "In winter snowtime–" The doors go shutting far in the distance, gently knocking like the pulse of a heart.

Nearer they come; cease at the doorway. The wind falls, the rain slides silver down the glass. Our eyes darken; we hear no steps beside us; we see no lady spread her ghostly cloak[9]. His hands shield[10] the lantern. "Look," he breathes. "Sound asleep. Love upon their lips."

Stooping[11], holding their silver lamp above us, long they look and deeply. Long they pause. The wind drives straightly; the flame stoops slightly. Wild beams of moonlight cross both floor and wall, and, meeting, stain[12] the faces bent; the faces pondering[13]; the faces that search the sleepers and seek their hidden joy.

"Safe, safe, safe," the heart of the house beats proudly. "Long years–" he sighs. "Again you found me." "Here," she murmurs, "sleeping; in the garden reading; laughing, rolling apples in the loft. Here we left our treasure–" Stooping, their light lifts[14] the lids upon my eyes. "Safe! safe! safe!" the pulse of the house beats wildly[15]. Waking I cry "Oh, is this *your* – buried treasure? The light in the heart."

**1. wood pigeons:** *des ramiers* **2. hum:** *bourdonnement* **3. a threshing machine:** *une batteuse* **4. a thrush:** *une grive* **5. the pulse:** *le pouls* **6. to spin:** *filer, tisser, inventer* **7. to seal:** *sceller, condamner* **8. the Downs:** chalk hills in Sussex **9. a cloak:** *une grande cape* **10. to shield:** *abriter* **11. to stoop:** *se pencher, se baisser* **12. to stain:** *teindre* **13. to ponder:** *réfléchir* **14. to lift:** *soulever* **15. wildly:** *à tout rompre*

## Zooming in

1. Where does the story take place? Pick out elements to illustrate your answer.
2. Who are the characters in the story and how are they related?
3. Whose feelings and impressions does the reader follow throughout the short story?
4. Two distinct worlds are represented. What are these worlds? What separates them? When do they converge?
5. Who is leading the quest? Where does this 'treasure hunt' take them in the house? What are they in search of?

# TEXT 2 Ernest HEMINGWAY ~ Indian Camp, 1924

**Ernest HEMINGWAY**
(1899-1961)

In his novels and stories, the protagonists are usually men who face extreme situations (war, bullfights, suffering) and react with a code of honour and masculinity (courage, loyalty, heroism, controlling emotions), perhaps because this is the only way to keep living in a world that has little meaning. His style is compressed and minimalist.

*This is the end of the short story. Nick's father, a doctor, accompanied by Nick and Nick's Uncle George, has been called to an Indian camp, where a woman is in labour[1]. Nick's father has to operate her, without an anesthetic and as best he can, while several men hold the woman down. But the operation is successful and a boy is born. The father is now in the bunk[2] above, having cut his foot.*

He bent over the Indian woman. She was quiet now and her eyes were closed. She looked very pale. She did not know what had become of the baby or anything.

"I'll be back in the morning," the doctor said, standing up. "The nurse should be here from St Ignace by noon and she'll bring anything we need."

He was feeling exalted and talkative as football players are in the dressing-room after a game. "That's one for the medical journal, George," he said. "Doing a Caesarean with a jack-knife[3] and sewing it up with nine-foot, tapered gut leaders[4]."

Uncle George was standing against the wall, looking at his arm. "Oh, you're a great man, all right," he said. "Ought to have a look at the proud father. They're usually the worst sufferers in these little affairs," the doctor said. "I must say he took it all pretty quietly." He pulled back the blanket from the Indian's head. His hand came away wet. He mounted on the edge of the lower bunk with the lamp in one hand and looked in. The Indian lay with his face towards the wall. His throat had been cut from ear to ear. The blood had flowed down into a pool where his body sagged[5] the bunk. His head rested on his left arm. The open razor lay, edge up, in the blankets.

Marsden HARTLEY, *Indian Fantasy*, 1914, Museum of Art, North Carolina

"Take Nick out of the shanty[6], George", the doctor said.

There was no need of that. Nick, standing in the door of the kitchen, had a good view of the upper bunk when his father, the lamp in one hand, tipped the Indian's head back.

It was just beginning to be daylight when they walked along the logging road[7] back towards the lake.

"I'm terribly sorry I brought you along, Nickie," said his father, all his post-operative exhilaration[8] gone. "It was an awful mess to put you through."

"Do ladies always have such a hard time having babies?" Nick asked.

"No, that was very, very exceptional."

"Why did he kill himself. Daddy?"

"I don't know. Nick. He couldn't stand things, I guess."

"Do many men kill themselves. Daddy?"

"Not very many. Nick."
"Do many women?"
"Hardly ever."
"Don't they ever?"
"Oh, yes. They do sometimes."
"Daddy?"
"Yes."
"Where did Uncle George go?"
"He'll turn up all right."
"Is dying hard, Daddy?"
"No, I think it's pretty easy, Nick. It all depends."

They were seated in the boat. Nick in the stern[9], his father rowing. The sun was coming up over the hills. A bass[10] jumped, making a circle in the water. Nick trailed his hand in the water. It felt warm in the sharp chill of the morning.

In the early morning on the lake sitting in the stern of the boat with his father rowing, he felt quite sure that he would never die.

**1. to be in labour:** *être en travail, sur le point d'accoucher* **2. a bunk:** *une couchette* **3. a jack-knife:** *un couteau de poche* **4. tapered gut leader:** *du fil à pêche* **5. to sag:** *s'affaisser (ici : former un creux dans)* **6. the shanty:** *la cabane* **7. a logging road:** *une route de bûcheron* **8. exhilaration:** *l'euphorie* **9. the stern:** *l'arrière* **10. a bass:** *une perche*

## Zooming in

**1** There are four main movements in this text. What are they? Choose a word, expression or sentence from that part that might sum it up.

- **a.** lines ... : ...
- **b.** lines ... : ...
- **c.** lines ... : ...
- **d.** lines ... : ...

**2** Why can you speak of stylistic experimentation?

- › How would you describe the sentences (think in terms of length and coordination)?

What effect is achieved by such syntax?

- › Is there any psychological analysis of the characters?
- › How is emotion nonetheless conveyed?

**3** Why is this an initiation story?

**4** Can you speak of an epiphany (a moment of revelation) at the end? What brings it about?

## TEXT 3 W. C. WILLIAMS ~ Landscape with the Fall of Icarus, 1949

**William Carlos WILLIAMS**
(1883-1963)

The poetry of W. C. Williams describes common subjects with clear images and a rhythm based on the music of the lines. What matters is the thing described, without any symbolism or comment.

According to Brueghel
when Icarus fell
it was spring

a farmer was ploughing
his field
the whole pageantry[1]

of the year was
awake tingling[2]
near

the edge of the sea
concerned
with itself

sweating in the sun
that melted
the wings' wax

unsignificantly
off the coast
there was

a splash[3] quite unnoticed
this was
Icarus drowning

Pieter Brueghel, *The Fall of Icarus*, 1560, Musées royaux des Beaux-Arts de Belgique, Bruxelles

1. **pageantry:** *l'apparat, la pompe* 2. **to tingle:** *vibrer, frissonner* 3. **a splash:** *un plouf*

## Zooming in

**1** **This poem alludes to the myth of Icarus. Read the following text and explain which part of the myth is mentioned.**

Daedalus was a legendary Athenian craftsman and inventor thought of as living in the age of King Minos. [...] Being afraid that his nephew and pupil Talos would outdo[1] him (for the latter invented the saw[2] and the potter's wheel), Daedalus threw him down from the Acropolis or into the sea [...]. Daedalus was condemned for his crime by the Areopagus and fled to Crete, where he constructed the labyrinth for king Minos. Afterwards, Minos would not let him go; Daedalus then made wings for himself and his son Icarus out of wax[3] and feathers, and they flew away. But Icarus flew too near the sun; the wax of his wings melted[4] and he fell into the sea and was drowned. Daedalus landed on the island in the Sporades now called Ikaria and buried his son's body. He then escaped to king Cocalus in Sicily, whither Minos pursued him; enticed[5] into Cocalus' palace, Minos was scalded[6] to death in a bath of Daedalus' invention.

*The Oxford Companion to Classical Literature*, 1989

1. **to outdo:** *surpasser* 2. **a saw:** *une scie* 3. **wax:** *la cire* 4. **to melt:** *fondre* 5. **to entice:** *entraîner* 6. **to scald:** *ébouillanter*

**2** **The title of the poem mentions both the landscape and Icarus. Study the way these two aspects are treated. What effect is thus created?**
- Number of lines devoted to each: ...
- What is emphasized in these two aspects? ...
- What main visual movement do we find? ...

**3** **Is the same effect to be found in Brueghel's painting?**

**4** **What is the meaning of Icarus falling unnoticed?**

**5** **How does the form of the poem contribute to its meaning?**

## TEXT 4 PAUL AUSTER ~ 'GHOSTS', IN THE NEW YORK TRILOGY, 1986

**Paul AUSTER**
(born 1947)

His novels blend genres (often using the form of thrillers) to convey the idea of a meaningless quest, of a world ruled by chance, mistakes and confusion (*The New York Trilogy*, 1986, *Moon Palace*, 1989, *The Music of Chance*, 1990).

*This is the incipit of the novel.*

FIRST OF ALL THERE IS BLUE. Later there is White, and then there is Black, and before the beginning there is Brown. Brown broke him in[1]. Brown taught him the ropes[2], and when Brown grew old, Blue took over. That is how it begins. The place is New York, the time is the present, and neither one will ever change. Blue goes to his office every day and sits at his desk, waiting for something to happen. For a long time nothing does, and then a man named White walks through the door, and that is how it begins.

The case seems simple enough. White wants Blue to follow a man named Black and to keep an eye on him for as long as necessary. While working for Brown, Blue did many tail jobs[3], and this one seems no different, perhaps even easier than most.

Blue needs the work, and so he listens to White and doesn't ask many questions. He assumes it's a marriage case and that White is a jealous husband. White doesn't elaborate. He wants a weekly report, he says, sent to such and such a postbox number, typed out in duplicate on pages so long and so wide. A cheque will be sent each week to Blue in the mail. White then tells Blue where Black lives, what he looks like, and so on. When Blue asks White how long he thinks the case will last. White says he doesn't know. Just keep sending the reports, he says, until further notice.

To be fair to Blue, he finds it all a little strange. But to say that he has misgivings[4] at this point would be going too far. Still, it's impossible for him not to notice certain things about White. The black beard, for example, and the overly[5] bushy eyebrows. And then there is the skin, which seems inordinately white, as though covered with powder. Blue is no amateur in the art of disguise, and it's not difficult for him to see through this one. Brown was his teacher, after all, and in his day Brown was the best in the business. So Blue begins to think he was wrong, that the case has nothing to do with marriage. But he gets no farther than this, for White is still speaking to him, and Blue must concentrate on following his words.

Everything has been arranged. White says. There's a small apartment directly across the street from Black's. I've already rented it, and you can move in there today. The rent will be paid for until the case is over.

Good idea, says Blue, taking the key from White. That will eliminate the legwork[6].

Exactly, White answers, stroking his beard.

And so it's settled. Blue agrees to take the job, and they shake hands on it. To show his good faith. White even gives Blue an advance of ten fifty-dollar bills.

That is how it begins, then. The young Blue and a man named White, who is obviously not the man he appears to be. It doesn't matter, Blue says to himself after White has left. I'm sure he has his reasons. And besides, it's not my problem. The only thing I have to worry about is doing my job.

It is 3 February 1947. Little does Blue know, of course, that the case will go on for years. But the present is no less dark than the past, and its mystery is equal to anything the future might hold. Such is the way of the world: one step at a time, one word and then the next. There are certain things that Blue cannot possibly know at this point. For knowledge comes slowly, and when it comes, it is often at great personal expense.

Times square, New York

White leaves the office, and a moment later Blue picks up the phone and calls the future Mrs Blue. I'm going under cover, he tells his sweetheart. Don't worry if I'm out of touch for a little while. I'll be thinking of you the whole time.

Blue takes a small grey satchel[7] down from the shelf and packs it with his thirty-eight[8], a pair of binoculars, a notebook, and other tools of the trade. Then he tidies his desk, puts his papers in order, and locks up the office. From there he goes to the apartment that White has rented for him. The address is unimportant. But let's say Brooklyn Heights, for the sake of argument. Some quiet, rarely travelled street not far from the bridge – Orange Street perhaps. Walt Whitman handset[9] the first edition of *Leaves of Grass* on this street in 1855, and it was here that Henry Ward Beecher railed[10] against slavery from the pulpit of his red-brick church. So much for local colour.

It's a small studio apartment on the third floor of a four-storey brownstone. Blue is happy to see that it's fully equipped, and as he walks around the room inspecting the furnishings, he discovers that everything in the place is new: the bed, the table, the chair, the rug, the linens, the kitchen supplies, everything. There is a complete set of clothes hanging in the closet, and Blue, wondering if the clothes are meant for him, tries them on and sees that they fit. It's not the biggest place I've ever been in, he says to himself, pacing from one end of the room to the other, but it's cosy[11] enough, cosy enough.

He goes back outside, crosses the street, and enters the opposite building. In the entryway he searches for Black's name on one of the mailboxes and finds it: Black – 3rd floor. So far so good. Then he returns to his room and gets down to business.

Parting the curtains of the window, he looks out and sees Black sitting at a table in his room across the street. To the extent that Blue can make out[12] what is happening, he gathers that Black is writing. A look through the binoculars confirms that he is. The lenses[13], however, are not powerful enough to pick up the writing itself, and even if they were, Blue doubts that he would be able to read the handwriting upside down. All he can say for certain, therefore, is that Black is writing in a notebook and writes: 3 Feb. 3pm. Black writing at his desk.

**1. to break so in:** *former quelqu'un* **2. to teach so the ropes:** *apprendre le métier à quelqu'un* **3. a tail job:** *une filature (suivre quelqu'un)* **4. misgivings:** *des doutes* **5. overly:** *trop* **6. the legwork:** *les déplacements* **7. a satchel:** *un cartable* **8. his thirty-eight:** *son revolver* **9. to handset:** *composer à la main (typographie)* **10. to rail against:** *s'indigner contre* **11. cosy:** *confortable* **12. to make out:** *distinguer.* **13. the lenses:** *l'objectif*

## Zooming in

**1** The situation
What is Blue's profession?
What is the role or function of each character?
- Brown: ...
- Blue: ...
- White: ...
- Black: ...

**2** List all the elements which confirm Blue's profession:
- The plot: ...
- His attitude: ...
- The vocabulary used: ...

**3** Are we going to read a novel which belongs to the genre described above, or a parody of that genre? What other elements are defamiliarizing and point to a post-modern novel?

**4** Who is the narrator? Whose point of view do we follow?

**5** What shows that Blue is soon going to lose his freedom and will become a mere puppet in White's hands?

## MOVING ON

***Watch***
- Karel Reisz's film *The French Lieutenant's Woman,* 1981 (adapted by Harold Pinter)
- Sam Wood's adaptation of Hemingway's *For Whom the Bell Tolls*, with Gary Cooper and Ingrid Bergman (1943)
- *The Dead* (1987) is an adaptation of James Joyce's story of the same name in *Dubliners*. It was John Huston's final film and a return to his roots in Ireland

***Read***
- Virginia Woolf's *Orlando* (1929) or *To the Lighthouse* (1927)
- James Joyce's *A Portrait of the Artist as a Young Man* (1914)
- Paul Auster's *The Book of Illusions* (2002)

***Look at***
Modernism and post-modernism in painting:
- Modernism: Cubism, futurism, abstraction,
- Post-Modernism: Hyper-realism, Magic realism

***Listen to***
William Carlos Williams reading his own poetry (Pennsound on the internet).

# The literature of the absurd

## The absurd

The notion of absurdity comes from Camus, who defined it as man's attempt to find purpose[1] in a world which has neither order nor intelligibility. It is based on a form of existentialism according to which there is no God and human beings come from nothingness and will go back to nothingness after death. The result is a sense of anguish, with all actions and aspirations becoming ironical. Qualities such as courage or heroism are therefore derisory and only reflect the fact that men take refuge in a world of illusion, which they prefer to reality.

## The theatre of the absurd

The term was originally applied to the plays of French playwrights such as Ionesco and Beckett, then flourished[2] in English with the works of **Beckett** (who writes in both French and English), **Pinter**, **Stoppard** and **Albee**.

A few works:

- Samuel Beckett (*Waiting for Godot*, 1954; *Endgame*, 1957; *Happy Days*, 1961)
- Harold Pinter (*The Room*, 1957; *The Dumb Waiter*, 1962)
- Tom Stoppard (*Rosencrantz and Guildenstern Are Dead*, 1967, *Arcadia*, 1993)
- Eward Albee (*Who's Afraid of Virginia Woolf*, 1962)

## A few characteristics of the theatre of the absurd

- People are isolated in an alien world and no significant communication is possible between human beings.
- No realistic settings: confronted with the meaninglessness of all actions, characters are symbolically imprisoned in reduced spaces (Winnie is half-buried in earth in *Happy Days*; Hamm is blind and cannot stand in *Endgame* – two of **Beckett**'s plays), frozen by their metaphysical situation.
- There is practically no plot.
- The protagonists have no depth and do not develop in the play.
- Language and reasoning are often illogical and pointless[3]. Characters talk for the sake of talking, to fill in time and forget their anguish.
- The sense of nothingness is sometimes reflected in moments of farce.

**William Shakespeare, *King Lear*, 1608**

*Even though there is nothing absurdist about Shakespeare's plays, some scenes reflect existential anguish.*

LEAR: Thou must be patient. We came crying hither:
Thou knowst[1] the first time that we smell the air
We wawl[2] and cry. I will preach to thee: mark me.
GLOUCESTER: Alack[3], alack the day
LEAR: When we are born we cry that we are come
To this great stage of fools.

1. **thou knowst:** *archaïque pour 'you know'*
2. **to wawl:** *crier (archaïque)* 3. **alack:** *hélas*

## The absurd in fiction

Several novelists transposed such existential absurdity to fiction, with black humour or absurd or nightmarish situations. This is the case in many of the novels of the American writers **Joseph Heller** (*Catch-22*, 1961), **Thomas Pynchon** (*The Crying of Lot 49*, 1966), and **Kurt Vonnegut** (*Slaughterhouse-Five*, 1969).

1. **a purpose:** *un but, un sens*
2. **to flourish:** *se développer, s'épanouir*
3. **pointless:** *qui ne rime à rien*

## TEXT 1 SAMUEL BECKETT ~ WAITING FOR GODOT, 1954

**Samuel BECKETT**

(1906-1989)

wrote his plays and novels in both French and English. His characters live in a universe of existential anguish where language and comedy are used to avoid thinking about the futility of existence.

*In* Waiting for Godot*, two characters, Vladimir and Estragon, vainly wait for Godot, someone they hardly know and who will never come. On each of the two days when the play takes place, a messenger comes and tells them that Godot won't be coming that day, but surely will on the next day.*

*Waiting for Godot*, directed by Christopher Gottschalk, 2010

*The landscape is bare[1] ('A country road. A tree.')*
*Estragon rises painfully, goes limping[2] to extreme left, halts, gazes into distance off with his hand screening[3] his eyes, turns, goes to extreme right, gazes into distance. Vladimir watches him, then goes and picks up the boot[4], peers[5] into it, drops it hastily.*

VLADIMIR: Pah!
*He spits[6]. Estragon moves to centre, halts with his back to auditorium.*
ESTRAGON: Charming spot. *(He turns, advances to front, halts facing auditorium.)* Inspiring prospects[7]. *(He turns to Vladimir.)* Let's go.
VLADIMIR: We can't.
ESTRAGON: Why not?
VLADIMIR: We're waiting for Godot.
ESTRAGON: *(despairingly)*. Ah! *(Pause.)* You're sure it was here?
VLADIMIR: What?
ESTRAGON: That we were to wait.
VLADIMIR: He said by the tree. *(They look at the tree.)* Do you see any others?
ESTRAGON: What is it?
VLADIMIR: I don't know. A willow[8].
ESTRAGON: Where are the leaves?
VLADIMIR: It must be dead.
ESTRAGON: No more weeping.
VLADIMIR: Or perhaps it's not the season.
ESTRAGON: Looks to me more like a bush[9].
VLADIMIR: A shrub[10].
ESTRAGON: A bush.
VLADIMIR: A—. What are you insinuating? That we've come to the wrong place?
ESTRAGON: He should be here.
VLADIMIR: He didn't say for sure he'd come.
ESTRAGON: And if he doesn't come?
VLADIMIR: We'll come back tomorrow.
ESTRAGON: And then the day after tomorrow.
VLADIMIR: Possibly.
ESTRAGON: And so on.
VLADIMIR: The point is—
ESTRAGON: Until he comes.

**VLADIMIR:** You're merciless[11].
**ESTRAGON:** We came here yesterday.
**VLADIMIR:** Ah no, there you're mistaken.
**ESTRAGON:** What did we do yesterday?
**VLADIMIR:** What did we do yesterday?
**ESTRAGON:** Yes.
**VLADIMIR:** Why... *(Angrily.)* Nothing is certain when you're about.
**ESTRAGON:** In my opinion we were here.
**VLADIMIR:** *(looking round)*. You recognize the place?
**ESTRAGON:** I didn't say that.
**VLADIMIR:** Well?
**ESTRAGON:** That makes no difference.
**VLADIMIR:** All the same... that tree... *(turning towards auditorium)* that bog[12]...
**ESTRAGON:** You're sure it was this evening?
**VLADIMIR:** What?
**ESTRAGON:** That we were to wait.
**VLADIMIR:** He said Saturday. *(Pause.)* I think.
**ESTRAGON:** You think.
**VLADIMIR:** I must have made a note of it. (He fumbles[13] in his pockets, bursting with[14] miscellaneous[15] rubbish.)
**ESTRAGON:** *(very insidious)*. But what Saturday? And is it Saturday? Is it not rather Sunday?
*(Pause.)* Or Monday? *(Pause.)* Or Friday?
**VLADIMIR:** *(looking wildly about him, as though the date was inscribed in the landscape.)* It's not possible!

**ESTRAGON:** Or Thursday?
**VLADIMIR:** What'll we do?
**ESTRAGON:** If he came yesterday and we weren't here you may be sure he won't come again today.
**VLADIMIR:** But you say we were here yesterday.
**ESTRAGON:** I may be mistaken. *(Pause.)* Let's stop talking for a minute, do you mind?
**VLADIMIR:** *(feebly)*. All right.
*(Estragon sits down on the mound. Vladimir paces agitatedly to and fro, halting from time to time to gaze into distance off. Estragon falls asleep. Vladimir halts finally before Estragon.)* Gogo!... Gogo!... GOGO!
*Estragon wakes with a start.*
**ESTRAGON:** *(restored to the horror of his situation)*. I was asleep! *(Despairingly.)* Why will you never let me sleep?

*Waiting for Godot*, directed by Bernard LEVY, Paris, 2009

TEXT 1 **SAMUEL BECKETT** ~ WAITING FOR GODOT, 1954

VLADIMIR: I felt lonely.

ESTRAGON: I had a dream.

VLADIMIR: Don't tell me!

ESTRAGON: I dreamt that—

VLADIMIR: DON'T TELL ME!

ESTRAGON *(gesture towards the universe)*: This one is enough for you? *(Silence.)* It's not nice of you, Didi. Who am I to tell my private nightmares to if I can't tell them to you?

VLADIMIR: Let them remain private. You know I can't bear that.

(From Act I)

1. **bare:** *dépouillé* 2. **to limp:** *boiter* 3. **to screen:** *protéger* 4. **a boot:** *une botte* 5. **to peer:** *regarder* 6. **to spit:** *cracher* 7. **prospects:** *des perspectives* 8. **a willow:** *un saule* 9. **a bush:** *un buisson* 10. **a shrub:** *un arbuste* 11. **merciless:** *impitoyable* 12. **a bog:** *un marécage* 13. **to fumble:** *fouiller* 14. **bursting with:** *pleines de* 15. **miscellaneous:** *divers*

## Zooming in

**1** The dialogue focuses on three main points in succession.
What are they?
- a. ...
- b. ...
- c. ...

**2** Show the meaninglessness of the dialogue by giving examples of:
- repetition: ...
- absurd discussion: ...
- pun: ...
- ready-made expressions, normally found in a more serious dialogue: ...
- assertions which are immediately contradicted: ...

Why is there such meaningless dialogue?

**3** Why are the stage directions so numerous compared to the dialogue?

**4** What do the following stand for?
- Gazing into the distance: ...
- The tree: ...
- Dreaming: ...

**5** What means are used to bring the audience into the situation of Vladimir and Estragon?

George TOOKER, *Landscape with Figures*, 1965-1966, Private collection

## TEXT 2 HAROLD PINTER ~ THE DUMB WAITER, 1960

**Harold PINTER**
(born 1930)

His plays have been described as 'comedies of menace' because their atmosphere is often one of fear. Relationships are tense or violent with racist insults, threats and violence giving the illusion of power and replacing real communication.

*The play takes place in a basement[1] room, where two professional killers are waiting for their orders concerning the next job. Strange things begin to happen: 'an envelope slides under the door' containing nothing but matches[2], just before this passage, then the dumb waiter[3] which is in the room begins to work, carrying orders for food. The last order will be to kill the first man who comes into the room – which will be Gus.*

*The Dumb Waiter*, Black Stripe Theater, 2007, Tokyo

GUS: Ben, look here.
BEN: What ?
GUS: Look.
*(Ben turns his head and sees the envelope. He stands.)*
BEN: What's that?
GUS: I don't know.
BEN: Where did it come from?
GUS: Under the door.
BEN: Well, what is it?
GUS: I don't know.
*(They stare at it.)*
BEN: Pick it up.
GUS: What do you mean?
BEN: Pick it up!
*(Gus slowly moves towards it, bends and picks it up.)*
What is it?
GUS: An envelope.
BEN: Is there anything on it?
GUS: No.
BEN: Is it sealed?
GUS: Yes.
BEN: Open it.
GUS: What?
BEN: Open it!
*(Gus opens it and looks inside.)*
What's in it?
*(Gus empties twelve matches into his hand.)*
GUS:. Matches.
BEN: Matches?
GUS: Yes.
BEN: Show it to me.
*(Gus passes the envelope. Ben examines it.)*
Nothing on it. Not a word.
GUS: That's funny, isn't it?
BEN: It came under the door?
GUS: Must have done.

BEN: Well, go on.
GUS: Go on where?
BEN: Open the door and see if you can catch anyone outside.
GUS: Who, me?
BEN: Go on!
*Gus stares at him, puts the matches in his pocket, goes to his bed and brings a revolver from under the pillow. He goes to the door, opens it, looks out and shuts it.*
GUS: No one.
*He replaces the revolver.*
BEN: What did you see?
GUS: Nothing.
BEN: They must have been pretty quick.
*Gus takes the matches from his pocket and looks at them.*
GUS: Well, they'll come in handy[4].
BEN: Yes.
GUS: Won't they?
BEN: Yes, you're always running out[5], aren't you?
GUS: All the time.
BEN: Well, they'll come in handy then.
GUS: Yes.
BEN: Won't they?
GUS: Yes, I could do with them. I could do with them too.
BEN: You could, eh?
GUS: Yes.
BEN: Why?
GUS: We haven't got any.
BEN: Well, you've got some now, haven't you?
GUS: I can light the kettle[6] now.
BEN: Yes, you're always cadging[7] matches. How many have you got there?
GUS: About a dozen.
BEN: Well, don't lose them. Red too. You don't even need a box.
*Gus probes his ear with a match.*
*(Slapping his hand.) Don't waste them! Go on, go and light it.*
GUS: Eh?
BEN: Go and light it.
GUS: Light what?
BEN: The kettle.
GUS: You mean the gas.
BEN: Who does?
GUS: You do.
BEN: *(His eyes narrowing.)* What do you mean, I mean the gas?
GUS: Well, that's what you mean, don't you? The gas.
BEN: *(Powerfully.)* If I say go and light the kettle I mean go and light the kettle.
GUS: How can you light a kettle?
BEN: It's a figure of speech! Light the kettle. It's a figure of speech[8]!
GUS: I've never heard it.
BEN: Light the kettle! It's common usage!
GUS: I think you've got it wrong.

## TEXT 2 HAROLD PINTER ~ The Dumb Waiter, 1960

**BEN:** *(Menacing.)* What do you mean?

**GUS:** They say put on the kettle.

**BEN:** *(Taut.)* Who says?

*They stare at each other, breathing hard.*

*(Deliberately.)* I have never in all my life heard anyone say put on the kettle.

**GUS:** I bet my mother used to say it.

**BEN:** Your mother? When did you last see your mother?

**GUS:** I don't know, about -

**BEN:** Well, what are you talking about your mother for?

*(They stare.)*

Gus, I'm not trying to be unreasonable. I'm just trying to point out something to you.

**GUS:** Yes, but –

**BEN:** Who's the senior partner here, me or you?

**GUS:** You.

**BEN:** I'm only looking after your interests, Gus. You've got to learn, mate[9].

**GUS:** Yes, but I've never heard-

**BEN:** *(Vehemently.)* Nobody says light the gas! What does the gas light?

**GUS:** What does the gas–?

**BEN:** *(Grabbing him with two hands by the throat, at arm's length.)*

THE KETTLE, YOU FOOL!

*Gus takes the hands from his throat.*

**GUS:** All right, all right.

*Pause.*

**BEN:** Well, what are you waiting for?

**GUS:** I want to see if they light.

**BEN:** What?

**GUS:** The matches.

*He takes out the flattened box and tries to strike[10].*

No.

*He throws the box under the bed.*

*Ben stares at him.*

*Gus raises his foot.*

Shall I try it on here?

*Ben stares, Gus strikes a match on his shoe. It lights.*

Here we are.

**BEN:** *(Wearily.)* Put on the bloody kettle, for Christ's sake.

*The Dumb Waiter*, directed by Adam Barnowski, The Abreact Performance Space, Detroit, 2006

*Ben goes to his bed, but, realising what he has said, stops and half turns. They look at each other.*

*Gus slowly exits, left. Ben slams his paper down on the bed and sits on it, head in hands.*

GUS: *(entering).* It's going.

BEN: What?

GUS: The stove[11].

*Gus goes to his bed and sits.*

I wonder who it'll be tonight.

*Silence.*

**1. a basement:** *un sous-sol* **2. a match:** *une allumette* **3. a dumb waiter:** *un monte charge* **4. to come in handy:** *être utile* **5. to run out of...:** *manquer de...* **6. the kettle:** *la bouilloire* **7. to cadge something:** *quémander quelquechose* **8. it's a figure of speech:** *c'est une façon de parler* **9. mate:** *mon vieux!* **10. to strike a match:** *faire craquer une allumette* **11. the stove:** *la cuisinière*

## Zooming in

1. Give examples of the way lack of communication is conveyed through:
   - meaningless remarks: ...
   - repetitions: ...
   - absurd quarrels: ...
   - sentence length: ...
2. Show the growing tension between the two men.
   - through the stage directions: ...
   - through their words: ...
3. What is the relationship between the two men?
4. Explain these two sentences:
   - 'realising what he has said': ...
   - 'I wonder who it'll be tonight.': ...
5. Find examples of emptiness and void in the text.
6. Comment on the title of the play.

# TEXT 3 JOSEPH HELLER ~ Catch-22, 1961

**Joseph HELLER**
(1923-1999)
became famous thanks to *Catch-22* (1961), a novel about the cruelty, hypocrisy and absurdity of war.

*Yossarian, the main character of* Catch-22, *is a US Army Air Force bombardier. His squadron is based in Italy towards the end of World War II. Yossarian is afraid of dying during one of the missions and goes to Doc Danneeka to ask if he can be grounded[1]. He will later pretend to be crazy in order not to be sent on more missions.*

"You're wasting your time," Doc Daneeka was forced to tell him.

"Can't you ground someone who's crazy?"

"Oh, sure. I have to. There's a rule saying I have to ground anyone who's crazy."

"Then why don't you ground me? I'm crazy. Ask Clevinger."

"Clevinger? Where is Clevinger? You find Clevinger and I'll ask him."

"Then ask any of the others. They'll tell you how crazy I am."

"They're crazy."

"Then why don't you ground them?"

"Why don't they ask me to ground them?"

"Because they're crazy, that's why."

"Of course they're crazy," Doc Daneeka replied. "I just told you they're crazy, didn't I? And you can't let crazy people decide whether you're crazy or not, can you?"

Roy LICHTENSTEIN, *Blam*, 1962, Yale University Art Gallery, New Haven

Lichtenstein, a pop artist, magnified[1] images from popular culture, such as comic strips here, to show the violence of mass culture.

1. to magnify: *amplifier, grossir*

Yossarian looked at him soberly and tried another approach. "Is Orr crazy?"

"He sure is," Doc Daneeka said.

"Can you ground him?".

"I sure can. But first he has to ask me to. That's part of the rule."

"Then why doesn't he ask you to?"

"Because he's crazy," Doc Daneeka said. "He has to be crazy to keep flying combat missions after all the close calls[2] he's had. Sure, I can ground Orr. But first he has to ask me to."

"That's all he has to do to be grounded?"

"That's all. Let him ask me."

"And then you can ground him?" Yossarian asked.

"No. Then I can't ground him."

"You mean there's a catch[3]?"

"Sure there's a catch," Doc Daneeka replied. "Catch-22. Anyone who wants to get out of combat duty isn't really crazy."

There was only one catch and that was Catch-22, which specified that a concern for one's own safety in the face of dangers that were real and immediate was the process of a rational mind. Orr was crazy and could be grounded. All he had to do was ask; and as soon as he did, he would no longer be crazy and would have to fly more missions. Orr would be crazy to fly more missions and sane if he didn't, but if he was sane he had to fly them. If he flew them he was crazy and didn't have to; but if he didn't want to he was sane and had to. Yossarian was moved very deeply by the absolute simplicity of this clause of Catch-22 and let out a respectful whistle[4].

"That's some catch, that Catch-22," he observed.

"It's the best there is," Doc Daneeka agreed.

(From chapter 5)

1. **to ground:** *interdire de voler, retenir au sol* 2. **it's a close call:** *il l'a échappé belle* 3. **a catch:** *une entourloupe, une clause 'attrape-nigaud'* 4. **a whistle:** *un sifflement*

## Zooming in

**1** Show the contrast between the logical development of the conversation and the absurd logic it reveals.
- the dialogue: ...
- absurd logic: ...

| | | Result | Why? |
|---|---|---|---|
| Someone is crazy → | asks to be grounded | ... | ... |
| → | does not ask to be grounded | ... | ... |
| Someone is sane → | asks to be grounded | ... | ... |

**2** Show that the effect produced is between horror and comedy.
- horror: ...
- comedy: ...

**3** Comment on the narrator's reactions.

**4** What is criticized in the text?

## MOVING ON

***Watch***

– Most of Samuel Beckett's and Harold Pinter's plays are available on DVD. You could compare several productions of the same play.
– Edward Albee's *Who's Afraid of Virginia Woolf* is also available on DVD.
– So is Tom Stoppard's *Rosencrantz and Guildenstern Are Dead*.

***Compare***

The French and English versions of Beckett's plays.

# Colonialism and post-colonialism

## Colonialism in Victorian and early 20th century literature

All through the 19th century, Britain enlarged its colonial possessions until "the sun never set on the British empire". The faraway countries of the empire constituted a source of wonder, curiosity or pride which are reflected in Victorian literature. The colonies often provided an exotic background for tales of adventure, for necessary long journeys abroad (Mr Bertram in Jane Austen's *Mansfield Park*) or for mysterious events (Rochester's marriage in *Jane Eyre*). But on the whole, the ideology of imperialism was never challenged. On the contrary, those colonies were seen as places were anything could happen and where the natives tended to be savage. It was the duty of the British to educate those people who were 'Half devil and half child' as Rudyard Kipling wrote in his poem "The White Man's Burden" (1910). Such insistence on the 'otherness' of the colonies seemed to legalize the colonizing enterprise.

In the first half of the 20th century, some writers such as Joseph Conrad or E. M. Forster began to expose the worst aspects of colonialism.

## A few examples of colonial writing

• Even though **Kipling** was often considered as the voice of imperialism, his novels, stories and poems offer a subtle picture of India and of the relationship between the population and the English colonizers.

• **Conrad** was one of the first novelists to denounce imperialism. He was born in the Polish Ukraine and learnt English as he worked on ships in the Merchant Service. His novels explore the often dark nature of man. *Heart of Darkness* (1902) relates a trip up the Congo and shows the absurdity, exploitation and horror which result from imperialism.

• **Forster** (1879-1970) is associated with the Bloomsbury Group and his novels reflect the need for tolerance and understanding in human relationships. *A Passage to India* (1924), shows the gap between East and West, which is partly caused by the prejudice of the English. See p. 25

## Post-colonial literature

The expression describes works which were written after the end of colonial rule (for instance after the independence of India in 1947) and which are about the effects of colonialism. Whereas English literature used to be sent to the colonies and read in schools, the reverse is now true and post-colonial literature is now widely sold in Britain. As **Salman Rushdie** put it: 'The Empire writes back to the centre'.

## Some recurrent themes and issues in post-colonial writings

• The problems faced in the countries after independence: crises and internal political and religious conflicts (in **Arundhati Roy**'s *The God of Small Things* (1997), for instance).

• The problem of writing in English, the language of the colonizer. Most of the time, the English language was adapted (in terms of vocabulary, syntax, rhythm), and therefore appropriated.

• Such writings often make use of the cultural and linguistic traditions of their native countries, oral traditions for instance. This may be the reason why many post-colonial novels use magic realism (as in many of Rushdie's novels) and hybrid language.

The British Empire in 1886

• Another way of asserting one's literary identity is to rewrite the English canon, that is to say the standard books in English literature. In doing so, post-colonial writers often invert the views which underlie[1] the original works. **J. M. Coetzee**'s *Foe* (1986), for instance, is a rewriting of Daniel Defoe's *Robinson Crusoe* (1719), from the point of view of his wife, who is not given a voice in Defoe's novel. With A *Harlot's Progress* (1999), the Caribbean writer **David Dabydeen** wrote a novel about the different characters in one of Hogarth's series of prints. **Jean Rhys**'s *Wide Sargasso Sea* (1966) is based on *Jane Eyre*.

## Post-colonial literature and feminism

Because most of the colonies tended to have a patriarchal system, women feel that they were doubly penalized – by the system of the colony and by the colonizer.

## The question of Ireland

Although Ireland does not correspond to the image of an emergent colonial nation, the long years of British domination were deeply resented as they led, for instance, to the gradual disappearance of the Irish language and to the integration of Irish literature into the British canon. The fight for independence in the early 20th century was reflected in the works of such writers as **Yeats** and **Synge**, and more indirectly in those of **Joyce**. All explored the meaning of Irish identity.

1. to underlie: *sous-tendre*

## TEXT 1 JAMES JOYCE ~ 'COUNTERPARTS', IN DUBLINERS, 1914

**James JOYCE**
(1882-1941)
He is best known as a modernist. Using stream of consciousness and a highly innovative use of language, he portrayed the deadening effects of Irish life. (*Dubliners*, 1914; *A Portrait of the Artist as a Young Man*, 1916, about the artistic development of a young man; *Ulysses*, 1922, which follows the thoughts of several characters during one day in Dublin.)

*Dubliners consists of 15 stories about the inhabitants of Dublin. There is little plot, but the stories show moments of intensity leading to 'moral, social or spiritual revelation.' The stories were written while Joyce was in exile and they are a justification for his leaving Ireland as well as a step towards its 'spiritual liberation'. Indeed, life in Dublin is seen as degraded or pitiful, and Joyce spoke of the 'paralysis' at the heart of the city. But his vision of drunks or perverts is not without affection.*

*In 'Counterparts', we have seen the main character, Farrington, getting drunk all through the day, hating his monotonous job in an office, vainly trying to look heroic, but finally being bullied[1] by everyone and humiliated by his boss. This is the end of the story, when he returns home.*

A VERY SULLEN-FACED[2] MAN stood at the corner of O'Connell Bridge waiting for the little Sandymount tram to take him home. He was full of smouldering[3] anger and revengefulness. He felt humiliated and discontented; he did not even feel drunk; and he had only twopence in his pocket. He cursed[4] everything. He had done for[5] himself in the office, pawned[6] his watch, spent all his money and he had not even got drunk. He began to feel thirsty again and he longed to be back again in the hot, reeking[7] public-house. He had lost his reputation as a strong man having been defeated twice by a mere boy. His heart swelled[8] with fury and, when he thought of the woman in the big hat who had brushed against him and said Pardon ! his fury nearly choked[9] him.

His tram let him down at Shelbourne Road and he steered[10] his great body along in the shadow of the wall of the barracks[11]. He loathed[12] returning to his home. When he went in by the side-door he found the kitchen empty and the kitchen fire nearly out. He bawled[13] upstairs:

"Ada! Ada!"

His wife was a little sharp-faced woman who bullied her husband when he was sober and was bullied by him when he was drunk. They had five children. A little boy came running down the stairs.

"Who is that?" said the man, peering through the darkness.

"Me, pa."

"Who are you ? Charlie ?"

"No, pa. Tom."

"Where's your mother ?"

"She's out at the chapel."

"That's right... Did she think of leaving any dinner for me?"

"Yes, pa. I —"

"Light the lamp. What do you mean by having the place in darkness? Are the other children in bed?"

The man sat down heavily on one of the chairs while the little boy lit the lamp. He began to mimic his son's flat accent,

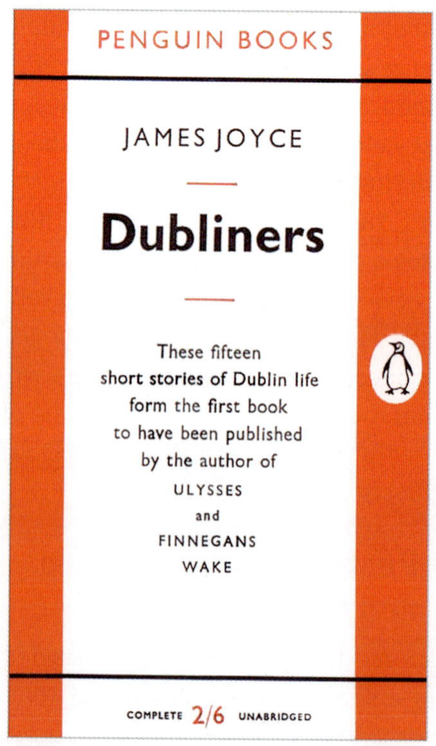

saying half to himself: "At the chapel. At the chapel if you please!" When the lamp was lit he banged his fist on the table and shouted:

"What's for my dinner?"

"I'm going... to cook it, pa," said the little boy.

The man jumped up furiously and pointed to the fire.

"On that fire! You let the fire out! By God, I'll teach you to do that again!" He took a step to the door and seized the walking-stick which was standing behind it.

"I'll teach you to let the fire out!" he said, rolling up his sleeve in order to give his arm free play.

The little boy cried "O, pa!" and ran whimpering[14] round the table, but the man followed him and caught him by the coat. The little boy looked about him wildly but, seeing no way of escape, fell upon his knees.

"Now, you'll let the fire out the next time!" said the man, striking at him vigorously with the stick. "Take that, you little whelp[15]!"

The boy uttered a squeal of pain as the stick cut his thigh. He clasped his hands together in the air and his voice shook with fright.

"O, pa!" he cried. "Don't beat me, pa! And I'll... I'll say a Hail Mary for you, I'll say a Hail Mary for you, pa, if you don't beat me... I'll say a Hail Mary..."

**1. to bully:** *tyranniser* **2. sullen-faced:** *à l'air maussade* **3. smouldering:** *qui couve* **4. to curse:** *maudire* **5. he had done for himself:** *il était fichu* **6. to pawn:** *mettre en gage* **7. to reek:** *puer, empester* **8. to swell:** *enfler* **9. to choke:** *étouffer* **10. to steer:** *diriger* **11. the barracks:** *la caserne* **12. to loathe:** *détester* **13. to bawl:** *hurler* **14. to whimper:** *gémir* **15. little whelp:** *petit morveux*

## Zooming in

1. Study the gradual rise of violence in this scene. How is violence underlined in each part?
   Part 1: fury: ... Lines: ...
   Part 2: growing tension: ... Lines: ...
   Part 3: physical violence ... Lines: ...

2. Who tells the story? Is there a progression in the way he talks about Farrington? What is Farrington called?

3. The title of the story, 'Counterparts' evokes both repetition and parallelism. Where can you see this in the passage? Think of the passage as the end of a story which has emphasized Farrington's humiliation. What is the effect of such repetitions and parallels?
   - Repetition: ...
   - Parallelism: ...

4. Study the references to light in this passage. What do they symbolize?

5. Dubliners are 'paralysed'. Could this also be said of the church?

## TEXT 2 E. M. FORSTER ~ A Passage to India, 1924

**E. M. FORSTER**
(1879-1970)
believed that only instincts and freedom between individuals can prevail against hypocrisy and conventions.
(*A Room With a View*, 1908; *Howards End*, 1910; *A Passage to India*, 1924).

*Mrs Moore, Ronny's mother, has come to India to visit her son, accompanied by Adela, who is engaged to Ronny. This conversation is between mother and son.*

"THERE'S NOTHING IN INDIA but the weather, my dear mother; it's the alpha and omega of the whole affair."

"Yes, as Mr McBryde was saying, but it's much more the Anglo-Indians themselves who are likely to get on Adela's nerves. She doesn't think they behave pleasantly to Indians, you see."

"What did I tell you?" he exclaimed, losing his gentle manner. "I knew it last week. Oh, how like a woman to worry over a side-issue[1]!"

She forgot about Adela in her surprise. "A side-issue, a side-issue?" she repeated. "How can it be that?"

"We're not out here for the purpose of behaving pleasantly!"

"What do you mean?"

"What I say. We're out here to do justice and keep the peace. Them's my sentiments. India isn't a drawing-room[2]."

"Your sentiments are those of a god," she said quietly, but it was his manner rather than his sentiments that annoyed her.

Trying to recover his temper, he said, "India likes gods."

"And Englishmen like posing as gods."

Queen Victoria in India

"There's no point in all this. Here we are, and we're going to stop[3], and the country's got to put up[4] with us, gods or no gods. Oh, look here," he broke out, rather pathetically, "what do you and Adela want me to do? Go against my class, against all the people I respect and admire out here? Lose such power as I have for doing good in this country, because my behaviour isn't pleasant? You neither of you understand what work is, or you'd never talk such eyewash[5]. I hate talking like this, but one must occasionally. It's morbidly sensitive to go on as Adela and you do. I noticed you both at the Club today - after the Collector had been at all that trouble to amuse you. I am out here to work, mind, to hold this wretched[6] country by force. I'm not a missionary or a Labour Member or a vague sentimental sympathetic literary man. I'm just a servant of the Government; it's the profession you wanted me to choose myself, and that's that. We're not pleasant in India, and we don't intend to be pleasant. We've something more important to do."

He spoke sincerely. Every day he worked hard in the court trying to decide which of two untrue accounts[7] was the less untrue, trying to dispense justice fearlessly, to protect the weak against the less weak, the incoherent against the plausible, surrounded by lies and flattery. That morning he had convicted[8] a railway clerk of overcharging[9] pilgrims for their tickets, and a Pathan[10] of attempted rape[11]. He expected no gratitude, no recognition for this, and both clerk and Pathan might appeal, bribe[12] their witnesses more effectually in the interval, and get their sentences reversed. It was his duty. But he did expect sympathy from his own people, and except from newcomers he obtained it. He did think he ought not to be worried about Bridge Parties when the day's work was over and he wanted to play tennis with his equals or rest his legs upon a long chair.

## TEXT 2 E. M. FORSTER ~ A Passage to India, 1924

He spoke sincerely, but she could have wished with less gusto[13]. How Ronny revelled[14] in the drawbacks[15] of his situation! How he did rub it in[16] that he was not in India to behave pleasantly, and derived positive satisfaction therefrom! He reminded her of his public-school days. The traces of young-man humanitarianism had sloughed off[17], and he talked like an intelligent and embittered[18] boy. His words without his voice might have impressed her, but when she heard the self-satisfied lilt[19] of them, when she saw the mouth moving so complacently[20] and competently beneath the little red nose, she felt, quite illogically, that this was not the last word on India. One touch of regret – not the canny[21] substitute but the true regret from the heart - would have made him a different man, and the British Empire a different institution.

"I'm going to argue, and indeed dictate," she said, clinking[22] her rings. "The English are out here to be pleasant."

"How do you make that out, mother?" he asked, speaking gently again, for he was ashamed of his irritability.

"Because India is part of the earth. And God has put us on the earth in order to be pleasant to each other. God ... is ... love." She hesitated, seeing how much he disliked the argument, but something made her go on. "God has put us on earth to love our neighbours and to show it, and He is omnipresent, even in India, to see how we are succeeding.

1. **a side-issue:** *une question secondaire* 2. **a drawing-room:** *un salon* 3. **to stop:** *(y) rester* 4. **to put up with:** *supporter* 5. **eyewash:** *des fadaises* 6. **wretched:** *malheureux* 7. **an account:** *un récit, un compte-rendu* 8. **to convict:** *déclarer coupable* 9. **to overcharge:** *faire trop payer* 10. **a Pathan:** *un membre d'une tribu du nord-ouest de l'Inde* 11. **a rape:** *un viol* 12. **to bribe:** *soudoyer* 13. **gusto:** *l'enthousiasme* 14. **to revel:** *se délecter de* 15. **the drawbacks:** *les inconvénients* 16. **to rub it in:** *insister* 17. **to slough off:** *disparaître, partir petit à petit* 18. **embittered:** *amer* 19. **the lilt:** *la cadence* 20. **complacently:** *avec suffisance* 21. **canny:** *prudent* 22. **to clink:** *faire tinter*

## Zooming in

**1** The structure of the text.
There are three main parts in this text. What are they? Show that the text has a very balanced structure.

What does this structure convey?

**2** Explain the main differences of opinion between Mrs Moore and her son by considering what the words "pleasantly" and "god" mean to them.

- 'pleasantly': Mrs Moore : ... Ronny: ...
- 'god': Mrs Moore : ... Ronny: ...

**3** What kind of narrator do we have here?

**4** 'Only connect' was in many ways Forster's motto (quite explicitly in his novel *Howards End*). How does it apply to the passage?

## TEXT 3 CHARLOTTE BRONTË ~ JANE EYRE, 1847

**Charlotte BRONTË**
(1816-55)
was one of three sisters brought up in a parsonage near the Yorkshire Moors. Her heroines are sensitive young women who assert their independence and put integrity and conscience before love. (*Jane Eyre*, 1847; *Villette*, 1853).

*Jane Eyre, an orphan girl, is brought up in an institution and becomes a governess at Thornfield Hall, Mr Rochester's home. They fall in love, but on the wedding day, the marriage is stopped when it is revealed that Rochester is already married to Bertha. Rochester now explains why he kept his marriage secret. Wood is the clergyman, Briggs a solicitor[1], Richard Mason is Bertha's brother.*

GENTLEMEN, MY PLAN IS BROKEN UP: — what this lawyer and his client say is true: I have been married, and the woman to whom I was married lives! You say you never heard of a Mrs. Rochester at the house up yonder[2], Wood; but I daresay you have many a time inclined your ear to gossip[3] about the mysterious lunatic[4] kept there under watch and ward[5]. Some have whispered to you that she is my bastard half-sister: some, my cast-off mistress. I now inform you that she is my wife, whom I married fifteen years ago, — Bertha Mason by name; sister of this resolute personage, who is now, with his quivering[6] limbs and white cheeks, showing you what a stout heart men may bear. Cheer up, Dick! — never fear me! — I'd almost as soon[7] strike a woman as you. Bertha Mason is mad; and she came of a mad family; idiots and maniacs through three generations! Her mother, the Creole, was both a madwoman and a drunkard! — as I found out after I had wed the daughter: for they were silent on family secrets before. Bertha, like a dutiful child, copied her parent in both points. I had a charming partner — pure, wise, modest: you can fancy I was a happy man. I went through rich scenes! Oh! my experience has been heavenly, if you only knew it! But I owe you no further explanation. Briggs, Wood, Mason, I invite you all to come up to the house and visit Mrs. Poole's patient, and my wife! You shall see what sort of a being I was cheated into espousing, and judge whether or not I had a right to break the compact[8], and seek sympathy with something at least human. This girl," he continued, looking at me, "knew no more than you, Wood, of the disgusting secret: she thought all was fair and legal and never dreamt she was going to be entrapped[9] into a feigned union with a defrauded wretch[10], already bound to a bad, mad, and embruted[11] partner! Come all of you — follow!"

**1. a solicitor:** *un notaire* **2. up yonder:** *là-bas* **3. gossip:** *des commérages* **4. a lunatic:** *un fou, une folle* **5. under watch and ward:** *bien surveillée* **6. quivering:** *tremblant* **7. I'd as soon:** *je préférerais* **8. the compact:** *le contrat* **9. entrapped:** *pris au piège* **10. a defrauded wretch:** *un malheureux qui s'est fait escroquer* **11. embruted:** *rendu à l'état de brute*

*Jane Eyre*, directed by Franco Zeffirelli, 1996

TEXT 4 # JEAN RHYS ~ WIDE SARGASSO SEA, 1966

**Jean RHYS**
(1890-1979)
was born in Dominica. Her novels describe lonely, vulnerable women, who are cut off from their roots and become alienated or exploited.
(*Wide Sargasso Sea*, 1966)

*Wide Sargasso Sea takes place in Jamaica in the 1830s and tells the story of Bertha (now called Antoinette) before she came to live at Thornfield Hall. Being neither English nor natives, her Creole family are despised by all, and their house is eventually attacked by blacks and burnt down, killing Antoinette's idiot brother and driving her mother mad. Being rich, she is married off to Rochester and loses control of her money. Rochester's love soon turns to hatred when he hears rumours of madness in her family and Antoinette becomes increasingly isolated and unbalanced. This passage is told by Rochester, who relates what Antoinette told him about her mother.*

"YOU WANT TO KNOW ABOUT MY MOTHER, I will tell you about her, the truth, not lies." Then she was silent for so long that I said gently, "I know that after your father died, she was very lonely and unhappy."

"And very poor," she said. "Don't forget that. For five years. Isn't it quick to say. And isn't it long to live. And lonely. She was so lonely that she grew away from other people. That happens. It happened to me too but it was easier for me because I hardly remembered anything else. For her it was strange and frightening. And then she was so lovely. I used to think that every time she looked in the glass she must have hoped and pretended. I pretended too. Different things of course. You can pretend for a long time, but one day it all falls away and you are alone. We were alone in the most beautiful place in the world, it is not possible that there can be anywhere else so beautiful as Coulibri. The sea was not far off but we never heard it, we always heard the river. No sea. It was an old-time house and once there was an avenue of royal palms but a lot of them had fallen and others had been cut down and the ones that were left looked lost. Lost trees. Then they poisoned her horse and she could not ride about anymore."

From part II See p. 49

## Zooming in

**1** Compare the two passages. Quote the text when necessary to justify your opinion and explain what the effect is.

- The main speaker: Jane Eyre: ... Wide Sargasso Sea: ...
- The way Antoinette's mother is described: Jane Eyre: ... Wide Sargasso Sea: ...
- The tone of voice: Jane Eyre: ... Wide Sargasso Sea: ...
- Sentence type: Jane Eyre: ... Wide Sargasso Sea: ...
- The setting: Jane Eyre: ... Wide Sargasso Sea: ...
- Would each text have the same effect on its own? Jane Eyre: ... Wide Sargasso Sea: ...

**2** In Victorian times, it was common for impoverished younger sons to marry rich Caribbean heiresses. What is Jean Rhys's view about this and how does *Wide Sargasso Sea* reflect upon colonialism?

# SALMAN RUSHDIE ~ MIDNIGHT'S CHILDREN, 1981

**Salman RUSHDIE**
(born 1947)

His novels and stories are often associated with magic realism, post-modern fiction and post-colonial fiction. His works combine mythical, realistic and fantastical elements, as well as a large variety of styles, and are often reminiscent of oral story telling. (*Midnight's Children*, 1981; *Haroun and the Sea of Stories*, 1990; *East, West*, 1994).

*Saleem Sinai, the narrator, relates the story of his life, which is also the history of post-independence India since he was born at midnight on 15 August 1947. This passage is about his family.*

A WOMAN WITH THE BICEPS OF A WRESTLER[1] was staring at him, beckoning[2] him to follow her into the room. The state of her sari told him that she was a servant; but she was not servile. "You look green as a fish," she said. "You young doctors. You come into a strange house and your liver[3] turns to jelly. Come, Doctor Sahib, they are waiting for you." Clutching[4] his bag a fraction too tightly, he followed her through the dark teak door.

... Into a spacious bedchamber that was as ill-lit as the rest of the house; although here there were shafts[5] of dusty sunlight seeping in through a fanlight[6] high on one wall. These fusty rays illuminated a scene as remarkable as anything the Doctor had ever witnessed: a tableau of such surpassing strangeness that his feet began to twitch[7] towards the door once again. Two more women, also built like professional wrestlers, stood stiffly in the light, each holding one corner of an enormous white bedsheet, their arms raised high above their heads so that the sheet hung between them like a curtain. Mr Ghani welled up[8] out of the murk[9] surrounding the sunlit sheet and permitted the nonplussed[10] Aadam to stare stupidly at the peculiar tableau for perhaps half a minute, at the end of which, and before a word had been spoken, the Doctor made a discovery:

In the very centre of the sheet, a hole had been cut, a crude circle about seven inches in diameter.

"Close the door, ayah[11]," Ghani instructed the first of the lady wrestlers, and then, turning to Aziz, became confidential. "This town contains many good-for-nothings who have on occasion tried to climb into my daughter's room. She needs," he nodded at the three musclebound women, 'protectors.'

Aziz was still looking at the perforated sheet. Ghani said, "All right, come on, you will examine my Naseem right now. *Pronto*."

My grandfather peered around the room. "But where is she, Ghani Sahib?" he blurted out[12] finally. The lady wrestlers adopted supercilious[13] expressions and, it seemed to him, tightened their musculatures, just in case he intended to try something fancy[14].

"Ah, I see your confusion," Ghani said, his poisonous smile broadening, "You Europe-returned chappies[15] forget certain things. Doctor Sahib, my daughter is a decent girl, it goes without saying. She does not flaunt[16] her body under the noses of strange men. You will understand that you cannot be permitted to see her, no, not in any circumstances; accordingly I have required her to be positioned behind that sheet. She stands there, like a good girl."

A frantic note had crept into Doctor Aziz's voice. "Ghani Sahib, tell me how I am to examine her without looking at her?" Ghani smiled on.

"You will kindly specify which portion of my daughter it is necessary to inspect. I will then issue her with my instructions to place the required segment against that hole which you see there. And so, in this fashion the thing may be achieved."

## TEXT 5 — Salman RUSHDIE ~ Midnight's Children, 1981

"But what, in any event, does the lady complain of?" — my grandfather, despairingly. To which Mr Ghani, his eyes rising upwards in their sockets[17], his smile twisting into a grimace of grief, replied: "The poor child! She has a terrible, a too dreadful stomach-ache."

"In that case," Doctor Aziz said with some restraint, "will she show me her stomach, please."

**1. a wrestler:** *un lutteur, un catcheur* **2. to beckon:** *faire signe de la main* **3. the liver:** *le foie* **4. to clutch:** *saisir* **5. shafts:** *rayons* **6. a fanlight:** *une petite fenêtre* **7. to twitch:** *remuer convulsivement* **8. to well up:** *apparaître* **9. the murk:** *l'obscurité* **10. nonplussed:** *déconcerté* **11. ayah:** *servante indienne* **12. to blurt out:** *lâcher (des paroles)* **13. supercilious:** *hautain* **14. something fancy:** *quelque chose d'intéressant, de recherché* **15. a chappy, a chap:** *un type* **16. to flaunt:** *exhiber* **17. the socket:** *l'orbite*

## Zooming in

1. The situation
   - Who is Mr Ghani?
   - Who is Aadam Aziz?
2. The structure of the text: what are its two main parts?
3. Theatricality: List all the elements that make the passage a theatrical one.
   - Some words: ...
   - The perforated sheet: ...
   - Line 46: ...
   - The setting: ...
4. Looking, peering, staring... List all the words that refer to ways of looking in the text. What effect do they achieve?
5. What point of view do we have in the passage? What is its effect?
6. Salman Rushdie often uses the technique of magic realism, which mixes fantasy and reality. Although it is not used here, a number of elements bring defamiliarization. What are they?
7. What aspects of Indian culture are reflected here?

### MOVING ON

**Watch**
- David Lean's *Lawrence of Arabia* (1962)
- Volker Schlöndorff's film based of Margaret Atwood's *The Handmaid's Tale*
- David Lean's film *A Passage to India* (1984)
- Sydney Pollack's *Out of Africa* (1985), adapted from a novel by Karen Von Blixen

**Read**
- The short stories of Somerset Maugham, many of which take place in British stations in Malaya.
- *Kim* (1901), by Rudyard Kipling

**Listen to**

A recording of some of Kipling's poems can be found on the internet.

# Drama[1]

## The stage

### 1 Compare a modern stage and an Elizabethan one.

A modern theatre

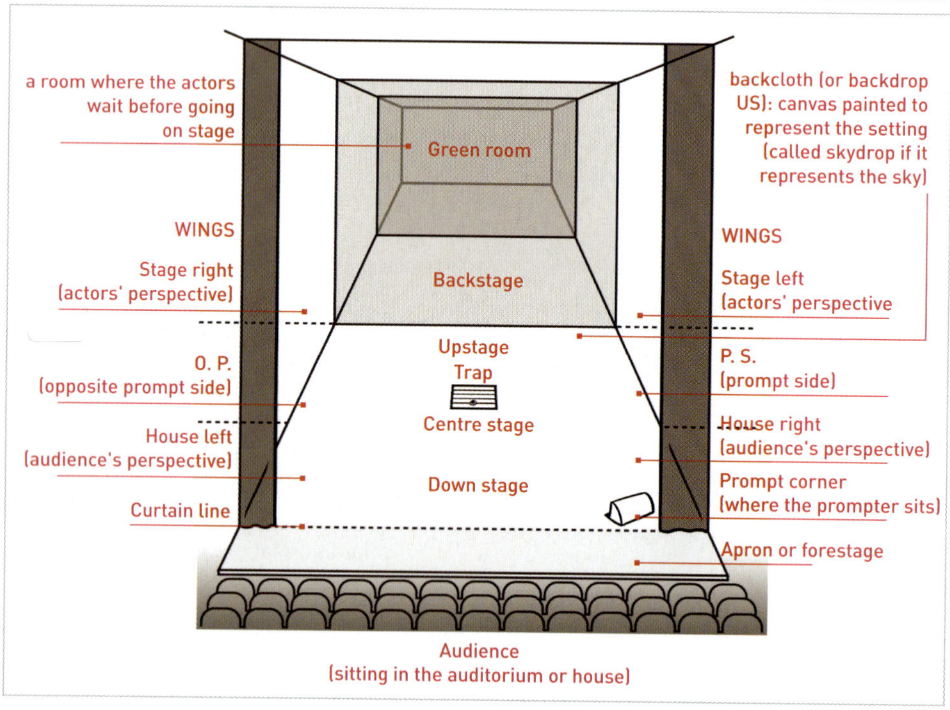


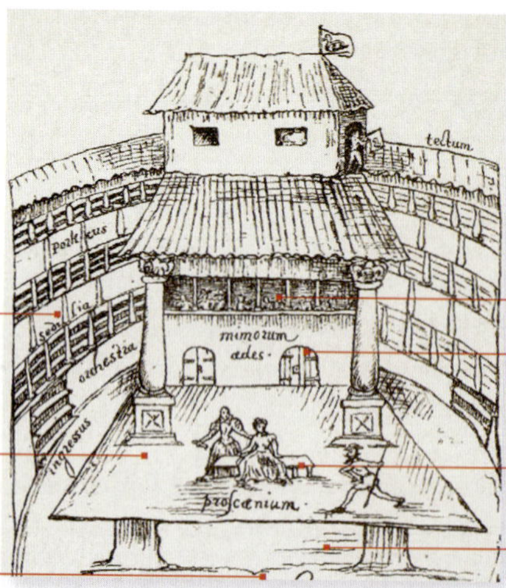


A sketch of the Swan theatre

1. **drama**: *le théâtre*
2. **a trap door**: *une trappe*

## The performance[1]

**2** **Which of the following words correspond to the definitions:**

**the scenery – the cast – costumes – the director – the dress rehearsal – the theatre – the props – the actors – the stage manager – the prompter – the rehearsal – the playwright – the audience – the wings – the stage**

a. The person who wrote the play.

b. The person who decides how the play should be acted.

c. The people who play the different roles in the play.

d. The people who watch the performance.

e. The building in which the performance takes place.

f. The place where the actors perform the play.

g. The place to the right or the left of the stage (not seen by the public).

h. The person responsible for the technical details of a performance.

i. Everything that is used to represent the place where the play takes place.

j. The objects which the characters use (*e.g.* a book, a handkerchief, a knife).

k. The clothes worn by the actors (particularly those of another period).

l. The person who stands in the wings and gives actors the lines they have forgotten.

m. A session when you repeat the text in order to prepare for the public performance.

n. All the actors who appear in a play.

o. The final rehearsal, in full costume.

## The play

**3** **Complete the following passage with the appropriate words from the list given below.**

**dialogue – monologue – acts – aside – speech – stage-directions – soliloquy – scenes**

Plays are usually divided into a number of ... (five in Greek tragedies or in Shakespeare's plays), themselves divided into ...

... describe the scenery, the atmosphere, the action or give information about the characters' appearance or their tone of voice. In some scenes, there is mainly conversation, or ... between several characters. Sometimes, a character is given a long ... which means that he speaks for a long time.

He can address other characters, address the audience (it is then called a ...), or talk to himself when alone on stage (it is then called a ...).

A few words said by an actor for the audience only, not to be heard by the other actors on stage, is called an ...

1. **a performance**: *une représentation*

# A few poetic genres

A poem is usually written in verse[1], and consists of a number of lines[2].
Several lines often form a stanza[3].
Note too:

the caesura

Speak of me as I am; nothing extenuate,
Nor set down aught in malice. Then must you speak ← an enjambment or run-on line
Of one that loved not wisely, but too well

William SHAKESPEARE, *Othello*

## Types of poem

- **A ballad**: a narrative poem (which tells a story) and may be meant to be sung. It consists of quatrains which usually alternate lines of 4 and 3 stresses. Lines 2 and 4 rhyme.
- **An elegy**: a poem of lament for someone who has died, or something which has disappeared.
- **An epic poem**: a long narrative poem describing the actions of a hero, actions which are important for his nation or race. It often involves superhuman deeds[4], battles, and the intervention of the gods.
- **Free verse**: verse without any particular form or rhythm.
- **An ode**: a lyric poem to celebrate someone or something. The tone is often elevated.
- **Pastoral**: a poem which describes the ideal life of shepherds and which praises a simple life in nature.
- **A sonnet**: a 14-line poem, used by Petrarch and very popular during the Elizabethan age. Petrarchan sonnets consist of 2 **quatrains** (a quatrain is a 4-line stanza) forming an **octave** + **two tercets** (a tercet is a three-line stanza) forming a **sestet**.
Shakespearean sonnets consist of 3 quatrains + a **couplet** (a couplet = two lines of verse).
- **An acrostic**: a poem in which some letters (usually at the beginning of the lines) form a word.
- **A visual poem**: a poem in which the lines are arranged in such a way that they form a shape which often evokes the subject of the poem.
- **Concrete poetry**: A poem with a layout[5] (or typeface[6], or colour) which is related to its meaning.

1. **verse**: *des vers, de la poésie*
2. **a line**: *un vers*
3. **a stanza**: *une strophe*
4. **a deed**: *une action*
5. **the layout**: *la disposition*
6. **the typeface**: *les caractères*

**1** **Read the following poems (a, b, c, d) and decide what genre they belong to. Justify your opinion.**

**a**

Come live with me and be my Love,
And we will all the pleasures prove
That hills and valleys, dale and field,
And all the craggy mountains yield.

There will we sit upon the rocks
And see the shepherds feed their flocks,
By shallow rivers, to whose falls
Melodious birds sing madrigals.

Christopher MARLOWE,
from *The Passionate Shepherd to His Love*, 1599

**b**

**Stroud**

**S**et among hills in the midst of five valley**S**,
**T**his peaceful little market town we inhabi**T**
**R**efuses (vociferously!) to be a conforme**R**.
**O**nce home of the cloth it gave its name t**O**,
**U**phill and down again its streets lead yo**U**.
**D**espite its faults it leaves us all charme**D**.

Paul HANSFORD, *Stroud*

**c**

He did not wear his scarlet[1] coat,
For blood and wine are red,
And blood and wine were on his hands
When they found him with the dead,
The poor dead woman whom he loved,
And murdered in her bed.

He walked amongst the Trial Men[2]
In a suit of shabby[3] grey;
A cricket cap was on his head,
And his step seemed light and gay;
But I never saw a man who looked
So wistfully[4] at the day.

I never saw a man who looked
With such a wistful eye
Upon that little tent of blue
Which prisoners call the sky,
And at every drifting[5] cloud that went
With sails[6] of silver by.

I walked, with other souls in pain,
Within another ring,
And was wondering if the man had done
A great or little thing,
When a voice behind me whispered low,
"That fellow's got to swing[7]."

Oscar WILDE, from *The Ballad of Reading Gaol*, 1898

1. **scarlet:** *écarlate* 2. **the Trial men:** *ses juges*
3. **shabby:** *miteux* 4. **wistfully:** *avec mélancolie*
5. **drifting:** passing 6. **a sail:** *une voile* 7. **to swing:** *être pendu*

**d**

l(a

le
af

fa
ll
s)

one
l
iness

e.e. CUMMINGS, *95 Poems*, 1958

**George HERBERT's visual poem, *Easter Wings*, 1633**

Lord, who createdst in wealth and store,
Though foolishly he lost the same,
Decaying more and more,
Till he became
Most poor:
With thee
O let me rise
As larks, harmoniously,
And sing this day thy victories:
Then shall the fall further the flight in me.

My tender age in sorrow did begin:
And still with sicknesses and shame
Thou didst so punish sin,
That I became
Most thin.
With thee
Let me combine,
And feel this day thy victory:
For, if I imp my wing on thine,
Affliction shall advance the flight in me.

**2** **Write an acrostic, with the first letters of the lines forming the name of a person (a friend? a public figure?), an animal or a concept.**

# Rhyme and sonorities

## Major types of rhyme

- **Couplet rhymes**: aa,bb,cc...
- **Alternate rhymes**: abab
- **Enclosing rhymes**: abba
- **Inner / internal rhyme**: two (or more) words rhyme inside a line, often the last word before the **caesura** and the last word in the line.
- **Eye rhyme**: words that look alike, but sound different and therefore cannot rhyme.

Be careful: when you decide what words rhyme, you need to listen to the words, not to look at the way they are written.

## Describing the sonorities of words, expressions or sentences

- **Alliteration**: the repetition of consonants at the beginning of words: fair and foul.
- **Consonance**: the repetition of consonants, but not at the beginning of words: pet and net.
- **Assonance**: the repetition of vocalic sounds : fish and chips.
- **Onomatopoeia**: words with a sound similar to what they mean: boom!

**1** **Decide if the following words rhyme or not. Remember that you need to listen to the words. Are there any example of eye rhyme?**

earth – birth　　write – fit　　laugh – calf
feminine – wine　　pain – vain

**2** **Do we find alliteration, assonance or consonance in the following expressions?**

Dances with the daffodils (W. Wordsworth)
The fair breeze blew, the white foam flew (S. T. Coleridge)
Time let me hail and climb (D. Thomas)
Fled from the childless land (D. Thomas)
And the salmon sing in the street (W. H. Auden)

## 3 Now read the following poem.

No longer mourn[1] for me when I am dead
Than you shall hear the surly[2] sullen[3] bell
Give warning[4] to the world that I am fled[5]
From this vile world, with vilest worms[6] to dwell[7]:
Nay[8], if you read this line, remember not
The hand that writ[9] it; for I love you so
That I in your sweet thoughts would be forgot
If thinking on me then should make you woe[10].
O, if, I say, you look upon this verse
When I perhaps compounded am[11] with clay[12],
Do not so much as my poor name rehearse[13],
But let your love even with my life decay[14],
Lest[15] the wise[16] world should look into your moan[17]
And mock you with me[18] after I am gone.

W. SHAKESPEARE, ***Sonnets LXXI***, 1609

**1. to mourn:** *pleurer quelqu'un* **2. surly:** *triste, maussade* **3. sullen:** *morne* **4. to warn:** *prévenir* **5. to flee, fled, fled:** *fuir* **6. a worm:** *un ver de terre* **7. to dwell:** *habiter* **8. nay:** archaic for no **9. writ: wrote** **10. should make you woe:** should make you sad **11. compounded am: am compounded:** *suis mélangé* **12. clay:** *l'argile* **13. to rehearse:** *répéter* **14. to decay:** *décliner, se décomposer* **15. lest:** *de peur que* **16. wise:** *sage* **17. a moan:** *une plainte* **18. mock you with me:** mock you because of me

**a.** What type of poem is it?

**b.** What is its rhyme scheme[1]?

**c.** How would you describe the rhymes?

In the first three stanzas: ...
In the couplet: ...

**d.** Find examples of alliteration, consonance, assonance and think about their effect.

**1. the rhyme scheme:** *l'agencement des rimes*

# Stress, metre and rhythm

## Stress

In spoken English, rhythm is to a large extent based on **stressed** and **unstressed** syllables.

**1** **Listen to the way the following words are pronounced: where do you put the stress in each of them? Put / above the stressed syllable.**

Europe – European a record – to record educate – education effect – effective

**2** **The following groups of words have the same stress pattern. What is it? Write it underneath each column using ˘ for unstressed syllables and / for stressed syllables.**

| | | | |
|---|---|---|---|
| sympathetic | character | satire | equality |
| enthusiastic | modesty | graceful | professional |
| inspiration | intimate | value | self-sacrifice |
| unimportant | library | traffic | disheartening |
| automatic | continent | active | |

**3** **Where is the stress in the following words?**

| | | | |
|---|---|---|---|
| contents | canal | damaged | interpretation |
| relative | recovery | relation | beginning |
| figure | professor | consequence | difficulty |
| responsibility | effort | ignore | ignorant |
| distinguish | | | |

## Rhythm

• **Metre** is the name given to the rhythm of poetry, that is to say the arrangement of stressed and unstressed syllables in its lines. All poems do not necessarily have regular metre, but it is usually possible to find a basic **metrical pattern**, with variations to avoid monotony and underline meaning.

**4** **The following lines are all regular. Decide where the stresses are. Grammatical words such as articles or prepositions are not usually stressed.**

**a.** Created half to rise, and half to fall (A. Pope)
**b.** Come live with me and be my love (C. Marlowe)
**c.** Tyger, tyger, burning bright (W. Blake)
**d.** A hand that can be clasped no more (Tennyson)

• The **iambic rhythm** (an unstressed syllable followed by a stressed syllable: ˘ /) has always been the most commonly used rhythm in English poetry. In the 18th century, it was often associated with lines of five feet (pentameters) which were therefore called **"iambic pentameters"**.

## 5 Which of the following lines is a regular iambic pentameter?

**a.** Here in the long unlovely street (A.E. HOUSMAN)
**b.** Thy beauty shall no more be found (A. MARVELL)
**c.** [a poor player]
That struts and frets his hour upon the stage (W. SHAKESPEARE)
**d.** Sweet spring, full of sweet days and roses (G. HERBERT)

• Here are the names of some well-known types of metrical feet and their description:

iamb: ˘ /  trochee: / ˘  anapest: ˘ ˘ /

## 6 The following lines all have regular rhythms.
### 1. Match each of them with the type of metrical feet it illustrates:

**a.** For the sky and the sea, and the sea and the sky (S. T. COLERIDGE)
**b.** Was a flash of golden fire (S. T. COLERIDGE)
**c.** I closed my lids, and kept them close (S. T. COLERIDGE)
**d.** Now until the break of day
Through this house each fairy stray. (W. SHAKESPEARE)
**e.** The cottage windows through the twilight blazed (W. WORDSWORTH)
**f.** If ever two were one, then surely we. (A. BRADSTREET)

### 2. Which of these three types of metrical feet (iamb, trochee, anapest) expresses rapidity?

• A **limerick** is a popular form of nonsense poetry. It often describes people's eccentricities.
Each line begins with an iamb and is followed by anapests.
Lines 1, 2 and 3 have three feet. Lines 3 and 4 have two feet.

There was an Old Man with a beard,
Who said, "It is just as I feared! –
Two Owls and a Hen,
Four Larks and a Wren,
Have all built their nests in my beard.

Edward LEAR

• Few lines are regularly iambic. In order to avoid monotony, it is common to start with a trochee, for example, in order to emphasize an important word.

/ ˘ ˘ / ˘ / ˘ / ˘ /
Seasons return; but not to me returns

/ ˘ ˘ / ˘ / ˘ / ˘ /
Day, or the sweet approach of ev'n or morn (J. MILTON)

• Nursery rhymes are usually the kind of poetry children first hear. They are often nonsensical and usually have a marked rhythm (often based on trochees) and a clear rhyming pattern.

**7** **Mark the stressed syllables (the lines do not always show a regular metrical pattern), show what the rhyme scheme is, then read the nursery rhymes aloud, emphasizing the stresses.**

**a**

Jack and Jill
Went up the hill,
To fetch a pail of water;
Jack fell down
And broke his crown,
And Jill came tumbling after.

**b**

Hickory dickory dock
The mouse went up the clock.
The clock struck one,
The mouse went down
Hickory dickory dock.

## Main technical words

**A few basic rhythms:**

• the **iambic** rhythm: an iamb = ˘ /

˘ / ˘ / ˘ / ˘ / ˘ /
*The Frost performs its secret ministry*

• the **trochaic** rhythm: a trochee = / ˘

/ ˘ / ˘ / ˘ / ˘
*How he must have cursed our revel*

• the **anapaestic** rhythm: an anapest = ˘ ˘ /

˘ ˘ / ˘ ˘ / ˘ ˘ /
*From the center all round to the sea*

**The rhythm can be:**

• regular, monotonous
• heavy, plodding
• light, sprightly

There can be a shift / a break in the rhythm.

# Rhetorical terms

Here are several rhetorical terms which are useful when talking about a text.

**Associate the term (column 1), its definition (column 2) and an example (column 3).**

| Words | Definitions | Examples |
|---|---|---|
| Anagram | 1. A mirror inversion of terms. | a. Feather of lead, bright smoke, cold fire, sick health! (W. SHAKESPEARE) |
| Anaphora | 2. A statement which seems contradictory but turns out to be true. | b. Madam, I'm Adam. |
| Antithesis | 3. A word used in such a way that its similarity to another word is evoked. | c. The child is father to the man. (W. WORDSWORTH) |
| Apostrophe | 4. A word, expression, or sentence which reads the same way backwards and forwards. | d. Blow, blow thou[1] winter wind. (W. SHAKESPEARE) |
| Chiasmus | 5. Addressing an absent person, concept or object as if it were present and alive. | e. Fitzwater: Thou liest[2]. Surrey: Dishonourable boy! That lie shall lie so heavy on my sword, That it shall render vengeance… (W. SHAKESPEARE) |
| Euphemism | 6. Contrasting words, expressions or ideas in parallel structures. | f. Nowhere → *Erewhon* (the title of a novel by S. BUTLER) |
| Hyperbole | 7. Denying the contrary, so that you say something in a more indirect way. It can be less offensive. | g. By failing to prepare, you are preparing to fail. (B. FRANKLIN) |
| Litotes, under-statement | 8. Exaggeration to obtain a comic or dramatic effect. | h. Singing my days, Singing the great achievements of the present, Singing the strong light works of engineers… (W. WHITMAN) |
| Oxymoron | 9. Giving human qualities to abstractions or objects. | i. To err is human, to forgive, divine. (A. POPE) |
| Palindrome | 10. Rearranging the letters of a word or an expression in order to form a new word or expression. | j. The cruel, crawling foam[3]. (J. RUSKIN) |
| Paradox | 11. The juxtaposition of contradictory terms. | k. He is no Hercules! |
| Personification | 12. The repetition of a word or words at the beginning of a line or sentence. | l. 'He passed away' instead of 'He died'. |
| Pun | 13. The use of a vague or pleasant expression to avoid mentioning something unpleasant or that might offend. | m. I wouldn't eat insects for a million pounds! |

**1. thou:** *you* **2. thou liest:** *you lie* **3. foam:** *l'écume*
If you wish to check the pronunciation of a word, look it up on the internet: on a website such as dictionary.com, you will find its phonetic transcription and hear it read.

# Prose and fiction: genres, plot and characters

## A few fictional genres

**1 Associate the type of novel with its definition.**

| | |
|---|---|
| 1. Bildungsroman (or Apprenticeship Novel) | a. a novel which describes the habits, behaviour and language of certain social groups, often with a mixture of realism and satire. |
| 2. Epistolary Novel | b. a novel which takes place in the future and includes robots, space travel, alien beings and different scientific laws. |
| 3. Gothic Novel | c. a narrative which is much shorter than a novel or a novella and which focuses on a moment of crisis or discovery. |
| 4. Historical Novel | d. a novel which shows a character's development from childhood to adulthood, his spiritual crises, the importance of his family background. |
| 5. Metafiction | e. a work of fiction which contains a reflection upon fiction, mainly to show how artificial narrative conventions are. |
| 6. Novel of Manners | f. a novel which consists of an exchange of letters, thus creating immediacy. |
| 7. Novella | g. a story full of excitement and suspense, about crime, mystery, or espionage. |
| 8. Picaresque Novel | h. a novel in which the hero travels in order to make his fortune and in the process moves from innocence to experience as he discovers society and a whole gallery of characters who lend themselves to satire. |
| 9. Science-fiction Novel | i. a very short novel. |
| 10. Short story | j. a novel full of suspense, mystery, blood-curdling or supernatural events See p. 58. |
| 11. Thriller | k. A text in which the characters and actions have another meaning outside the text. |
| 12. Allegory | l. a novel set in a past which is described realistically. |

## 2 Here are very short passages from different kinds of stories or novels. What genres do they belong to?

**a**

Tomorrow would be Christmas, and even while the three of them rode to the rocket port the mother and father were worried. It was the boy's first flight into space, his very first time in a rocket, and they wanted everything to be perfect.

A. R. Bradbury, "The Gift" in *A Medicine for Melancholy*, 1959

**b**

As she mused[1], she saw the door slowly open; and a rustling[2] sound in a remote part of the room startled her. Through the dusk she thought she perceived something move. The subject she had been considering, and the present state of her spirits, which made her imagination respond to every impression on her senses, gave her a sudden terror of something supernatural.

B. A. Radcliffe, *The Mysteries of Udolpho*, 1794

1. to muse: *rêver* 2. rustling: *bruit de froissement*

**c**

My dear Parents,
O let me take up my complaint, and say, "Never was poor creature so unhappy and so barbarously used as poor Pamela." Indeed, my dear father and mother, my heart's just broke! I can neither write as I should, nor let it alone: to whom but you can I vent[1] my griefs, and keep my poor heart from bursting?

C. S. Richardson, *Pamela*, 1740-1

1. to vent: *donner libre cours à*

**d**

And now, having brought this fiction to a thoroughly traditional ending, I had better explain that although all I have described in the last two chapters happened, it did not happen quite in the way you may have been led to believe.

E. J. Fowles, *The French Lieutenant's Woman*, Jonathan Cape, 1969

## The plot, the characters

## 3 Complete the text with the following words.

**climax – foreshadow – flat – plot – twists – embedded – story – analepsis – suspense – round – subplot – prolepsis – denouement**

When you talk about the chronological events of a novel, you talk of its ... The word ... is very similar but refers to the way the events are related to each other, the causal links between them. In many novels, there are two plots: the main plot and the ..., often with parallels between the two. In several 18th century novels, there are stories told within the novel: they are called ... stories.

The events of a novel usually move towards a ..., or moment of maximum intensity before the ... at the end of the novel. There can be many turning points and narrative ... before the action comes to a conclusion, all of them creating ... Events are not always told chronologically in a novel. Sometimes we find ... or flashbacks into the past; but events can also be described before they actually happen, thus revealing the future: one then speaks of ... Some scenes, actions, or images also simply announce or ... future events. The novelist E.M. Forster divided characters into two groups. ... characters are complex, capable of change and capable of surprising us. On the contrary, ... characters are types, which can easily be summed up, reduced to one idea or characteristic.

# Point of view

• Point of view is another way of saying: Who tells the story?
– With a **first-person point of view**, we follow the thoughts and vision of a character who can only tell us what (s)he can see and think and no more.
– With a **third-person point of view**, the narrator follows the thoughts and vision of one or several characters.

• Another distinction can be made between:
– a narrator who is a character in the story: you speak of **internal focalization**;
– an outside narrator who is exterior to the story and observes the characters from above: you speak of **external focalization**.

Some narrators (particularly in 19th century novels) are called **omniscient**: they are like God and know everything about the characters' thoughts and actions, even when no one is there to watch them.

**1** **Here are the beginnings of novels or stories. Read them carefully, then answer the questions that follow.**

**a**

It was about three o'clock on a Friday afternoon when Annette decided to leave school. An Italian lesson was in progress. In an affected high-pitched voice the Italian tutor was reading aloud from the twelfth canto of the *Inferno*. She had just reached the passage about the Minotaur. Annette disliked the *Inferno*. It seemed to her a cruel and unpleasant book. Why should the poor Minotaur be suffering in hell? It was not the Minotaur's fault that it had been born a monster.

I. MURDOCH, *The Flight from the Enchanter*, Chatto & Windus, 1956

**b**

Mr Bennet was so odd[1] a mixture of quick parts[2], sarcastic humour, reserve, and caprice, that the experience of three and twenty years had been insufficient to make his wife understand his character. Her mind was less difficult to develop. She was a woman of mean[3] understanding, little information, and uncertain temper. When she was discontented she fancied[4] herself nervous. The business of her life was to get her daughters married; its solace[5] was visiting and news.

Jane AUSTEN, *Pride and Prejudice*, 1813

1. **odd:** *étrange* 2. **quick parts:** *intelligence et vivacité*
3. **mean understanding:** *peu d'intelligence*
4. **fancied herself:** *s'imaginait* 5. **solace:** *consolation*

**c**

In the late summer of that year we lived in a house in a village that looked across the river and the plain to the mountains. In the bed of the river there were pebbles and boulders, dry and white in the sun, and the water was clear and swiftly moving and blue in the channels.

Ernest HEMINGWAY, *A Farewell to Arms*, 1932

**d**

When I came out of the church and crunched back down the gravel path towards the plot where my grandparents were buried, I found that Gill was still standing by their gravestone, staring across the churchyard with a strange, frozen look in her eye.

Jonathan COE, *Ivy and Her Nonsense*, Penguin Books, 1995

**a. Decide which category each passage above belongs to:**

| | Internal focalization | External focalisation |
|---|---|---|
| **First-person point of view** | ... | ... |
| **Third-person point of view** | ... | ... |

**b. Underline all the elements which made you decide in favour of an "internal" or "external" point of view.**

**c. What do you think are the advantages and disadvantages of...**

| | Advantages | Disadvantages |
|---|---|---|
| **Internal point of view** | ... | ... |
| **External point of view** | ... | ... |

*See Part 4: Tasks p. 183*

• An extreme form of internal focalization is **stream of consciousness**, a technique used by several modernist novelists *See p. 114*, who tried to render the chaos of thoughts, impressions or memories that can go through someone's mind at a particular time and before they can be reorganized by reason. Stream of consciousness can take many different forms.

Here is the end of Molly Bloom's monologue in James Joyce's *Ulysses*, a fifty-page monologue without any punctuation.

> the queer little streets and pink and blue and yellow houses and the rosegardens and the jessamine and geranium and cactuses and Gibraltar as a girl where I was a Flower of the mountain yes when I put the rose in my hair like the Andalusian used or shall I wear a red yes and how he kissed me under the Moorish wall and I thought well as well him as another and then I asked him with my eyes to ask again yes and then he asked me would I yes to say yes my mountain flower and first I put my arms around him yes and drew him down to me so he could feel my breasts all perfume yes and his heart was going like mad and yes I said yes I will Yes
>
> J. JOYCE, *Ulysses*, 1922

# Reporting words and thoughts

The following worksheet will help you remember the techniques used to report someone's words or thoughts in a narrative and will give you further vocabulary.

## Direct speech

The exact words used by the person are given. *"Don't forget to give John a ring", she said.*

When you use this technique, remember that:

– one does not use dashes (–...–) in English to introduce someone's words, but the words themselves appear between inverted commas ("..."). The reporting verb (e.g. *he said / she answered...*) is not between inverted commas;

– the reporting verb normally appears after the subject (*"he said"*), though you can sometimes find *"said/answered + pronoun"*.

## Indirect speech

- **The words are reported by someone else.** *She said she would be late.*
- **The most common reporting verbs are:**

| Verb + that | Verb + name of person / pronoun + that | Verb used with both structures |
|---|---|---|
| answer | tell | say (to someone) that |
| believe | remind | admit (to someone) that |
| claim | persuade | suggest (to someone) that |
| deny | convince | mention (to someone) that |
| hope | | explain (to someone) that |
| knew | | point out (to someone) that |
| expect | | promise (someone) that |
| think | | show (someone) that |
| regret | | confess (to someone) that |
| | | shout (to someone) that |
| | | whisper (to someone) that |
| **Reporting** verbs in questions: *ask / wonder + if / whether / how / when / what* | | |

- **If the reporting verb is in the past, you will have to make the following changes:**

Present → preterit: *"I'm leaving tonight." → She said she was leaving tonight /that night.*

Preterit or present perfect → pluperfect: *"I've won a prize." → She said she had won a prize.*

will or shall → would: *"He'll come." → They said he would come.*

- **When reporting a question, the inversion disappears:**

*"When will you come?" → They asked when we would come.*

- **When reporting an imperative, the name of the person addressed or a pronoun appears:**
  *"Bring another chair!"* → She asked him to bring another chair.
- **Some other words may have to change too:**
  Here → there (if the words are reported in a different place).
  Now → then / tomorrow → (on) the next day / yesterday → (on) the preceding day...
  (if the words are reported some time later).

## Free indirect speech

A narrator reporting words or thoughts in indirect speech can occasionally leave out the reporting verbs after a few sentences, so that we feel we hear the words directly. But the form is that of indirect speech.

| | |
|---|---|
| *She promised to come back. She said she would write soon.* | = indirect speech |
| *It had been such a wonderful week, so peaceful and happy.* | = free indirect speech<br>→ *(She said) it had been...* |

## Narration

The words are summarized rather than given exactly.

*He seemed happy and kept joking all evening.*

**1 The following four passages report the words of one or several people.**

| | |
|---|---|
| **A.** Jane came to tell me that Peter wants you to know that he's got the postcard and it has the stamp you want on it. I'm not sure what he means but he insisted that I tell you. | **Exact words:** Yes ?<br>No ... |
| **B.** "So you paid the money but you never received the records?", Philip said.<br>"That's right, and the telephone number he gave is constantly engaged," Dora said. | **Exact words:** Yes ?<br>No ... |
| **C.** Betty apologised for being late and told them what had happened to her that afternoon. | **Exact words:** Yes ?<br>No ... |
| **D.** She was sorry she couldn't come. But she'd come back later, if they still wanted her then. She'd bake a cake for the children. | **Exact words:** Yes ?<br>No ... |

**a.** Match each passage with the technique used in it:

- direct speech
- narrative
- indirect speech
- free indirect speech

**b.** Read them carefully and decide whether or not it is possible to tell the exact words they used. If you think it is, write down these words underneath.

**c.** Classify these four ways of reporting speech or thoughts to show which form most gives the impression that the narrator has disappeared and which one shows the narrator most in control.

| Telling | | | Showing |
|---|---|---|---|
| narrator most in control | | | narrator almost forgotten |

**2** **a. Here is a passage from a play. Report the dialogue as if it were part of a novel, choosing narration, direct speech or indirect speech.**

JACK: The fact is, Lady Bracknell, I said I had lost my parents. It would be nearer the truth to say that my parents seem to have lost me… I don't actually know who I am by birth. I was… well, I was found.

LADY BRACKNELL: Found!

JACK: The late[1] Mr Thomas Cardew, an old gentleman of a very charitable and kindly disposition, found me, and gave me the name of Worthing, because he happened to have a first-class ticket for Worthing in his pocket at the time. Worthing is a place in Sussex. It is a seaside resort[2].

LADY BRACKNELL: Where did the charitable gentleman who had a first-class ticket for this seaside resort find you?

JACK: *(Gravely.)* In a handbag.

LADY BRACKNELL: A handbag?

JACK: *(Very seriously.)* Yes, Lady Bracknell. I was in a handbag – a somewhat large, black leather handbag, with handles to it - an ordinary handbag, in fact.

Oscar Wilde, *The Importance of Being Earnest*, 1895

**1. late:** *défunt* **2. a seaside resort:** *une station balnéaire*

**b.** Compare the different passages written in the class. Are all the narrative passages similar? Which tend more towards summary and which tend to relate many details? Are there as many differences in the passages in direct speech or indirect speech?

# Images[1]

The word "imagery" is used in literature to describe all the images produced by a text in the reader's mind. Many come from the scene which is described, but others come from the description of something in terms of something else.

- In ordinary speech and writing as well as in literature, one often uses **similes** and **metaphors** to compare things that are unlike.
– In comparisons (or similes), the comparison is introduced by words such as *like, as, similar to, seem, resemble*.
– In metaphors, there is no such term, so that one thing is directly identified with the other.

- If you describe a sensation in terms of another sensation, it is **synaesthesia**. (ex: *a cool colour*, or a *warm colour*).

- Instead of using a particular word, one can also use a word which is closely associated to it: it is **metonymy** (If you say: "I've been reading all Shakespeare", Shakespeare stands for 'the works of Shakespeare'.)
A particular form of metonymy is **synecdoche**, where a part is used for the whole or vice versa. (For example: 'a hand' for a worker).

## 1 Read the following quotations and decide:

**a.** Whether they contain comparisons or metaphors.

**b.** Which of the two is more striking? Why?

**a**

I wandered lonely as a cloud
That floats on high o'er vales[1] and hills
When all at once I saw a crowd,
A host[2] of golden daffodils[3],
Fluttering[4] and dancing in the breeze.

W. Wordsworth

1. **a vale:** *une vallée* 2. **a host of:** *une foule de*
3. **a daffodil:** *une jonquille* 4. **to flutter:** *palpiter, trembler*

**b**

O, my love is like a red, red rose,
That is newly sprung in June.

R. Burns

**c**

O, beware[1], my lord, of jealousy!
It is the green-eyed monster…

W. Shakespeare

1. **beware:** *be careful*

**d**

My father's body was a globe of fear
His body was a town we never knew.

M. Ondaatje

1. If you wish to check the pronunciation of a word, look it up on the internet: on a website such as dictionary.com, you will find its phonetic transcription and hear it read.

• Comparisons and metaphors are ways of stimulating the reader's imagination and emotion through evocation. A further way of doing so is through the use of symbols. A **symbol** is an object, an image, an action... which means more than it is itself. A tree, for instance, may be a symbol of life, of growth, of the regenerative process.

**2** **a. What would you say the following things symbolize?**

key lamp rain ring wings steps island candle

**b.** Compare your answers.

**3** **Complete the following poem.**

**Autumn**

A touch of cold in the Autumn night –
I walked abroad[1],
And saw the ruddy[2] moon lean over a hedge[3]
Like ...
I did not stop to speak, but nodded[4],
And round about were the wistful[5] stars
With white faces like ...

T. E. HULME (reproduced in *The Forms of Poetry*, CUP)

1. abroad: *dehors* 2. ruddy: *rougeâtre* 3. a hedge: *une haie*
4. to nod: *incliner la tête* 5. wistful: *mélancolique*

**4** **Now think about the different passages you have read and ask yourself why writers use similes, metaphors and symbolism instead of stating things more directly.**

**a.** Draw up a list of five reasons.

**b.** Then list all the reasons given in the class.

**c.** Do you agree with all of them? Which seem more important than others?

# Tone

Tone is the speaker's or the writer's attitude to what is said. In drama, the characters' tone of voice is often conveyed through stage directions. Here are, for instance, some stage-directions (adjectives, adverbs and past participles) which point to tone in Arthur Miller's *Death of a Salesman*: anxiously / angry, humiliated / urgently / furiously / accusing / angered / shocked / impressed / timidly / decidedly / interestedly / longingly...

- In fiction and in poetry, the attitude and tone of the characters and of the narrator are not usually explained so clearly and it is important to sense and evaluate them.
- Here is a list of words that can be useful when describing the tone of an utterance or text:

| | | |
|---|---|---|
| calm | indignant | sarcastic |
| detached | ironic | sardonic |
| enthusiastic | joyful | serious |
| excited | lyrical | shy |
| flat | mocking | solemn |
| humble | playful | surprised |
| humorous | resentful[1] | wild |
| impersonal | | |

- We will now focus more particularly on humour, irony and satire, which are often used in literature.

## 1 Match each word with its definition.

| | |
|---|---|
| 1. **Humour** | a. Saying the contrary of what you mean: *Are you pleased now?* when someone has done something stupid. Dramatic irony is the contrast between what a character says and what the reader knows e.g. in Shakespeare's *Macbeth*, King Duncan admires the harmony of nature when he arrives at Macbeth's castle, but the reader knows he will be murdered there. |
| 2. **Irony** | b. The use of humour, wit, absurdity or irony in order to criticise someone or something. |
| 3. **Satire** | c. An original, brilliant way of expressing ideas, often based on puns or paradox. |
| 4. **Wit** | d. A type of writing which provokes smiles or laughter. It results from a comic perception of life. It is kind and sympathetic, not critical. |

1. **resentful**: *amer*

**2** **Read the following passages and decide whether they are ironic, humorous or satirical. Explain why. What do these short passages tell you about the speakers?**

**a**

It's over and can't be helped... and that's one consolation, as they always say in Turkey, when they cut the wrong man's head off.

C. DICKENS, *The Pickwick Papers*, 1836-1837

**b**

"Do you get to see many plays, Mr Wutherspoon?" [...]
"No, but I do love the movies. I'm a real fan. One trouble with books is that they're not so thoroughly safeguarded[1] by intelligent censors as the movies are, and when you drop into the library and take out a book you never know what you're wasting your time on... Why, once I started a novel by this fellow Balzac that you read about, and it told you how a lady wasn't living with her husband. I mean she wasn't his wife. It went into details, disgustingly! And the English was real poor..."

S. LEWIS, *Main Street*, 1920

1. **safeguarded:** *protégés*

**c**

The only way to get rid of temptation is to yield[1] to it.

O. WILDE, *The Picture of Dorian Gray*, 1895

1. **to yield:** *céder*

**d**

Heark ye[1], Clinker, you are a most notorious offender – You stand convicted of sickness, hunger, wretchedness, and want.

T. SMOLLETT, *Humphry Clinker*, 1771

1. **heark ye:** *écoutez (archaïque)*

**3** **Associate each word with its definition.**

| | |
|---|---|
| **1. A burlesque** | **a.** the comic imitation of a literary form or genre. |
| **2. A parody** | **b.** a work that ridicules an elevated subject by dealing with it in a low or absurd way. |
| **3. A travesty** | **c.** the humorous or satirical imitation of a work or author. |

To be, or not to be: that is the question:
Whether 'tis nobler in the mind to suffer
The slings and arrows of outrageous fortune,
Or to take arms against a sea of troubles,
And by opposing end them? To die: to sleep;
No more; and by a sleep to say we end
The heart-ache and the thousand natural shocks
That flesh is heir to, 'tis a consummation
Devoutly to be wish'd.

W. SHAKESPEARE, *Hamlet*, 1600-1601

**Toothache**

To have it out or not? that is the question –
Whether 'tis better for the jaws to suffer
The pangs and torments of an aching tooth,
Or to take steel against a host of troubles,
And, by extracting, end them? To pull– to tug! –
No more: and by a tug to say we end
The tooth-ache, and a thousand natural ills
The jaw is heir to. 'Tis a consummation
Devoutly to be wished!

(Anonymous)

A passage from Shakespeare and its parody (Anonymous)

• In 1729, Jonathan Swift wrote a pamphlet entitled *A Modest Proposal* in order to tackle the problem of misery in Ireland. In it, he advocated eating young children who would thus become useful instead of being a burden to their families. It is a masterpiece of irony, in which the reader only gradually understands that the text is ironic and not serious; it is only after two pages that the reader is told that children will make proper food for the landlords who have already "devoured" the parents.

**4 Choose a subject you feel is important socially or culturally and write a short pamphlet to defend your view, using irony as a method.**

You should be careful not to:
– be too obvious: part of the effect will be lost if it is immediately clear that you do not literally mean what you say;
– be too subtle, or it may not be clear, even at the end, that there is irony. (In 1703, Daniel Defoe was arrested and sentenced to stand in the pillory when people misunderstood the irony of his pamphlet *The Shortest Way with the Dissenters*, which attacked High Church intolerance !)

TASKS

# You are a publisher

→ You have studied a short story or a novel.

**1** **Imagine you are a publisher and have to write the blurb[1] which will appear on the back of the book. In order to do so you must:**

**a.** Ask yourself what you found really important, interesting or original in the story

**b.** Think of what will make people buy the book (you are the publisher...), so you may want to create some suspense.

If you look at such blurbs, they often include:

- a summary of the beginning of the plot (but not of the end!)
- the main interest of the story
- a few quotations from press reviews, the most laudatory[2] ones, of course.

**Two examples of blurbs**

MEET BALRAM HALWAÏ, THE « WHITE TIGER »: SERVANT, PHILOSOPHER, ENTREPRENEUR, MURDERER...

'Dazzling... With The White Tiger, Adiga sets out to show us a part of [India] that we hear about infrequently: its underbelly... Welcome... to an India where Micro soft call-centre workers tread the same pavement as beggars who burn street rubbish for warmth... It's a thrilling ride'

*David Mattin, Independent on Sunday.*

'[An] extraordinary and brilliant first novel... At first, this novel seems like a straightforward pulled-up-by-your-bootstraps tale, albeit given a dazzling twist by the narrator's sharp and satirical eye for the realities of life for India's poor... But as the narrative draws the reader further in, and darkens, it becomes clear that Adiga is playing a bigger game...'

*Adam Lively, Sunday Times*

'Blazingly savage and brilliant... What Adiga lifts the lid on is also inexorably true: not a single detail in this novel rings false or feels confected. The White Tiger is an excoriating piece of work [that] also manages to be suffused with mordant wit, modulating to clear-eyed pathos'.

*Neel Mukherjee*

**£ 6.99**
**Fiction**
**www.atlantic-books.co.uk**

ATLANTIC BOOKS • COVER ILLUSTRATION BY PETRA BORNER/DUTCH UNCLE • COVER DESIGN BY GHOST

Aravind ADIGA, *The White Tiger*, Atlantic Books

*'Spectacular, heartbreaking, beautifully written. Rosamond's story is one of the most extraordinary and compelling you will ever read. Impossible to put down. I loved every moment of it.'*
Sunday Express

Deeply moving and compelling. "The Rain Before It Falls" is the story of three generations of one family riven by tragedy. When Rosamond, a reluctant bearer of family secrets, dies suddenly, a mystery is left for her niece Gill to unravel. Some photograph albums and tapes point towards a blind girl named Imogen whom no one has seen in twenty years. The search for Imogen and the truth of her inheritance becomes a shocking story of mothers and daughters and of how sadness, like a musical refrain, may haunt us down the years.

*'A sad, often very moving story of mothers and daughters'*
Guardian

*'Entirely compelling... the plot will keep you rapt... reminiscent of Ian McEwan at his most effective'*
New Statesman

read more
www.penguin.com
Cover photograph c. General Photographic Agency/Hulton Archive/Getty Images

Jonathan COE, *The Rain Before It Falls*, Penguin Books

**1. the blurb:** *le texte de quatrième de couverture*
**2. laudatory:** *élogieux*

**Here is a list of adjectives you might use when praising a book**

| | | | | |
|---|---|---|---|---|
| unforgettable | intriguing | funny | a story of | a gifted writer |
| moving | inventive | hilarious | a portrait of | (S)he has a genius for |
| heart-wrenching[1] | enjoyable | witty[6] | | (S)he is a master of |
| absorbing | convincing | | | |
| inspiring | compelling[5] | | | |
| dazzling[2] | impressive | | | |
| breathtaking[3] | | | | |
| exhilarating[4] | | | | |
| delightful | | | | |

**2** **You now have to choose a picture for the cover of the book. This could be:**

- a painting
- one of you own photographs
- a more abstract design[7]

Remember that this picture should:

- evoke the book in some way (one of its characters, the atmosphere...)
- catch people's attention and make them want to buy the book.

Bring the picture you have chosen to the class, and be ready to defend it against other proposals[8].

## You are a critic

→ **You have read or studied a short story or a novel.**

**1** **Imagine you work as a critic for a newspaper or magazine and write a review[9] of the story for that magazine or newspaper. The required[10] length is of 200 words.**

Remember that:

**a.** You need to mention the subject of the story, but should not reveal all of the plot[11] or what happens at the end.

**b.** You must give your opinion, which may not always be positive.

**c.** The length of your book review is limited to 200 words. Get a rough idea[12] of the length that is required, then write your text. Count the words and then rewrite[13] some sentences in order to obtain the right length.

**1. heart-wrenching:** *déchirant*
**2. dazzling:** *éblouissant*
**3. breathtaking:** *époustouflant*
**4. exhilarating:** *stimulant*
**5. compelling:** *irresistible*
**6. witty:** *spirituel (plein d'esprit)*
**7. a design:** *un motif*
**8. a proposal:** *une proposition*
**9. a review:** *un article critique*
**10. required:** *exigé*
**11. the plot:** *l'intrigue*
**12. a rough idea:** *une idée approximative*
**13. rewrite:** *récrire, reformuler*

**Here are a few expressions you can use**

| Praise | Criticism |
|---|---|
| • The book is concerned with ...<br>• As the title suggests, this book is about ...<br>• The book opens with ...<br>• What is particularly moving (engrossing[6] / gripping[7] / convincing / enjoyable / powerful / original ...) about this book is ...<br>• Interesting as ... may be, it is ... which most fascinates (appeals to / intrigues / absorbs ...) the reader<br>• The style is marked by ... | • What is disappointing about it is ...<br>• It is difficult to like ...<br>• ... does not work as well as ...<br>• The end is rather flat.<br>• It lacks ...<br>• The book / end / plot ... is flawed[8] in a number of ways: ...<br>• Is this plausible? Can we really believe that ...?<br>• The story / plot is too conventional<br>• A predictable[9] ending<br>• A tedious[10] thriller / melodrama ...<br>• It is unfortunate that...<br>• ... serves no purpose<br>• BUT the book is redeemed[11] by.... |

Another possibility is to imagine that you work for a literary programme on the radio. In your programme, you present a series of books.

**2** **Choose a book you have read or from which you have read a passage.**

**a.** Present it briefly (without revealing the end), explaining why you liked it or found it interesting. Books chosen to be discussed on such programmes are usually books you like.

**b.** Choose to read one or two short extracts. You need to choose them carefully in order to make your listeners want to read them.

**c.** Then present your programme to the rest of the class.

6. **engrossing:** *captivant*
7. **gripping:** *passionnant, palpitant*
8. **flawed:** *gâché*
9. **predictable:** *prévisible*
10. **tedious:** *ennuyeux*
11. **redeemed by:** *racheté, sauvé par*

# You are a film/stage director

→ You have studied a long text, a short story or a novel.

**1** **Imagine you are a stage or film-director. You intend to transpose the text to the stage[1] or the screen[2]. You must choose the ideal actors for the main roles.**

**a.** You can choose pictures of real actors, but any picture cut out from a magazine will do[3] if you find a person whose face, expression or general attitude seems to correspond to that of the character in the text.

**b.** Bring the picture to the class. You will of course have to be prepared to justify and defend your choice against those of other students.

**Here are a few expressions you may need**

| To describe someone | To express comparison |
|---|---|
| • (S)he looks too ... / not ... enough / not as ... as X is in the story.<br>• (S)he doesn't look like a ...<br>• (S)he doesn't look as if (s)he ... + preterit<br>• I find her/him quite ... / rather... / perfectly ...<br>• She reminds me of ...<br>• Her/his face / mouth / nose ... is rather ...<br>• She/he is fair-haired / blue-eyed / dark-skinned | • Comparatives and superlatives (He looks more frightening than ...... / She is the most pleasant of them all.)<br>• They're very similar. He's similar to...<br>• They're almost alike, only this one is more...<br>• In comparison to/with....., he is.....<br>• Compared to/with....., he is....<br>• Unlike.....<br>• (S)he is not at all like what I imagined... |

**2** **As a film director, you are also responsible for camera angles and sets[4]. Choose a scene you particulary like in the text you have read and decide how you would film it.**

– Where would it take place?

– What sort on lighting would you have? A harsh[5], intense light? A faint[6], subdued[7] one? Would the colours be warm or cold? Would you use special effects?

– What sort of shots[8] and camera angles would you use for the different moments of your scene?

› a long shot[9]? › A close-up[10]? › A zoom shot?

› a wide angle shot? › A bird's eye view[11]?

Then explain your choices to the rest of the class, and answer the questions they might have. If several students in your class choose to work on the same scene, compare and discuss your versions of it.

1. **the stage:** *la scène, au théâtre*
2. **the screen:** *l'écran, au cinéma*
3. **will do:** *conviendra*
4. **sets:** *les décors*
5. **a harsh light:** *une lumière crue, dure*
6. **faint:** *faible*
7. **a subdued light:** *une lumière douce, atténuée*
8. **a shot:** *un plan*
9. **a long shot:** *un plan général*
10. **a close-up:** *un gros plan*
11. **a bird's eye view:** *une vue d'ensemble*

## You are a script writer

→ You have read a long text or a short story.

**1** **Imagine you are a script writer.**

The film director wishes to produce a court métrage of that story. You therefore need to write the script, or part of the script (for one scene only for example). This means going through the short story again in order to decide which scenes you will keep and which dialogues you will select.

In order to get an idea of what a script looks like, here is a short passage from the script of *Rear Window* (Hitchcock, 1954, from a story by Cornell Woolrich).

*Context: Jeff, with his leg in a cast[1], spends his time watching the lives of his neighbors through the window, particularly that of a salesman, whose suspicious behaviour leads him to believe that the salesman has killed his wife. Stella is Jeff's girl friend.*

Int[2]. Jeff's Apartment – Day – Semi-Closeup
*He quickly turns his wheelchair around to the window until he is in profile.*

Ext[3]. Neighborhood – Day – Semi-Long Shot
*The salesman, having just raised the shades[4] in the living room, is now looking out the window. It is not a casual[5] look, but a long, careful, searching appraisal[6] of all the apartment house windows in his neighborhood, starting from his left to his right. His eyes move closer toward Jeff's apartment.*

Int. Jeff's Apartment – Day – Medium Shot
*Jeff in his chair, facing the window, Stella beside him. Jeff nearly knocks the startled[7] Stella off her feet[8] with his arm.*

JEFF: Get back! Out of sight! Quick!
*He propels[9] his chair backward quickly, and Stella moves to the side with surprising agility. They are both in shadow.*

STELLA: *(A startled whisper)* What is it? What's the matter?
*Jeff keeps his eyes trained on[10] the window.*

JEFF: *(Quietly)* The salesman's looking out his window.

*Stella relaxes, gives Jeff a disgusted look, and starts to move out of the shadows.*

STELLA: A Federal offense.

JEFF: *(Sharply)* Get back there! He'll see you!

*She moves back into the shadows.*

STELLA: I'm not shy. I've been looked at before.

JEFF: *(Still peering toward window)* It's not an ordinary look. It's the kind of look a man gives when he's afraid somebody might be watching him.

A. HITCHCOCK, *Rear Window*, 1954

**1. with his leg in a cast:** *la jambe dans le plâtre* **2. INT.:** *abréviation de 'Interior'*. **3. EXT.:** *abréviation de 'Exterior'* **4. the shades:** *les stores* **5. casual:** *au hasard, sans but précis* **6. appraisal:** *étude, examen* **7. startled:** *ahuri* **8. to knock someone off his / her feet:** *faire tomber quelqu'un* **9. to propel:** *propulser, pousser* **10. his eyes trained on:** *le regard dirigé vers*

**a.** Read this script and underline:

- the dialogue in red (direct speech),
- the stage directions in blue (for example: Quietly),
- the description of the scene (or instructions to the cameraman) in green (for example: He quickly turns his wheelchair...).

**b.** Note also the following indications:

- **a long shot:** *un plan général*,
- **a semi-long shot,**
- **a medium shot,**
- **a semi-close up,**
- **a close up:** *un gros plan.*

**c.** Remember that for your dialogue you can:

- use the dialogue, or part of the dialogue of the story you started from,
- transform indirect speech in the story into direct speech,
- invent new dialogue.

**2** **Then present the script to the class, and have them act out the scene.** Does it lead you to change some of the dialogue, and if so, why? Are the stage directions clear enough?

**3** **As the script writer, you need to write a 30-word advertisement to make people want to see the film. Write this advert.**

# You are a comic strip writer

→ You have read a text or a short story.

**1** **Imagine you are a comic strip writer and have been asked to turn the story or part of the story into a comic strip.** Working in groups, first select a passage from the story.

Remember that:

**a.** You can use some of the sentences of your text (from dialogues or narrative), keeping only what seems most important to you.

**b.** You can also summarize passages that would be too long or could not easily be transposed into a comic strip.

**c.** You can transpose reported speech into direct speech and vice versa.

Here is an example of such a transposition

[Quinn] climbed out of bed, walked naked to the telephone, and picked up the receiver on the second ring.
'Yes?'
There was a long pause on the other end, and for a moment Quinn thought the caller had hung up[1]. Then, as if from a great distance, there came the sound of a voice unlike[2] any he had ever heard. It was at once mechanical and filled with feeling, hardly more than a whisper[3] and yet perfectly audible, and so even in tone that he was unable to tell if it belonged to a man or a woman.
'Hello?' said the voice.
'Who is this?' asked Quinn.
'Hello?' said the voice again.
'I'm listening,' said Quinn. 'Who is this?'
'Is this Paul Auster' asked the voice. 'I would like to speak to Mr Paul Auster.'
'There's no one here by that name.'
'Paul Auster. Of the Auster Detective Agency.'
'I'm sorry,' said Quinn. 'You must have the wrong number.'
'This is a matter of utmost[4] urgency,' said the voice.
'There's nothing I can do for you,' said Quinn. 'There is no Paul Auster here.'
'You don't understand,' said the voice. 'Time is running out[5].'
'Then I suggest you dial[6] again. This is not a detective agency.'
Quinn hung up the phone.

Paul AUSTER, *City of Glass*, Faber & Faber, 1987

1. **to hang up:** *raccrocher* 2. **unlike:** *différent de* 3. **a whisper:** *un soupir* 4. **utmost:** *extrême*
5. **time is running out:** *il n'y a plus beaucoup de temps* 6. **to dial:** *composer le numéro*

And here is some vocabulary you may want to use:

A speech balloon (or speech bubble)

A caption (for the narrative)

P. Karasik & D. Mazzucchelli, *City of Glass*, Faber & Faber, 2004

## You are a journalist

**→ You have studied a text.**

**Imagine you are a journalist, who is asked to interview the author of the book from which your text was taken.**

**a.** You first need to prepare your interview and decide what questions you wish to ask. The questions will of course depend on what you found interesting in the text, but here are a few possibilities:

- Why did you write the book?
- Can you explain why you gave it that title?
- Is there a political / social / moral ... message in your book?
- Can you explain the behaviour of ... (a character) ? Why does he/she ...?
- What did you find most difficult when writing the book?

**b.** The interview is then held in class.

- In groups of two: one is the journalist, the other the author.
- Or with the whole class, divided into two groups.

**c.** You could record or film the interview.

## Changing the text

→ **There are several ways in which you can change a text that you have read.**

Here are a few possibilities.

**1 Adding stage directions to a scene from a play.**

You will need to understand the scene well before you can do so. Here is an example.

**a.** Read the following excerpt from Arthur Miller's *Death of a Salesman* and provide stage directions for each line.

*Willy, a travelling salesman[1], is close to mental breakdown[2], and has just asked his boss, Howard, to get him a job in New York as he no longer wants to travel. Howard says he has no job in New York for him...*

HOWARD (... ): Willy, look...

WILLY (... ): I'll go to Boston.

HOWARD (... ): Willy, you can't go to Boston for us.

WILLY (... ): Why can't I go?

HOWARD (... ): I don't want you to represent us. I've been meaning to tell you for a long time now.

WILLY (... ): Howard, are you firing[3] me?

HOWARD (... ): I think you need a good long rest, Willy.

WILLY (... ): Howard –

HOWARD (... ): And when you feel better, come back, and we'll see if we can work something out.

WILLY (... ): But I gotta earn[4] money, Howard. I'm in no position to –

HOWARD (... ): Where are your sons? Why don't your sons give you a hand?

Willy (... ): They're working on a very big deal.

WILLY (... ): This is no time for false pride, Willy. You go to your sons and you tell them that you're tired. You've got two great boys, haven't you?

WILLY (... ): Oh, no question, no question, but in the meantime...

HOWARD (... ): Then that's that, heh?

WILLY (... ): All right, I'll go to Boston tomorrow.

HOWARD (... ): No, no.

WILLY (... ): I can't throw myself on my sons. I'm not a cripple[5]!

HOWARD (... ): Look, kid, I'm busy this morning.

Arthur MILLER, *Death of a Salesman*, 1949, Viking Penguin Inc.

**1. a travelling salesman:** *un voyageur de commerce* **2. a mental breakdown:** *une dépression* **3. to fire:** *renvoyer* **4. I gotta earn:** I've got to earn **5. a cripple:** *un infirme*

**b.** You could then try to act out the scene, respecting the stage directions.

## 2 Adding adverbs.

Read the following text and add as many adverbs as you can to it. No blank spaces are provided here and you should think of as many places as you can to add adverbs (at the beginning or end of a sentence, to qualify the whole sentence; to qualify adjectives or verbs, etc.)

Here are examples of different types of adverbs:

**fortunately – quite – rather – besides – however – hardly – surely – almost – somewhere – too – finally...**

We were sitting towards the rear[1] of the aircraft, behind the wing. He had the window seat, and I was next to him. About ten minutes out of Genoa, they were getting ready to serve drinks, you could hear the clink of bottles from the back of the plane, when this salesman chap turned away from the window, and tapped me on the arm and said, "Excuse me, but would you mind having a look out there. Is it my imagination or is that engine on fire? So I leaned across him and looked out of the window. It was dark, but I could see flames licking round the engine. Well, I'd never looked at a jet engine at night before, for all I knew that was always the effect they gave. I mean you might expect to see a kind of fiery glow[2] coming out of the engine at night. On the other hand, these were flames, and they weren't coming out of the hole at the back. "I don't know what to think," I said. "It doesn't look right." "Do you think we should tell somebody?" he said. "Well, they must have seen it for themselves, mustn't they?" I said. The fact was, neither of us wanted to look a fool by suggesting that something was wrong, and then being told that it wasn't. A chap on the other side of the aisle noticed that we were exercised[3] about something, and came across to have a look for himself. "Christ!" he said and pushed the button to call the stewardess. I think he was some sort of engineer. The stewardess came by with the drinks trolley at that moment. "If it's a drink you want, you'll have to wait your turn," she said. The cabin staff were snappish[4] because of the long delay[5]. "Does the captain know that his starboard engine is on fire?" said the engineer. She gaped at him, squinted out of the window, then ran up the aisle, pushing her trolley in front of her, like a nursemaid running with a pram[6].

Adapted from: David Lodge, *Small World*, Martin Secker & Warburg, 1984

**1. the rear:** the back **2. a glow:** *une lumière rougeâtre* **3. exercised:** *préoccupés*
**4. snappish:** *irritable* **5. a delay:** *retard* **6. a pram:** *un landau*

## 3 Changing the plot.

Starting with the previous text by David Lodge, imagine a change at some point, for example, instead of the 'chap on the other side' who intervenes, imagine someone else does and write the rest of the text.

## 4 Reducing the text by a number of words.

**a.** You have written a short text to be published in a magazine. Unfortunately, they tell you that it is too long and that you must reduce it by 20 or 50 words.

**b.** If your text was the following article, what words would you take out (20 or 50) without rewriting the text?

Remember that you can remove:

- an adjective or an adverb
- a whole sentence
- a relative clause.

But you must be careful this does not change the meaning of the sentence or text.

### More snow looms[1] as Britain suffers winter chaos

Heavy snowfall and freezing conditions caused major disruption across almost all of Britain today with a warning tonight of more snow on the way.

Bitter easterly winds continued to bring Arctic conditions and forecasters[2] warned there is little chance of an early reprieve[3].

Many commuters worked from home, thousands of children could not go to school and motorists faced travel chaos as a number of roads were impassable.

Almost every corner of the UK woke up to between 0.8in (2 cm) and 4in (10 cm) of snow this morning, with the east coast worst hit by flurries[4] and sub-zero temperatures.

Some places in the south of England saw up to 10cm of snow due to a brisk wind pushing the showers inland.

In Scotland, Kinloss in Moray saw temperatures plunge to minus 13C° overnight and during the day the highest temperature recorded there was minus 2C°. (...)

Forecasters have warned that more snow showers are expected across England, Wales and eastern Scotland tomorrow. (...)

As driving conditions were described as hazardous[5], the AA[6] recorded one of its busiest days on record yesterday with almost 20,000 breakdowns.

Today it received an average of 1,350 calls an hour, a spokesman said.

The RAC said callouts to breakdowns had peaked at 2,000 an hour so far today.

*The Independent*, Tuesday 30 November 2010

1. **to loom:** *surgir, menacer* 2. **a forecaster:** *un météorologue* 3. **a reprieve:** *un sursis*
4. **a flurry:** *une rafale de neige* 5. **hazardous:** *dangereux*
6. **AA:** Automobile Association 7. **RAC:** Royal Automobile Club

# Adding and comparing

→ **You have read a short story or a passage from a novel or a play.**

One of the best ways of appreciating it is to compare it with another text or document. Here are a few possibilities.

## 1 Compare the story with a film version of it.

Even if you have read a short passage only, you can watch the corresponding part of the film and, without looking at the text decide:

**a.** Has there been any change in the plot itself?
**b.** Is the dialogue the same in the film and in the text? Has any been omitted, added or changed? What do you think of such changes?
**c.** Are the characters as you imagined them? Why or why not?
**d.** What about photography? What effects are used to express the atmosphere of the text?

› For example, many of Hitchcock's films were inspired by short stories e.g. "Rear Window" was based on a story by Cornell Woolrich, and the film by Robert Altman was inspired by Raymond Carver's "Short Cuts" (short stories).

## 2 Whenever possible, you could compare two film versions of the play or book.

The comparison will lead you to explain why you prefer one version to the other, and to justify your opinion by referring to the text.

› For example many performances of Shakespeare's plays are easily available, or you could compare two versions of Jane Austen's *Pride and Prejudice* – the BBC version and the film by Joe Wright.

## 3 Compare a short story with another short story by the same writer.

If the two short stories have a similar structure, you should find out what that structure is, and what other common points can be found between the two stories, in terms of style for example.

› For instance, if you compare the following stories by Somerset Maugham: 'The Luncheon' and 'The Escape', you find the following structure common to the two stories:

starting point a mistake → the difference between the man and the woman → how he tries to repair the mistake → the result → the final twist

## 4 Compare a story with a poem on the same subject.

Traditional tales lend themselves particularly well to this task since they have often been rewritten. There are, for example, very many modern versions of some of Perrault's tales, for instance in James Thurber's *Fables for our time* or in Angela Carter's *The Bloody Chamber*.

## Comparing readings of a text

**→ You have read a short text or part of a text that you find interesting. You should now prepare to give a dramatised reading aloud of it.**

**1** **a.** First make sure that you understand the text perfectly well and ask yourself:
- What the situation exactly is.
- How many voices can be heard in the text.
- Whether you can draw a portrait of the characters involved.
- What their moods are in the text.
- Whether there are any changes in their tone during the conversation (if so where does it take place and what is it?).
- Whether there are gestures or body movements that should underline what you say.

**b.** Practise reading the text aloud, as expressively as possible. If you do not know how to pronounce a word, look it up in the dictionary. Several internet sites (for example dictionary.com) give you the phonetic pronunciation of words and you can also hear them pronounced.

**c.** Then read the text aloud in class and compare your "performance" with those of other students.

The following excerpts would lend themselves very well to this activity.

*He rises painfully, goes limping to extreme left, halts, gazes into distance off with his hand screening his eyes, turns, goes to extreme right, gazes into distance. Vladimir watches him, then goes and picks up the boot, peers into it, drops it hastily.*
VLADIMIR: Pah!
*(He spits. Estragon moves to centre, halts with his back to auditorium.)*
ESTRAGON: Charming spot. *(He turns, advances to front, halts facing auditorium.)* Inspiring prospects. *(He turns to Vladimir.)* Let's go.
VLADIMIR: We can't.
ESTRAGON: Why not?
VLADIMIR: We're waiting for Godot.
ESTRAGON *(despairingly)*: Ah! *(Pause.)* You're sure it was here?
VLADIMIR: What?
ESTRAGON: That we were to wait.
VLADIMIR: He said by the tree. *(They look at the tree.)* Do you see any others?
ESTRAGON: What is it?
VLADIMIR: I don't know. A willow.

ESTRAGON: Where are the leaves?
VLADIMIR: It must be dead.
ESTRAGON: No more weeping.
VLADIMIR: Or perhaps it's not the season.
ESTRAGON: Looks to me more like a bush.
VLADIMIR: A shrub.
ESTRAGON: A bush.
VLADIMIR: A ______. What are you insinuating? That we've come to the wrong place?
ESTRAGON: He should be here.
VLADIMIR: He didn't say for sure he'd come.
ESTRAGON: And if he doesn't come?
VLADIMIR: We'll come back tomorrow.
ESTRAGON: And then the day after tomorrow.

S. BECKETT, *Waiting for Godot*, Faber & Faber, 1954

*Albert is 28 and lives with his mother.*

MOTHER: Now why don't you go and put a bulb in Grandma's room and by the time you come down I'll have your dinner on the table.
ALBERT: I can't go down to the cellar, I've got my best trousers on, I've got a white shirt on.
MOTHER: You're dressing up tonight, aren't you? Dressing up, cleaning your shoes, anyone would think you were going to the Ritz.
ALBERT: I'm not going to the Ritz.
MOTHER *(suspiciously)*: What do you mean, you're not going to the Ritz?
ALBERT: What do you mean?
MOTHER: The way you said you're not going to the Ritz, it sounded like you were going somewhere else.
ALBERT *(wearily)*: I am.
MOTHER *(shocked surprise)*: You're going out?
ALBERT: You know I'm going out. I told you I was going out. I told you last week. I told you this morning. Look, where's my tie? I'm late already. Come on, Mum, where'd you put it?
MOTHER: What about your dinner?
ALBERT *(searching)*: Look... I told you... I haven't got the... wait a minute... ah, here it is.
MOTHER: You can't wear that tie. I haven't pressed it.
ALBERT: You have. Look at it. Of course you have. It's beautifully pressed. It's fine. *(He ties the tie.)*
MOTHER: Where are you going?
ALBERT: Mother, I've told you, honestly, three times.

Harold PINTER, *A Night Out*, from *Act I*, *Methuen*, 1961

## 2 You can also compare various readings of the same scene.

The *Sourcebook Shakespeare* (Methuen Drama), for example, gives the text of the play as well as an audio CD which includes key scenes from well-known performances; so that the same speech is heard spoken by two or three different actors.

# Imitating a text

**You have read a text with a clear style or structure.**

You are going to write a pastiche of it.

The first thing you need to do is to study the text carefully and make a note of its main stylistic characteristics.

1 **In the first passage** given below, for example, you could write another nonsense story, keeping lines 3 and 6 and one or two rhymes.

2 **In the second example** (a passage from a short play), it is clear that Clifford keeps on talking without listening to Charmian's answers. As for Charmian, she tries to answer him but, because of the noise, can't hear properly what he says. So that instead of "everyone's saying" she understands "insane", and "God" becomes "odd".

In this particular case, you should first imagine what a character says, then think of the way his/her words might be misheard, and therefore lead to incongruous answers.

3 **In the third example** (a poem by Brian Patten), it is the very short sentences of the dialogue, each followed by 'she said' or 'he said', which give the text its originality. But the poem also tells a story with a twist in it.
In this case, you should think of a dialogue with a twist in it at the end and tell it using the same kind of structures.

**a**

There was an old man,
And he had a calf[1],
And that's half;
He took him out of the stall[2],
And put him on the wall,
And that's all.

*Traditional nursery rhyme*[3]

**1. a calf:** *un veau* **2. a stall:** *une stalle d'étable* **3. a nursery rhyme:** *une comptine*

**b**

*The two characters, Charmian and Clifford, are standing at a party, holding glasses. The confused roar[1] of conversation around them makes it impossible to hear anything.*

CLIFFORD: I suppose there's one person who must be able to hear what everyone's saying.

CHARMIAN: Completely insane[2]!

CLIFFORD: And that's God!

CHARMIAN: Very odd[3], when you come to think about it.

CLIFFORD: He just tunes out[4] everybody else, and there's you and me, say, as clear as a bell[5]!

CHARMIAN: Such hell! Why do we do it?

CLIFFORD: Everyone smiling and nodding away.

CHARMIAN: Away? Yes, we have. To Egypt, which was rather a lark[6]!

M. Frayn, *"Heart to Heart"*, in *Alarms and Excursions*, Methuen, 1998

**1. a roar:** *clameur, bruit très fort* **2. insane:** *fou* **3. odd:** *étrange* **4. to tune out:** *ne plus faire attention à, ne plus entendre* **5. as clear as a bell:** *parfaitement clair* **6. it was a lark:** *c'était amusant*

**c**

### Hair Today, No Her Tomorrow

'I've been upstairs,' she said.
'Oh yes?' I said.
'I found a hair,' she said.
'A hair?' I said.
'In the bed,' she said.
'From a head?' I said.
'It's not mine,' she said.
"Was it black?' I said.
'It was,' she said.
'I'll explain,' I said.
'You swine[1],' she said.
'Not quite,' I said.
'I'm going,' she said.
'Please don't,' I said.
'I hate you!' she said.
'You do?' I said.
'Of course,' she said.
'But why?' I said.
'That black hair', she said.
'A pity,' I said.

'Time for truth,' she said.
'For confession?' I said.
"Me too,' she said.
'You what?' I said.
'Someone else,' she said.
'Oh dear,' I said.
'So there![2]' she said.
'Ah well,' I said.
'Guess who?' she said.
'Don't say,' I said.
'I will,' she said.
'You would[3],' I said.
'Your friend,' she said.
'Oh damn,' I said.
'And his friend,' she said.
'Him too?' I said.
'And the rest,' she said.
'Good God,' I said.
'What's that?' she said.
'What's what?' I said.
'That noise?' she said.
"Upstairs?' I said.
'Yes,' she said.
'The new cat,' I said.
'A cat?' she said.
'It's black,' I said.
'Black?' she said.
'Long-haired,' I said.
'Oh no,' she said.
'Oh yes,' I said.
'Oh shit!' she said.
'Goodbye,' I said.

'I lied,' she said.
'You lied?' I said.
'Of course,' she said.
'About my friend?' I said.
'Y-ess,' she said.
'And the others?' I said.
'Ugh,' she said.
'How odd,' I said.
'I'm forgiven?' she said.
'Of course,' I said.
'I'll stay?' she said.
'Please don't,' I said.
'But why?' she said.
'I lied,' I said.
'About what?' she said.
'The new cat,' I said.
'It's white,' I said.

B. Patten, from *Storm Damage*,
Harper & Collins, 1988

1. **a swine:** *un salaud* 2. **So there!:** *Eh bien voilà* 3. **You would!:** *C'est bien de toi !*

# TASKS

## Into another genre

→ You have read a poem, a passage from fiction or from a play.

**1** **Starting from that text, transform it into another text belonging to a different genre.**

**a.** You can, for instance, transform a passage from a novel or a longer poem into a haiku, an epitaph, an elegy, a ballad, a short story, an article, etc... But you should of course try to fit the form to the contents.

**b.** Or you can use the text you have read as the basis for a text belonging to another genre, as in the example of a letter given below.

**Here are a few prose or poetic forms you can choose from**

apprenticeship novel – autobiography – detective story – diary – blog – detective story – epistolary novel – fable – fairy tale – picaresque novel – science fiction – utopia – epitaph – acrostic – haiku – nursery rhyme – elegy – visual poem – free verse – ballad – epic – ode – sonnet – limerick

Make sure you know the characteristics of the genre you have chosen. See part 3

My dear Chris,

You will never believe what I have discovered! As you know Betty and I have come on a cycling tour of Wiltshire: B&Bs, good food, a lot of reading for me (my thesis is beginning to take shape) and brass rubbing[1] for Betty. A couple of days ago, I walked with her to the church where she intended to work on the lovely brass plate of a knight, then walked around in that tiny village church, and that's when I saw the epitaph.

Of course, it was the name that first caught my attention – a coincidence surely. But then I remembered that Grandfather Charles always said that we had family in Wiltshire and I vaguely remember that he mentioned this village. The name stuck in my mind because it is such an amusing one. I wonder whether you could check in the family files. If it is the right village, then they must be our ancestors, for it's such a tiny place. Wouldn't it be lovely to have all these pious people for our ancestors?

Do check!

Much love,

Anne

1. **brass rubbing:** *action qui consiste à frotter une feuille sur une plaque de cuivre afin d'en décalquer le motif*

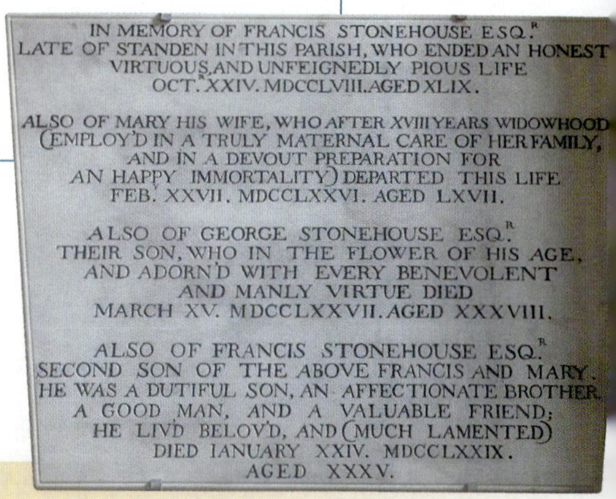

# Choosing a point of view

**1** **a.** In this activity, you will have to choose a particular point of view when writing your story.

- Start with a picture (a painting, an advertisement, a photograph...) involving several characters in an interesting situation.
- Study the picture carefully and decide who the characters are, what the relationship between them is, and what is actually happening in the picture or how the scene will develop immediately afterwards.

**b.** You should then tell the story, choosing one of the following points of view:

- A first person narrative, choosing to follow the thoughts of one of the characters.
- A third-person narrative, also following the point of view of one of the characters.
- A third-person narrative, with an exterior and omniscient point of view, that is to say with a narrator who is almighty and can enter the thoughts of all the characters.

A painting such as the following one by Georges de La Tour (*Le Tricheur*, 1647, Musée du Louvre) lends itself particularly well to this activity.

G. de La Tour, *Le Tricheur*, 1647, Musée du Louvre

**2** **Write your story then read it or tell it to the rest of the class.** They will have to guess who is speaking and what the point of view is.

**3** **Another possibility is to start from a text you have studied in class.**

**a.** What point of view do we follow in the text? That of one of the characters? That of an omniscient narrator? Is it a first or third person narrative?

**b.** Then re-write the passage, changing the point of view.

**c.** Read your new version to the rest of the class, who will have to guess what the point of view is.

## Playing with style

→You have read a story or studied a picture.

Starting from the very short summary of a story, or from a picture you must interpret, or from any story you want to tell, try and write that story, using a stylistic constraint[1].

**a.** Imagine that you start from the following picture. Study it carefully, look at its title, and try to think of the story behind the picture. It does not matter if it is not what actually[2] inspired the painting.

W. F. YEAMES, *And When Did You Last See Your Father?*, 1878, National Museum Liverpool

**b.** You must now tell this story in an original way. You could for instance:

- Tell it without using adjectives, or without using adverbs.
- Use dialogue only, or reported speech only.
- Use as many modals as possible.
- Use a relative clause in each sentence.
- Use free indirect speech only.
- Mention a colour in each sentence.

But you could use another idea of your own.

**c.** Then tell your story to the rest of the class, and see if they can guess what choice you made.

**1. a constraint:** *une contrainte*
**2. actually:** *en fait*

# Desert Island Books

Desert Island Discs is a well-known Radio 4 programme in which a celebrity is interviewed and asked to choose his or her eight favourite pieces of music – those he/she would take to a desert island. The guest is also asked questions about his/her life and has to justify the choice of each piece of music briefly, usually by explaining what memories it holds for him/her or what associations it has in his/her mind.

**Imagine a similar type of programme called Desert Island Books.**

**a.** Draw up a list of books you would choose to take away with you on a desert island.

**b.** Next to each book, you might write a few words to remind you of how you would justify each choice.

**c.** Remember that you will be interviewed by one or several students in the class.

This may be a good opportunity to revise the use of tenses, particularly present, past and present perfect. *e.g.*:

I read it first when I was...

I've read it several times since then.

I've never read another book which was so...

I always think of it as...

# Fifty-five word stories

This activity is inspired by an American literary competition in which the participants have to write very short stories of exactly 55 words. The best of them are then published (*The World's Shortest Stories*, ed. by Steve Moss, Running Press, 1998, 1995). It is an "exercise in literary minimalism", which requires imagination and concision, but can be quite amusing.

**a.** You will find two examples below. Read them and note that they both finish with a twist[1] in the last line.

**1. a twist**: *un retournement de situation, un rebondissement*

**a**

"Careful, honey, it's loaded[1]," he said, re-entering the bedroom.
Her back rested against the headboard[2]. "This for your wife?"
"No. Too chancy[3]. I'm hiring[4] a professional."
"How about me?"
He smirked[5]. "Cute[6]. But who'd be dumb[7] enough to hire a lady hit man[8]?"
She wet her lips, sighting[9] along the barrel[10].
"Your wife."

J. WHITMORE, *Bedtime story*, in *The World's Shortest Stories*, ed. by Steve Moss, Running Press, 1998, 1995

**1. loaded:** *chargé (pistolet)* **2. the headboard:** *la tête de lit* **3. chancy:** *risqué* **4. to hire:** *engager les services de* **5. to smirk:** *sourire de façon suffisante* **6. cute:** *malin, fûté* **7. dumb:** *bête* **8. a hit man:** *un tueur à gages* **9. to sight:** *viser* **10. the barrel:** *le canon du pistolet*

**b**

"Old Grapplemeyer died broke[1].
The reading of this will[2] is over."
"That old fraud[3]," sobbed Lydia,
Grapplemeyer's mistress of 30 years.
"I've wasted my life."
"You?" shouted David. "I was his
secretary, valet, and more!"
"I was only the cook, but I'll miss dear
Mr. Grapplemeyer," said Rosemary,
fingering[4] a huge diamond ring.

S. POWELL, *Grapplemeyer*, in *The World's Shortest Stories*, ed. by Steve Moss, Running Press, 1998, 1995

**1. broke:** *fauché* **2. a will:** *un testament*
**3. a fraud:** *un imposteur* **3. to finger:** *tripoter*

**b.** Now try and write your own 55-word story.

Here is how you can go about it:

- Think of a plot, or at least of an unexpected outcome to a particular situation.
- Write a very short story about it – perhaps about half a page –, using dialogue or narration, and not paying too much attention to its length at this point.
- Read your story over again, looking out for mistakes or points that are not clear.
- Then count the number of words you have. If your story is too short, add a sentence or a few adverbs or adjectives, carefully choosing those that will best contribute to the atmosphere or the clarity of the situation. If, on the contrary, it is too long (which is more likely), look at each sentence and ask yourself whether it is really necessary. Or try to replace two sentences by just one. Try to delete a few adjectives or adverbs. In each case, you will have to weigh words carefully in order to reach maximum effect with the smallest number of words.
- Then read and compare your stories.

# Write a fairy tale

You know that most fairy tales follow a number of conventions.

**a.** You are now going to write one, using the traditional characters and motifs of such tales.

You are given:

- The first sentence.
- The last sentence.
- And in between a list of elements which are characteristic of fairy tales.

You should use at least five elements from each category, but can add others as well.

**b.** Try to invent your own story rather than tell one you already know, like *Cinderella* or *Bluebeard*.

Once upon a time, there was a... who...

| Characters | Places | Motifs | Objects |
|---|---|---|---|
| a fairy | a poor farm | marriage | a dress |
| a prince | a palace | inheriting the crown | shoes |
| a goblin[1] | a dark forest | beauty | a ring |
| a talking animal | a tower | ugliness | a sword |
| a princess | a prison | an ordeal[3] | a letter |
| a demon | a cave | being persecuted | a key |
| a witch | a large city | helping someone | a long rope |
| a dwarf[2] | a church | breaking a prohibition | a cake |
| a youngest son | a field | being cruel to someone | a hidden treasure |
| an ogre | a ballroom | turning something/ someone into something/ someone else | a boat |
| a youngest daughter | a kitchen | a strange meeting | a rose |
| a giant | a lake or river | a spell[4] | a magic wand[5] |
| a dragon | | being transported to another place | |
| a sister | | | |
| a stepmother | | | |
| a poor servant | | | |

They married and lived happily ever after.

**1. a goblin:** *un lutin*
**2. a dwarf:** *un nain*
**3. an ordeal:** *une épreuve*
**4. a spell:** *un sort, un sortilège*
**5. a magic wand:** *une baguette magique*

As an example, this is the beginning of *Sleeping Beauty*, by the Brothers Grimm.

A long time ago there were a King and Queen who said every day, "Ah, if only we had a child!" but they never had one. But it happened that once when the Queen was bathing, a frog[1] crept out of the water on to the land, and said to her, "Your wish shall be fulfilled[2]; before a year has gone by, you shall have a daughter."
What the frog had said came true, and the Queen had a little girl who was so pretty that the King could not contain himself for joy, and ordered a great feast. He invited not only his kindred[3], friends and acquaintances, but also the Wise[4] Women, in order that they might be kind and well-disposed towards the child. There were thirteen of them in his kingdom, but, as he had only twelve golden plates for them to eat out of, one of them had to be left at home. The feast was held with all manner of splendour and when it came to an end the Wise Women bestowed[5] their magic gifts upon the baby: one gave virtue, another beauty, a third riches, and so on with everything in the world that one can wish for. When eleven of them had made their promises, suddenly the thirteenth came in. She wished to avenge herself for not having been invited, and without greeting, or even looking at anyone, she cried with a loud voice, "The King's daughter shall in her fifteenth year prick herself with a spindle[6], and fall down dead." And, without saying a word more, she turned round and left the room.

Brothers Grimm, *Sleeping Beauty*, 1812

**1. a frog:** *une grenouille* **2. to fulfill:** *réaliser, accomplir*
**3. his kindred:** his family **4. wise:** *sage, intelligente*
**5. to bestow:** *accorder, conférer* **6. a spindle:** *un fuseau (pour filer)*

**c.** Tell your story to the rest of the class, who should decide:
- Which elements you have chosen from each column,
- Whether or not it is a good fairy tale. If it is not, explain why. Is it original in some other way?

# Index

**Shakespeare**: writer
*Macbeth*: work
Beat writers: movement, period, genre, etc.
31: page numbers
**55**: text proposed for study

## A-B



## C-D



## E-G



## H-K

## L-O



## P-R



## S-U



## V-Y

## Crédits photographiques

Couverture : collection Christophel (ht); Mary Evans/Rue des Archives (bas)
Rabat (de ht en bas et de gauche à droite) : Archivio L.A.R.A. / Planeta; Bis/Ph Eleen Tweedy/ Archives Labor; Archivio L.A.R.A. / Planeta (2 documents); Bristol City Museum and Art Gallery; © Adagp, Paris, 2011; Archivio L.A.R.A. / Planeta © The Estate of Francis Bacon/All rights reserved/ADAGP, Paris 2011; National Portrait Gallery, Smithsonian Institution; Archivio L.A.R.A. / Planeta (4 documents); Bis/ Leo Castelli Gallery, New York, ©Jasper Johns / ADAGP, Paris 2011; Archivio L.A.R.A. / Planeta © 1998 Rothko Prizel & Christopher Rothko - ADAGP, Paris 2011
p. 6 g: Bis/Ph Eileen Tweddy/Archives Labor; p. 6 m: Victoria and Albert Museum; p. 6 d: Archivio L.A.R.A./Planeta; p. 7: The Bridgeman Art Library; p. 8: BIS/Archives Nathan; p. 9 ht: BIS/ Ph. Jeanbor/Archives Larbor; p. 9 bas: Archivio Arici/Leemage; p. 10 g: Archivio L.A.R.A./Planeta; p. 10 d: Archivio L.A.R.A./ Planeta; p. 12 g: Archivio L.A.R.A./Planeta; p. 12 m: Archivio L.A.R.A./Planeta; p. 12 d: BIS/Ph. H. Josse/Archives Labor; p. 13: Archivio L.A.R.A. / Planeta; p. 14: Archivio L.A.R.A./ Planeta; p. 15: Fitzwilliam Museum, University of Cambridge, UK/The Bridgeman Art Library; p. 16: BIS/Ph. Eileen Tweedy/ Archives Larbor; p. 17: Bis/Ph Eleen Tweedy/Archives Labor; p. 18: Archivio L.A.R.A./Planeta; p. 19: Bis/Archives Larbor; p. 20: La Collection/Artothek; p. 21: The Maas Gallery, London/ The Bridgeman Art Library; p. 23 g: Bis/Ph coll Archives Bordas; p. 23 d: Bis/Courtesy Bernard Jacobson Gallery © ADAGP, Paris 2011; p. 24 ht: The Bridgeman Art Library; p. 24 bas: The Bridgeman Art Library; p. 25: Sotheby's/akg-images © The Estate of Vanessa Bell; p. 26: Henry Moore Foundation/ The Bridgeman Art Library; p. 27: BIS / Ph. Eileen Tweedy/ Archives Larbor; p. 29: Archivio L.A.R.A./Planeta; p. 30 g bas: The Bridgeman Art Library © ADAGP, Paris 2011; p. 30 d ht: collection Christophel; p. 32 g: Corbis; p. 32 m: Archivio L.A.R.A./Planeta; p. 32 d: DeAgostini/Leemage; p. 34 Christie's Images/The Bridgeman Art Library; p. 35: Butler Institute of American Art, Youngstown/Museum Purchase 1955/The Bridgeman Art Library; p. 36: The Bridgeman Art Library; p. 37 g: Archivio L.A.R.A./Planeta; p. 37 d: Archivio L.A.R.A./Planeta; p. 38: John Held, Jr.; p. 39: Archivio L.A.R.A./Planeta; p. 40: collection Christophel; p. 41 ht: Reed College; p. 41 bas: coll. particulière; p. 43 g: Archivio L.A.R.A./Planeta © 1998 Rothko Prizel & Christopher Rothko - ADAGP, Paris 2011; p. 43 d: BIS/Ph. Coll. Archives Larbor © Adagp, Paris.; p. 44: Archivio L.A.R.A./Planeta © Robert Rauschenberg/ADAGP, Paris 2011; p. 45 :©Jasper Johns/ADAGP, Paris 2011; p. 46: Akg-images/© 2011 Andy Warhol Foundation/ADAGP, Paris/Licensed by Campbell's Soup Co. All rights reserved; p. 47: The Bridgeman Art Library; p. 48 ht: The Bridgeman Art Library; p. 49: The Bridgeman Art Library; p. 50: coll. particulière; p. 52: Archivio L.A.R.A./Planeta; p. 53: akg-images © The Estate of Francis Bacon/All rights reserved/ADAGP, Paris 2011; p. 54: Archivio L.A.R.A./Planeta; p. 55: Archivio L.A.R.A./Planet; p. 56: BIS/ Ph. Coll. Archives Nathan; p. 57: collection Christophel; p. 59 ht: collection Christophel; p. 59 bas: BIS/Ph. Coll. Archives Nathan; p. 60 g: Mary Evans/Rue des Archives; p. 60 d: Private Collection/The Bridgeman Art Library; p. 61: Hulton Archive/ Getty Images; p. 62: PrismaArchivo/Leemage; p. 63: BIS/ Goethe Museum, Francfort/Ph. Coll. Archives Nathan; p. 64 ht: BIS/Ph. Coll. Archives Larbor; p. 64 bas: coll. particulière; p. 66: Mike Laye/Corbis; p. 69 ht: The Bridgeman Art Library; p. 69 bas: coll. particulière; p. 70: Archivio L.A.R.A./Planeta; p. 71 g: Archivio L.A.R.A./Planeta; p. 71 d: The Charles Dickens Museum; p. 73 g: BIS/Ph. Brentano's/Archives Larbor; p. 73 d: collection Christophel; p. 74: BIS/Ph. Coll. Farm Security Administration/Coll. Archives Bordas; p. 76: akg-images/ ullstein bild; p. 77 g: Fred Stein Archive/adoc-photos; p. 77 d: collection Christophel; p. 78: collection Christophel; p. 80: akg-images/ullstein bild; p. 81: collection Christophel; p. 83 g: Archivio L.A.R.A./Planeta; p. 83 d: The Granger Collection NYC/Rue des Archives; p. 85: Archivio L.A.R.A./Planeta; p. 87 ht: Archivio L.A.R.A./Planeta; p. 87 bas: Geraint Lewis/Alamy/ Photo12; p. 89: Lebrecht/Leemage; p. 91 ht: Bettmann/ Corbis; p. 91 bas: collection Christophel; p. 93 g: photo by J. A. Scholten, St. Louis, 1870. Missouri History Museum; p. 93 d: Heritage Images/Leemage; p. 96: Writer Pictures/Leemage; p. 98 ht: coll. particulière; p. 99: collection Christophel; p. 101: © 1992 Soraida Martinez; p. 102 g: North Wind Pictures/ Leemage; p. 102 d: collection GB; p. 104 ht: Bettmann/Corbis; p. 104 bas: © ADAGP, Paris 2011; p. 105 g: Bettmann/Corbis; p. 105 d: Getty Images/Panoramic Images; p. 107: Writer Pictures/Leemage; p. 109: Effigie/Leemage; p. 111 g: Photo McCabe /Lebrecht/Leemage; p. 112: David Corio/Michael Ochs Archive/Getty Images; p. 113: collection Christophel; p. 114: collection GB 115 © ADAGP, Paris 2011; p. 116 ht: Archivio L.A.R.A./Planeta; p. 116 bas: Archivio L.A.R.A./ Planeta; p. 118 ht: Archivio L.A.R.A./Planeta; p. 118 bas: North Carolina Museum of Art/Corbis; p. 120 g: Lisa Larsen/Time Life Pictures/Getty Image; p. 120 d: Musées royaux des beaux-arts de Belgique, Bruxelles, Archives Nathan; p. 121 d: Lein/Writer Pictures/Leemage; p. 122: Emin Kuliyev Shutterstock; p. 123: collection Christophel; p. 125 g: Archivio L.A.R.A./Planeta; p. 125 d: coll. particulière; p. 126: Agathe Poupeney; p. 127: DR; p. 128 g: Photo lewis /Lebrecht/Leemage; p. 128 d: Black Stripe Theater; p. 130: Abreact Performance Space; p. 132 ht: Effigie/Leemage; p. 132 bas: akg-images © Estate of Roy lichtenstein New York /ADAGP, Paris 2011;-p. 135: Boston Public Library; p. 136 ht: Selva/Leemage; p. 138 ht: Mirrorpix/ Lebrecht/Leemage; p. 138 bas: Hills & Saunders, National Portrait Gallery, London; p. 140 ht: Archivio L.A.R.A./Planeta; p. 140 bas: collection Christophel; p. 141: Archive Modernista; p. 142 g: Sheehan/Writer Pictures/Leemage; p. 143: collection Christophel; p. 144: The Stapleton Collection/The Bridgeman Art Library; p. 183: BIS/Archives Larbor; p. 184: Walker Art Gallery, National Museums Liverpool/The Bridgeman Art Library.



## Crédits textes

p. 26: W.H. Auden, 'Funeral Blues', in *Collected Shorter Poems*, Faber & Faber, 1966 DR; p. 30: Philip Larkin, 'This be the Verse', in *Collected Poems*, 1988, The Marvell Press and Faber & Faber. DR; p. 38: Robert Frost, 'The Road not Taken', in *Complete Poems of Robert Frost*, c. 1967 by Holt, Rinehart and Winston DR; p. 40: John Dos Passos, 'The Big Money', in *USA*, 1936 DR; p. 41: Langston Hughes, 'Mother to Son', in *Selected Poems*, c. 1926, 1954, Alfred A. Knopf DR; p. 44: Lawrence Ferlinghetti, 'I am Waiting', in *A Coney Island of the Mind*, New Directions, 1958 DR; p. 46: John Updike, *Rabbit, Run*, 1961 DR; p. 51: Vikram Seth, *A Suitable Boy*, III. 18, Phoenix House, 1993; p. 55: *Brave New World* by Aldous Huxley. Copyright © 1932, 1946 by Aldous Huxley. Reprinted by permission of Georges Borchardt, Inc., on behalf of the Aldous and Laura Huxley Trust. All rights reserved.; p. 56: *Nineteen Eighty Four* by George Orwell (Copyright © George Orwell, 1949) by permission of Bill Hamilton as the Literary Executor of the Estate of the Late Sonia Brownell Orwell and Secker & Warburg Ltd. For US print rights contact Harcourt Brace ; p. 66 : Angela Carter, 'The Werewolf', in *The Bloody Chamber*, Victor Gollancz, 1979 © Angela Carter DR ; p. 73 : John Steinbeck, *The Grapes of Wrath*, William Heinemann, 1939 © John Steinbeck 1939 DR ; p. 76 : W. H. Auden, *The Unknown Citizen*, in *Collected Shorter Poems*, Faber & Faber, 1966 DR ; p. 77 : Arthur Miller, *The Crucible* (1953), The Cresset Press, 1956 ; p. 80 : Seamus Heaney, *Digging* (1966) in *New Selected Poems*, Faber & Faber, 1990 ; p. 89 : Craig Raine, 'A Martian Sends a Postcard Home', © Craig Raine, 1979, O.U.P. ; p. 98 : Carson McCullers, *The Heart is a Lonely Hunter* (1940), The Cresset Press, 1943 DR ; p. 104 : Gwendolyn Brooks, 'We Real Cool' from *Selected Poems*. Copyright © 1963 by Gwendolyn Brooks DR ; p. 105 : N. Scott Momaday, House Made of Dawn , Harper & Row, 1968 DR ; p. 107 : Alice Walker, *The Color Purple* (1982), The Women's Press, 1983 ; p. 109 : Wole Soyinka, 'Telephone Conversation' (1980), in Gerald Moore and Ulli Beier (eds), *Modern Poetry from Africa*, Hardmondsworth, 1963 DR ; p. 110 : Wole Soyinka, From *Nobel Lectures, Literature 1981-1990*, World Scientific Publishing Co., Singapore, 1993 © The Nobel Foundation 1986 DR ; p. 111 : Zadie Smith, *White Teeth*, Hamish Hamilton, 2000 DR ; p. 115 : John Fowles, *The French Lieutenant's Woman*, Jonathan Cape, 1969 ©John Fowles ; p. 120 : William Carlos Williams, 'Landscape with the Fall of Icarus', in *Pictures from Brueghel*, New Directions, 1949 DR ; p. 121 : Paul Auster, *Ghosts* (1986) in *The New York Trilogy*, Faber & Faber, 1987© Paul Auster ; p. 125 et p. 179 : Samuel Beckett, *Waiting for Godot* (1954), Faber & Faber, 1972 ; p. 128 : Harold Pinter, *The Dumb Waiter*, Methuen, 1960, Faber & Faber, 1991 DR ; p. 132 : Joseph Heller, *Catch-22* (1961), Jonathan Cape, 1962 DR ; p. 141 : Jean Rhys, *Wide Sargasso Sea*, André Deutsch, 1966 DR ; p. 142 : Salman Rusdie, *Midnight's Children*, Jonathan Cape, 1981© Salman Rushdie 1981 ; p. 147 : Paul Hansford, Stroud © Paul Hansford 1958 DR ; p. 170 : Alfred Hitchkock, *Roar Window*, © Hitchkock, 1954 DR ; p. 172 : Paul Auster, *City of Glass*, Faber & Faber, 1987 © Paul Auster ; p. 173 : P. Karasik & D. Mazzucchelli, Paul Auster, *City of Glass* Faber & Faber, 2004 DR ; p. 174 : Arthur Miller, *Death of a Salesman*, © 1949, Arthur Miller, Viking Penguin Inc ; p. 175 : Adapted from : David Lodge, *Small World*, Martin Secker & Warburg, 1984 DR ; p. 176 : *The Independent*, Tuesday 30 November 2010, ©Independent.co.uk DR ; p. 179 : Harold Pinter, *A Night Out*, from Act I, Methuen, 1961, DR ; p. 181 : Brian Patten, from *Storm Damage*, Flamingo, Harper & Collins, 1988 DR ; p. 186 : *The world's shortest stories*, ed by Steve Moss, Running Press, 1995-1998



FSC
www.fsc.org
MIXTE
Papier issu de sources responsables
FSC® C022030

N° d'éditeur 10180606 - Dépôt legal Août 2011
Imprimé en Espagne par Dédalo Offset, S. L.